# Natural Language Processing

Harry Tennant

# Natural Language Processing

An Introduction to an
Emerging Technology

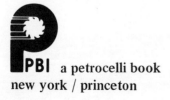

PBI   a petrocelli book
new york / princeton

*Designed by Bruce Campbell*
*Typesetting by Backes Graphics*

**Library of Congress Cataloging in Publication Data**
Tennant, Harry.
    Natual language processing.

    "A Petrocelli book."
    Includes index.
    1. Linguistics  Data processing.  I. Title.
p98.T4    410'.72    81-4559
ISBN 0-89433-100-0    AACR2

To Julie with my love
and my thanks for all the help.

# Contents

Preface                                                                    vii

1  Natural Languages                                                        1
   1.1 Motivation / 1.2 Research Strategies / 1.3 Methodology
   1.4 Case Study: The Automatic Advisor / 1.5 Critique of
   the Automatic Advisor / References and Further Reading

2  Early Natural Language Programs                                         19
   2.1 Computation-Based Natural Language Processing /
   2.2 Case Study: BASEBALL / 2.3 Case Study: SAD-SAM /
   2.4 Case Study: SYNTHEX / 2.5 Case Study: STUDENT /
   2.6 Case Study: DEACON / 2.7 Case Study: DOCTOR /
   References and Further Reading

3  Syntax                                                                  49
   3.1 Structural Constraints in English / 3.2 Transition
   Networks / 3.3 Case Study: The LUNAR ATN Parser /
   3.4 Bottom-Up Parsing / 3.5 Combining Top-Down and
   Bottom-Up Parsing / 3.6 Computational Linguistic Models
   of Syntax / References and Further Reading

4  Semantics                                                              101
   4.1 Multiple Word Senses / 4.2 Modifier Attachement /
   4.3 Noun-Noun Modification / 4.4 Pronouns /
   4.5 Determiners and Noun Phrases / 4.6 Ellipsis and
   Substitution / 4.7 Case Frames / 4.8 Concept
   Decomposition / References and Further Reading

**5 Implemented Semantic Analyzers**     **139**

5.1 Case Study: SHRDLU / 5.2 Airline Guide /
5.3 LUNAR / 5.4 ROBOT / 5.5 Case Study: Preference
Semantics / 5.6 Case Study: SOPHIE / 5.7 Case Study:
LIFER / 5.8 Case Study: The Linguistic String Project /
5.9 Case Study: PLANES / 5.10 Case Study: RENDEZ-
VOUS / 5.11 Case Study: ELI / References and Further
Reading

**6 Representing Knowledge about Objects and Events**     **217**

6.1 The Structure of Frames / 6.2 Matching / 6.3 Frame
Activation / 6.4 Viewpoints / 6.5 Case Study: FRL /
6.6 Case Study: KLONE / 6.7 Case Study: KRL /
6.8 Case Study: GUS / 6.9 Case Study: SAM and PAM /
References and Further Reading

**7 Discourse**     **241**

7.1 Speech Acts / 7.2 Speech Acts in Question-Answering
Dialogs / 7.3 Rules for Organizing Discourse / 7.4 Rules
for Dialogs / 7.5 Rules of Written Discourse / References
and Further Reading

**Glossary**     **267**

**Index**     **271**

# Preface

This book is intended to introduce the reader to the developing technology of natural language processing. It is organized primarily around case studies of implemented natural language processors. For clarity, the various aspects of language analysis, syntax, semantics, discourse, and knowledge representation are considered separately, but they are, in fact, interdependent. The case study approach illustrates the mutual dependence of the various aspects through examples. In addition, case studies give the reader indirect exposure to the areas of application to which natural language systems have been applied. To some degree, case studies can also give an indication of the extent of coverage that the systems have over their domains of discourse. Finally, the case studies illustrate some of the open questions of natural language processing.

In this book, a number of concepts will be defined. This specialized vocabulary facilitates later reference. It should also familiarize readers with the nomenclature of the field so that they can follow later developments in the technical literature if they wish to.

Although new vocabulary is defined, no prior familiarity with natural language processing or other branches of artificial intelligence is presupposed. The book is written only with the expectation that the reader is familiar with concepts of general computer science. As for linguistics, the level of sophistication required of readers is about the level one attains in a high school grammar class.

This is a relatively short book. It is intended as an introduction to the field, not as a comprehensive survey covering every facet. It could be read with one of two goals: to familiarize the reader with the directions and status of ongoing research, or to serve as a starting point leading to deeper investigation. This introductory book concentrates on the issues central to natural language processing technology. Many related topics are not covered, topics the interested reader may wish to consider. There is a great deal of natural language research currently being conducted in linguistics and psychology. In artificial intelligence, there is related work in language generation, speech understanding, problem solving and knowledge representation. Knowledge representation is discussed to some extent, but thorough coverage would require a book in itself. The emerging discipline of cognitive science is meant to study cognition through the methodologies of linguistics, psychology, artificial intelligence, and other disciplines. In computer science, related work is going on in database technology, interactive system design, and human factors design; these are not covered here.

The material presented here is based primarily on reports of research in the open literature. To a lesser extent, some of the material is based on my personal experience of research in natural language processing. Available sources are not always as complete or detailed as one might wish, but I have made an attempt to discuss each system and its relation to others as fairly and accurately as possible. There are bound to be some errors, and for these, I apologize in advance.

Finally, I hope the readers enjoy reading about this technology as much as I have enjoyed working on it and writing about it.

HRT
*Urbana, Illinois*
*1981*

# 1. Natural Languages

Natural languages are the languages used by people in the course of their daily affairs, for example, English, French, Serbo-Croation, Swahili. Users of natural languages can express a broad range of ideas to others through them. Given enough attention, nearly any concept that comes to mind can be conveyed to another person through a common natural language. Some ideas are easy to express, such as, "I stubbed my toe," whereas others may require hours of explanation. The prime characteristic of natural languages is that they can be used to express nearly all the concepts that occur to the people who speak and understand them.

The word *natural* emphasizes a contrast with artificial languages. Artificial languages are those that have been designed to be highly expressive over a limited range of ideas. Musical notation is an artificial language; it is wonderfully concise for expressing which notes should be played at which times and for how long. These are the only concepts, however, that can be communicated through it. Musical notation cannot help me express the fact that I have stubbed my toe. Another set of artificial languages is programming languages. These are an interesting case because, like natural languages, they can be used to express a broad range of ideas. LISP, for instance, is an extendable language; thus, if an idea is difficult to express in its current form, it can be improved at will. But programming languages have been designed with their application to computers in mind, and this has affected their form. Programming languages have been written so as to be analyzed easily by computers.

1

### ⋅ 1.1 Motivation

Research in natural language processing is concerned with making computers capable of using natural languages. There are two reasons for this. First, computers that can use natural languages would undeniably be a useful tool. It would mean that a person in need of information retrieval or information processing on a computer could obtain it without having to go through an intermediary. He or she would not have to learn the nuances of a programming language and would not need to worry about forgetting it during long periods of disuse. A computer that could use natural languages could read normal text, providing users with access to computer-generated summaries or reports synthesized from reading several text sources.

The second motivation for natural language research is that it will increase our understanding of how human languages and minds work. To develop the technology for a computer to use language, we must first be able to say specifically what language is. We must be able to say precisely how the concepts we wish to express can be represented in the computer. Building computer programs requires this precision and attention to detail. A programmed implementation of a theory of language can be used to identify flaws, inconsistencies and areas of incompleteness that may otherwise go unnoticed.

### 1.2 Research Strategies

Two research strategies are in use for conducting natural language processing research: the isolated phenomena strategy and the entire system strategy. The first strategy tests specialized theories of restricted language phenomena, for example, analysis of syntactic structure of sentences or identifying the referents for pronouns. Programs are written to show that the theory can make some contribution to language understanding in the proper context. This strategy works best when isolated phenomena are being considered. Studying isolated phenomena promotes a deep understanding of them. One criticism of the isolated phenomena strategy is that in focusing on a subproblem of natural language processing, other subproblems must be assumed solvable by some other methods. Sometimes the other problems, whose solutions have been "assumed away," are difficult to solve. The danger is that attention may unwittingly be focused on the easy or less crucial problems, leaving the difficult ones unattended.

Another criticism of the isolated phenomena strategy is that success is difficult to measure. Evaluation must rely primarily on plausibility arguments. Without demonstrative evaluation, deficiencies and inconsistencies in a large piece of work may easily go undetected.

The second research strategy designs and builds entire natural language processing programs. This strategy is closer to engineering research than to pure science. For a given allotment of research resources, less can be applied to particular subproblems than with the isolated phenomena strategy. It may also become mired in implementing many mundane programs, as well as numerous interesting ones. The entire system strategy, however, is protected against assuming away the major problems or concentrating on nonessentials. Because the entire system strategy requires some attention to the complete range of language analysis, major problems receive attention first. Another advantage of this strategy is that it lends itself to impartial evaluation. Because an entire system must be built to "do something"—whether answering questions, generating summaries, or conducting fact searches—some way must be found to test whether it can do it and to measure how well it is done.

## 1.3 Methodology

The methodology of natural language processing research is straightforward: develop a theory and program it, then study the behavior of the resulting program for flaws in the theory. The cycle starts again with a revised or altogether new theory and a corresponding program.

It sounds much easier than it is. One is not entirely free in forming his or her theories, because the theories will have to be programmed. The human brain is much more complex than any computer in existence, so computer implementations must, at best, be partial models of how the human mind works. The programs written to implement theories of language and cognition tend to be as large as the computer technology will readily allow. As a result, the programming arc of the cycle may require several man-years of effort. Finally, it is not clear how we should study the behavior of the resulting programs, to characterize their achievements and understand their flaws.

To help give the flavor of the methodology of natural language research, a case study of one rather straightforward question-answering program written by the author several years ago will be presented. It is given not for the value of the natural language processor itself, but as a vehicle for discussing how research is done in the field. Following the description is a critique of its performance. The program description concentrates primarily on its positive aspects, as, for the most part, do all the case studies in this book. The critique of the Automatic Advisor should put it into better perspective.

### 1.4 Case Study: The Automatic Advisor

The Automatic Advisor is a natural language processor that got its name from the first application of the system. It was designed to be a natural language processing system that could easily be applied to different domains of discourse. The first domain was a database consisting of the course descriptions and requirements of the engineering college of a university. The system was designed to operate on databases in the form of a simplified semantic net, a network of items (nodes in the network), with relationships between the items (directed links between nodes). Implementation of the system is totally restricted to this database structure, but the general architecture could be adapted to other database organizations. A small fragment of the database is shown in Figure 1.1.

The language processor works by first scanning the input sentence for words and phrases that correspond to the named items and relations. An item and a relation pair indicate an item (or a set of them) to return as an answer. For example, if the sentence

1) What is the name of the infe 210?

were given, the relation NAME OF and the item INFE 210 would be identified. The rest of the words in the sentence are examined and all

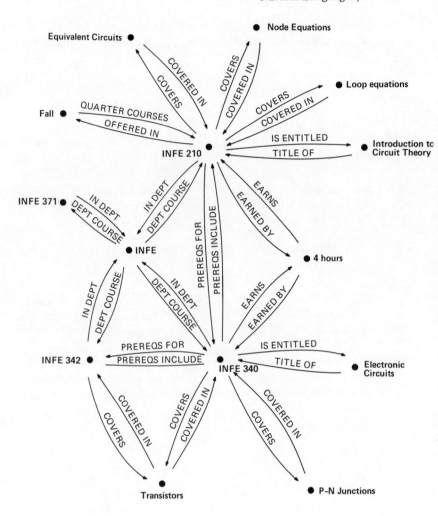

**Figure 1.1**

must conform to a syntax (sentence grammar). By checking the syntax and accounting for the function of all the words in the sentence, one has some assurance that the sentences that can be analyzed at all are analyzed correctly. If the program picked out only the item and relation names, and ignored the rest of the sentence, it would be easy to misinterpret sentences. Sentence 1 indicates a network fragment:

● ————————→ ●

?   NAME OF   INFE 210

To find the answer to this query , the inverse relation of NAME OF is found in the dictionary. It is IS ENTITLED. Then, the set of nodes linked to the node named INFE 210, through the link named IS ENTITLED, is returned as the answer. In the case of IS ENTITLED, there is only one node—the title—whose name is INTRODUCTION TO CIRCUIT THEORY. The Automatic Advisor then concatenates the names in the node, link, node triple to return the answer:

2) INTRODUCTION TO CIRCUIT THEORY IS THE TITLE OF INFE 210.

When the answer is generated, synonyms for the node and link names that are more amenable to the syntax of the answer are used. In this question, IS THE TITLE OF has been substituted for NAME OF.

In spite of the simple design of this natural language processor, it does allow several interesting modes of question answering. First, although it is checked, the syntax of the sentence is not as important as the occurrence of phrases corresponding to items and relations. Users commonly abbreviate their questions to forms that violate the rules of formal syntax with inputs such as:

3) INFE 210 NAME
4) COVERED IN INFE 212
5) INFE 240

These questions are handled by recognizing an item (INFE 210) and a relation (NAME), a relation (COVERED IN) and an item (INFE 212), or just an item (INFE 240). When a sentence consists of only an item, everything that is known about the item is displayed. It should be pointed out here that NAME and NAME OF are not synonyms. A NAME relation points from a course to a title, while NAME OF points from a title to a course. The synonym used for NAME when generating answers is IS ENTITLED, whereas for NAME OF it is IS THE TITLE OF. Figure 1.2 illustrates this difference.

Notice that after a question with an item and a relation is answered, the result is a new set of items. This consistency allows the system to handle embedded clauses. This is a powerful capability, since data elements whose names are not known to the user are often specified by their descriptions. In

6) What is the name of the course that covers p-n junctions?

The user has not specified a course by name, but by what it covers. The relative clause, "that covers p-n junctions," consists of the relation COVERS and the item P-N JUNCTIONS. This inner clause (relation-item pair) is resolved, and the user is informed:

7) INFE 240 COVERS P-N JUNCTIONS.

The set of answer items—in this case, just INFE 240—is used in place of the relative clause and noun, with "infe 240" being used in place of "course" to make the new sentence:

8) What is the name of infe 240?

The question is then answered with

9) INTRODUCTION TO SOLID STATE DEVICES IS THE TITLE OF INFE 240.

Relative clauses can modify nouns, as in the example above. Another common method of description is noun-noun modification. The

Figure 1.2

question in the example above would have had the same meaning if stated as:

10) What is the name of the p-n junction course?

In this phrasing, the item name P-N JUNCTION is modifying the noun *course*. To handle this sort of modification, there must be a method of deducing that "the p-n junction course" is a reference to INFE 240. This is done by using semantic markers. Each relation in the system is assigned a pair of item types that it connects. The relation IS THE TITLE OF connects a [TITLE] type item to a [COURSE] item. IS ENTITLED connects a [COURSE] to a [TITLE], IS COVERED IN connects a [TOPIC] and [COURSE]. Every noun in the system that is not an item name is also given a semantic marker. The noun *course* has the marker [COURSE]. The noun *lectures* also has the marker [COURSE]. When an item name is found modifying a noun, like "p-n junction course," the pair of semantic markers of this item name, in this case [TOPIC], and noun, in this case [COURSE], specifies a set of relations. Any of the relations that relate [TOPIC] and [COURSE] items could be implied by this phrase. In this domain, only one relation connects a [TOPIC] to a [COURSE], and that is IS COVERED IN. The meaning of "p-n junction course" is assumed to be "p-n junction is covered in." This item-relation pair is replaced with the answer set INFE 240. The original question becomes "what is the name of infe 240" as with the relative clause. This relation-item pair is then resolved and the answer is generated.

The marker-specifying noun is sometimes deleted. A course covering transistors may be referred to informally as "transistors" rather than "the transistor course" or its formal name, "Introduction to Electronic Devices." When a relation-item pair is found, the appropriate one of the pair of semantic markers of the relation is compared to the marker of the item. In

11) What does transistors earn?

the relation EARN is expected to connect a [COURSE] to a [CREDIT]. Instead of a [COURSE], it finds a [TOPIC] item, "transistors."

A relation that can link a [TOPIC] to a course . . . is searched for. IS COVERED IN is found, and the question changed so that the credit earned by each course that has TRANSISTORS as a topic is printed along with the course. Using one semantic type where a different type is expected is called coercion.

Pronouns can be handled in the Automatic Advisor using the same semantic marker mechanism. Whenever an item is encountered by the system, either in a user's question or as a set of answer items, it is entered on a list. If a set of items is encountered, the entire set is added to the list as a unit. This list of items and sets of items are used to find what pronouns refer to.

12) What is the name of infe 210?

13) INTRODUCTION TO CIRCUIT THEORY IS THE TITLE OF INFE 210.

14) What does it earn?

In the dialog above, three items have been referred to. INFE 210 has been referred to twice, INTRODUCTION TO CIRCUIT THEORY has been referred to, and some as yet undetermined item has been referred to by "it." In sentence 14 "earn" is recognized as a relation relating a [COURSE] to a [CREDIT] item. The syntax of the question specifies that the user wants to know what the [CREDIT] is of the item referred to by "it." Consequently, "it" must refer to a [COURSE]. The list of items most recently referred to is checked for the last reference to a [COURSE], which in this case is INFE 210. The question can now be answered:

15) INFE 210 EARNS 4 HOURS.

The Automatic Advisor can   also deal with embedded relations and relations and items joined with conjunctions. For example,

16) What are the names of the prerequisites of infe 375?

is handled by finding the set of prerequisites of INFE 375 first, and then finding the names of each course in that set.

17) What are the names of and prerequisites of infe 375 and
· infe 340

This question is answered by forming a set of items consisting of INFE 375 and INFE 340. The prerequisites of both members of this set are found and a response is printed; then the same is done for the names of both courses in the set.

The Automatic Advisor worked reasonably well in its domain of engineering courses (more about this in the next section). Most of the linguistic mechanisms deal only with relations and items. Therefore, a natural language processor of the same power, but for another database with a similar structure, can be built in just the time it takes to make the database. This was done for a bibliographic database, allowing reference to sources by author, title, source, date, and content. Within four hours from the conception of the project, the adapted Automatic Advisor was answering English questions pertaining to the bibliographic database.

## 1.5 Critique of the Automatic Advisor

Since the author wrote the Automatic Advisor and has used it, this section will discuss some of its many shortcomings. Unfortunately, the same kind of criticism is not possible for the other natural language programs found in this book. They all have their shortcomings—just as the Automatic Advisor does—but it has not been common practice for the designers to discuss the limitations of natural language programs. When reading the literature on natural language processors, readers are presented with a discussion much like the one above for the Automatic Advisor. Readers should be aware that the kind of criticisms made here about the Automatic Advisor could be made about all current natural language processors; they must therefore beware when reading about other systems. The faults are there—they just have not been identified by the program designers. Furthermore, programs written as research projects tend to be short lived. They are resident on computers whose hardware, operating system, and compilers are being changed constantly. Inevitably, some of these changes will render a large program like a natural language processor unusable. If there is not sufficient interest in the program to constantly keep it compatible with the system on which it resides, it soon becomes unusable. The half-life is about a year for very large programs. As a result, if the description of natural language processors does not discuss their performance limitations, they will probably never be known.

The author performed an experiment with the Automatic Advisor. Several problems were constructed that should have been answerable from the database. In one problem, the subject was given copies of the title page and table of contents of several textbooks used in some of the engineering courses covered by the Automatic Advisor. The subject's problem was to identify the courses that would probably use these books as texts. A second problem was concerned with scheduling. The subject was asked if three particular courses could be taken in the same quarter. They were upper-level courses, and the subject was directed to take into account that all prerequisites had to be taken in proper sequence and a maximum load of 12 hours was allowed per quarter. A third problem asked the user to find a three-hour course to take in the spring semester.

The database problems were used primarily to give the subjects something to talk about to the program. Transcripts of the conversations were analyzed to get an idea of where the weaknesses of the Automatic Advisor were. One class of errors was that the test subjects had many ways of phrasing their questions and statements that the program could not understand. If the utterances had been reworded appropriately, the equivalent rewordings could have been understood. These errors represent inadequacies in what is called the linguistic coverage of the program. Another class of errors involved the subjects saying things that could not have been understood, no matter how they were reworded. The subjects were referring to concepts that the Automatic Advisor simply could not deal with. This second class of errors are inadequacies in the conceptual coverage of the program.

The minimal requirement for a natural language processor is that users can express themselves within the domain of the system. This is a minimal requirement for all natural language processors that are going to be used. All of the programs described in this book are research exercises, and so one might excuse them from not meeting it (which they do not). Instead, a program developed for research should demonstrate the *capability* of meeting the minimal requirement. The assumption is that all of the necessary machinery could be programmed into a natural language processor, but large and uninteresting tasks like expanding the vocabulary from 2,000 words to 10,000 words have not been done. Unfortunately, no method other than actual use has yet been devised that could determine whether a program is based on a sufficiently sophisticated design so that it could be capable of meeting the minimal requirement.

The Automatic Advisor does not meet the minimal requirement. When subjects attempted to use it, they usually had great difficulties in doing so.

Table 1.1 gives a list of sentences that have been interpreted properly by the Automatic Advisor. They appear to represent a fairly broad range of natural language processing capabilities. One finds simple questions (1), elliptical phrases (3, 4), conjunctions (5), pronouns (7), and embedded queries (9, 10). These examples suggest that they might be representative of a useful natural language processor, but do not be misled!

---

**Table 1.1  Sample sentences handled by the Automatic Advisor**

---

1. What courses deal with communications?
2. Give me the Fourier transform courses that are offered in the fall.
3. Courses on communications.
4. Cover communications.
5. What are the prerequisites of infe 210 and math 195?
6. Do any courses cover p-n junctions?
7. When are they offered?
8. How many courses cover computers?
9. What is covered by the courses that they are prerequisites for?
10. Courses that are prerequisites of courses that cover information theory.
11. I have taken infe 340 and infe 341.
12. Can I take infe 371?

---

FAILURES DUE TO LINGUISTIC COVERAGE

1) What courses cover digital computers?
2) What courses cover digital design?
3) What courses deal with control systems?

All three sentences failed because of an inadequate vocabulary. "Digital computers" is unknown, but use of "computers" alone would have worked. (It does not know about analog computers.) There are also synonyms for "digital design" and "control systems." Performance could be improved by adding more synonyms to the dictionary. This would decrease the probability of a user typing in words or phrases that are unknown to the program. It is not a certain cure, however. For one thing, there are many synonyms for most concepts. Attempting to enumerate all of them for all the concepts in the system is a rather ambitious goal. Also, synonyms rarely have precisely the same meaning; they may be synonymous in one context, but not another. The Automatic Advisor is not prepared to take the context into account, so a large number of synonyms could cause new problems. The more synonyms that are in the dictionary, the higher the probability of misinterpretation in context.

Notice that the examples of failures look very much like the sentences that were handled appropriately. Without the explanatory narrative, one might not be able to tell them apart. This means that the users would have significant difficulty trying to determine what language they can use confidently.

4) Aren't there any courses on control?

The analysis of sentence 4 failed because the "aren't there" construction is not included in the syntax rules. This form could be added rather easily. The syntactic analysis capabilities of the Automatic Advisor, while not simplistic, is far from sophisticated. There is some evidence for extending the linguistic coverage of the Automatic Advisor by adding more syntactic rules. It could probably be made nearly complete for syntax, that is, the probability of a user entering a sentence considered syntactically acceptable but the program failing to handle it because of its syntax could be a few percent or less. It may be possible, but it would still be a major task and probably not worth doing, given the other limitations of the program.

5) What is covered in infe 311 and 312?
6) What are the prerequisites of infe 340, infe 376 and math 324?

The Automatic Advisor failed on sentences 5 and 6 because of the conjunctions. In sentence 5, there is an implied "infe" as in, "infe 311 and (infe) 312." The program could be extended to handle such cases, and probably even be made nearly complete. Sentence 6 failed because the program requires an "and" between each member of a conjoined list (e.g., "infe 340 and infe 376 and math 324"). This change would be almost trivial.

7) Are any of them worth 3 hours?
8) What is the credit given for them?

The pronouns in sentences 7 and 8, "them" in both cases, were unresolvable. It would be straightforward to accommodate the pronouns in these examples. The problem of pronominal reference in general is rather difficult (see chapter 4). The Automatic Advisor presents an inhospitable environment for implementing a more complete treatment. Although the pronoun resolution techniques in the implementation described here work sometimes, they do fail quite frequently.

## FAILURES DUE TO CONCEPTUAL COVERAGE

The sentences in this section failed because the Automatic Advisor did not know what the user was talking about. They are conceptual coverage failures. In some cases the sentences would have failed for linguistic coverage reasons, in spite of the conceptual coverage problems.

9) Linear analysis

The first query, "linear analysis," meaning, "tell me what you know about linear analysis," failed because there is no such concept in the program. That is due to the fact that the database was written from catalog descriptions of courses. Linear analysis is an idea germane to several of the courses described in the database, but since it was not in the catalog, it is not in the database. This is certainly a poor way to approach the problem of defining the conceptual coverage for a natural language program, but it is not uncommon. A more reasonable approach may include using the textbooks for the courses or interviewing a sample of the expected user population.

10a) What do infe 210 and infe 211 cover? [handled appropriately]
10b) What are the prerequisites? [not handled]

Question 10b is an interesting failure. It refers to the context established in 10a but notice that 10a does not even mention prerequisites. "*The* prerequisites" implies that there are some particular prerequisites that the user has in mind. If 10a had been followed by something like, "When are *the courses* offered" (which would also have failed), the problem would have been easier. "*The* courses" implies some particular courses; the ones mentioned in the previous sentence are the obvious choices. The proper selection can be made in the same way that pronoun resolution is done.

Instead, the user asked for "the prerequisites." In order to understand the query, the analyzer must recognize that nothing has been mentioned as a prerequisite, but the focus of the conversation is on courses, and courses have prerequisites. The user probably means the prerequisites of the courses that were just mentioned. It would take considerable toil to enable the Automatic Advisor to handle references like the one in 10b, and the completeness of the result is doubtful. Mechanisms developed for this sort of reference are mentioned in chapter 6.

11) What courses have to come before infe 340?
12) What courses have to be taken before infe 340?
13) What must I take in order to be able to take infe 340?
14) What comes before math 195?

The above questions form an interesting series. The subject started out by asking for the prerequisites for infe 340, but misspelled "prerequisite." The question was rejected on that basis (many natural language programs have incorporated spelling correction procedures to guard against this common problem, but the Automatic Advisor˙ does not have one). The hapless subject did not notice the spelling error, but assumed that the program did not know what "prerequisite" meant. The subject tried to clarify it, but only got in deeper.

The Automatic Advisor attempts to capitalize on its limited realm of discourse by assuming that users will restrict their vocabulary to the information-rich domain specific words. Nearly all natural language processors do effectively the same thing in one form or another, but perhaps not always to the same degree as this one. The rephrasings that the user intended as simplifications could only work if the concept referenced by the word "prerequisite" were a structure similar to the structure synthesized from all phrases like "what one must take before he is able to take." Two phrases with similar conceptual structures would be synonymous. The conceptual representation in the Automatic Advisor is so simple as to be incapable of representing the necessary degree of detail.

15) The other ones I just mentioned.
16) Let's see the infe courses offered in the spring again.
17) Is that everything on infe 347?

The dialog between a question-answering system and a user is not limited to asking about the database. Once the dialog begins, the dialog itself, or components of it, may become a topic of conversation. Sentences 15-17 each refer to concepts that are defined by the fact that the user and the program have been conducting a dialog. Dialog events have occurred sequentially in time, and there are objects that are meaningful only in the dialog context. "That" in sentence 17 referred to an entire video screen full of data which had been accumulated through a series of questions and answers. That chunk of data was a meaningful unit only in terms of the dialog which generated it. These questions are far beyond the conceptual coverage of the Automatic Advisor. It has no representation of the concept of a dialog.

    18) You mean you do not know when math 195 is offered
    19) So all I need is junior standing and math 195

When people conduct dialogs to get information, they do more than just a semi-infinite loop of ask a question, get an answer, ask a question. . . . There is more give and take involved as the questioner tries to understand the answer he or she has been given. The answerer tries to make sure he or she has been understood. The questioner considers the implications of the answer and composes follow-up questions accordingly. Sentences 18 and 19 failed because the Automatic Advisor is not prepared to conduct dialogs the way people want to conduct them. As far as it is concerned, once it has printed the answer to a query it is finished. If the user cannot understand the response, that is too bad for the user. But the whole motivation for a computer system for information retrieval is ultimately to facilitate *understanding* of the information, not just retrieval. Developing a technology directed toward facilitating understanding is really what this whole book is about.

### References and Further Reading

Mann, W.C. "Improving Methodology in Natural Language Processing." In *Theoretical Issues in Natural Language Processing*. Cambridge, Mass.: Bolt Beranek and Newman Inc., June 1975.

Petrick, S.R. "On Natural Language Based Computer Systems." *IBM Journal of Research and Development* (July 1976): 314-25.

Tennant, H.R. "Experience with the Evaluation of Natural Language Question Answerers," to appear in *Proceedings of the International Joint Conference on Artificial Intelligence*. 1979.

_____. "The Automatic Advisor." M.S. Thesis, University of Illinois at Chicago Circle, 1977.

Watt, W.C. "Habitability." *American Documentations* (July 1968): 338-51.

Wilks, Y. "Methodology in A1 and Natural Language Understanding." In *Theoretical Issues in Natural Language Processing*. Cambridge, Mass: Bolt Beranek and Newman Inc., June 1975.

Woods, W.A. "A Personal View of Natural Language Understanding." *Sigart Newsletter*, No. 61, Feb., 1977.

____. "Some Methodological Issues in Natural Language Understanding." In *Theoretical Issues in Natural Language Processing*. Cambridge, Mass.: Bolt Beranek and Newman Inc., June 1975.

# 2. Early Natural Language Programs

Early attempts at natural language processing were concerned with finding small sets of general rules for understanding language. This is contrasted with more recent programs (from about 1970 to the present) which were more concerned with the subtle nuances of language and with finding a large number of specific rules which take more of the special cases into account. The appeal of finding a small set of general rules is obvious, but it did not work very well. The change in the point of view of intelligence as primarily computation based to primarily memory based (as a large set of rules must be) occurred not only in natural language work, but in artificial intelligence in general.

Another fundamental difference between the early programs and the later ones was the way in which computer technology had changed. A researcher in 1960 who had wanted to model language as memory based would have had little support from the computer. Primary memory was typically measured in the thousands of words as opposed to the millions of words. Not only was it not possible to store a large knowledge structure in primary memory, but often much of the program itself was stored on secondary memory.

Until the middle or end of the 1960s secondary storage was typically magnetic tape. Virtual memory was nonexistent. This contrasts with current secondary storage implemented on much faster disks. Today a user may enjoy a virtual address space of more than 1 billion words, a six-order of magnitude difference; access time is about five orders of magnitude faster. Many computer users also have access to archival memory, adding a couple more orders of magnitude to the total.

The researcher's task was made even more difficult in the early days by the comparative dearth of software support. Debugging was something done on punched cards while hunched over a line printer watching a core dump being printed out. Languages were much less sophisticated—LISP was just being developed.

A present-day hobbyist who bought a computer under the guise of gaining information processing services like balancing checkbooks or computing income tax, has better hardware to study natural language than the researcher had in the early 1960s.

## 2.1 Computation-Based Natural Language Processing

Computation-based language processing, although seldom the subject of current research, does have some positive attributes. Part of the natural language processing problem can be approached from this point of view.

The task of understanding language can be considered to have two components: recognizing the concepts that are referred to, and being able to deal with the diverse ways in which users refer to concepts. Representing a range of concepts is primarily a memory-based task. It is often possible, however, to embody some knowledge in general deduction rules, trading memory for computation. For example, let us say that all dogs are expected to have four legs and a tail, and Sheba and Tip are dogs. We could duplicate the leg and tail information in the attributes of Sheba and Tip. It is preferable, however, to factor out the commonalities of the class of dogs and store them all in one place, among the description of what a dog is. The descriptions of Sheba and Tip include the fact that they are dogs. A deduction rule is needed that says that if A is an element in the set B, then A inherits the attributes of B that define the set. So some memory can be traded for computation, but if the range of concepts known to the system is large, it will probably still use a lot of memory.

On the other hand, much of the grammar of English is computation based. The grammar specifies that a sentence is composed of a noun phrase and verb phrase. A noun phrase is composed of adjectives, a noun, and prepositional phrases or relative clauses (e.g., the boy *who burned down the barn*). The grammar, for the most part, works with parts of speech—noun, verb, adjective, etc. Since it uses few data elements, it could be mainly computation based. A complete grammar of English would, of course, be a forbidding task, but a small portion could be programmed on a small computer to handle a majority of the grammatical constructs of sentences given to it.

To summarize, a computation-based program could be written to accept from users statements or questions that have a limited conceptual range. A limited conceptual range can be thought of as a limited vocabulary. However, the syntax (grammar) employed by the users could be quite free.

The early natural language programs had to differ from the programs that came 15 to 20 years later, because of the computing technology on which they were implemented. In 1962, using an IBM 650, it would have been absurd to consider building the kind of programs that are being built today. This is a humbling thought with respect to current natural language work. Computation is becoming less costly today at as fast a rate as ever. Memory is quickly getting cheaper, so large memories by today's standards will certainly seem pitifully inadequate a few decades from now.

## Machine Translation

As soon as computers became available in the early 1950s, there was a strong interest in using them for translating text from one language to another. Claims for the proficiency of machine translation, as it is called, proliferated. The United States federal government was enthusiastic and funded the research heavily. Attention in the United States concentrated on translating newspapers and technical material from Russian, French or German to English. A similar effort was under way in the Soviet Union and in Europe. Research in the Soviet Union was particularly interesting. They had made a strong commitment to the field, with a large number of researchers actively involved in the field. In addition, where United States machine translation dealt with translating three source languages into English, research in the Soviet Union studied the translation of about twenty languages—both from these languages into Russian and from Russian into the other languages. Remarkably, this enthusiasm for machine translation was maintained in spite of the fact that they had very few computers available for testing their theories. Much of the work was done by hand simulating translation programs!

Knowledge of the nature of language has increased dramatically in the past thirty years. When the machine translation effort was started, however, little linguistic theory relevant to machine translation was available. What was available was sometimes either ignored because of the impracticality of programming it on the limited machines of the day or ignored in favor of finding a quicker solution using the brute computing power of the machine.

Translation was viewed largely as word by word substitution with complications. When translating from Russian to English, for example, each Russian word would be looked up in a dictionary and its English equivalent added to the translation. The complications included differences in the grammatical structures and word meanings between the languages. Given any pair of languages, many words in one language will not have an exact equivalent in the other. The Eskimo language, for example, has seven words for "snow," each describing a different kind of snow. One can imagine that a language of Indians of the Amazon jungle may not have any words for snow, never having seen it; translating a text on snow conditions from Eskimo to Amazon Indian would obviously not be straight word by word substitution. This example is extreme, of course, but the principle holds for nearly all pairs of languages.

Languages differ structurally. Russian has no articles, so a translator must insert "a," "an" or "the" in the English translation when the text indicates that they are necessary.

Most words have more than one meaning or sense. A word-by-word translation does not give any clue as to which sense is intended; that must be determined from context. Furthermore, the set of senses for a word in one language may not be the same as the set of senses for a corresponding word in another language. The most familiar example of this sort of failure is in translating the aphorism "The spirit is willing but the flesh is weak" from English to Russian, then back to English. One result was "The wine is agreeable, but the meat has spoiled."

The complications to word-by-word translation were largely handled in the early systems with special rules for structural- or meaning-related problems. However, they were neither sufficiently powerful nor sufficiently general to make machine translation effective.

In spite of these difficulties, machine translation gained momentum. Researchers were claiming that fully automatic high-quality translators were near at hand. They were encouraged by their partial successes, the rapid increase in computer capacity and perhaps ignorance of the true difficulties of the problem. Commercial ventures were started, and the claims became even stronger. Many were actively taking orders, but few were able to deliver high quality translations. By the mid-1960s United States federal funding had reached $20 million, and a study was done of the effectiveness of machine translation. The results of the study indicated that machine translation could not match its claims. The study also concluded that there was no immediate prospect for the emergence of a high-quality, fully automatic machine translator. It was concluded that the high level of funding was not justified.

This study was highly controversial. Claims were made that it had used the results of outdated research and had been oriented toward immediately useful systems rather than progress in a field of research. In spite of the controversy, the effect of the study was to reduce drastically the level of funding for machine translation in the United States. Machine translation in Europe and the Soviet Union have continued.

Some attempts at machine translation have been made in the United States recently, but with much more modest claims; these will be discussed in later chapters under Preference Semantics and SAM. Other work in machine translation, not discussed further in this book, has taken the more modest goal of man-machine symbiosis in translation.

## 2.2 Case Study: BASEBALL

### QUERY LANGUAGE

BASEBALL (Green, et al. 1963) was a question-answering program that answered questions on the month, day, place, teams and scores for each American League baseball game in one year. The data was organized into fields as follows:

    Month
    Place
    Day
    Game serial number
    (Team, score)
    (Team, score)

The parentheses around (team, score) indicate that each team is associated with its own score.

The database was queried by specifying a number of attribute-value pairs. For example,

    Place = ?
    Team = Red Sox
    Month = July
    Day = 7

retrieved all the places that the Red Sox played on July 7.

Attaching modifiers to attribute names increased the power of the query language significantly. For example, the attribute Team has a team name value. Team modified by "number of" has an integer value—it counts the number of teams in a list. The query language also allowed embedded queries. With this facility, the result of one query could be used in answering a second query. For example,

    DAY = EACH
    MONTH = JULY
    TEAM = ?

prepared 31 lists, one for each day in July. The list for a particular day was composed of all the teams that played on that day. The subsequent query

    DAY = ?
    MONTH = JULY
    TEAM (NUMBER OF) = 8

used the result of the previous query to prepare a list of all the days on which the list of teams that played equals 8. These queries were used to answer the question

"(on how many days) (in July) did (eight (teams)) play?"

> DAY (NUMBER OF) = ?
> MONTH = JULY
> TEAM (NUMBER OF) = 8

## SYNTAX

Syntactic analysis proceeded first by scanning the sentence for idioms like "New York" and "Red Sox." The idioms (or compound words, as they are sometimes called) were replaced by single words that represented them. The sentence was then scanned *from right to left* to bracket noun phrases, prepositional phrases and adverbial phrases. Any prepositions that were left without objects were attached to the first noun phrase in the sentence. The subject and object were then located. This was done differently for active and passive verbs. If the last verb in the sentence was a main verb (not an auxiliary) and if it was preceded by a form of "be," then the sentence was considered to be passive. Otherwise it was active. The subject of sentences with passive verbs were the noun phrases that were objects of the preposition "by." The object of passive sentences was the first noun phrase that was not the object of a preposition. In,

1) What teams were beaten by the Red Sox?

"were beaten" indicates passive, "by" indicates that "Red Sox" is the subject and "teams" is the object. For active verbs, the subject was the noun phrase between the main verb and auxiliary, if there was such a noun phrase. The first noun phrase not in a prepositional phrase was the object.

2) How many games did the Yankees play in July?

"The Yankees" is the subject of sentence 2 and "how many games" is the object. If there was not a noun phrase between the auxiliaries and main verb of an active sentence, the first free noun phrase is the subject and the second the object:

3) What teams won 10 games in July?

Subject: "what teams"; object: 10 games.

## SEMANTICS

After syntactic analysis, the question was analyzed for semantic components. First, if there were words whose meaning depended on context, procedures associated with those words were run to determine the intended meanings. In

4) Did Boston beat Cincinnati on July 7?

Boston and Cincinnati are taken to indicate teams. In another context they could indicate where a game was played.

Next, procedures associated with modifiers were run to take the modifiers into account in the query.

| | |
|---|---|
| team | TEAM = |
| what team | TEAM = ? |
| winning team | TEAM (winning) = |
| each team | TEAM = EACH |

Verbs could also modify the meanings of constituents of the query. "Beat" had an associated procedure so that the subject and object were designated as the winning and losing teams. The query constituents for the sentence,

"Who beat the Yankees on July 4?"

are shown below before and after the application of the "beat" procedure:

| *Before* | | *After* |
|---|---|---|
| WHO | → TEAM = ? | TEAM(winning) = ? |
| YANKEES | → TEAM = YANKEES | TEAM(losing) = YANKEES |
| JULY | → MONTH = JULY | MONTH = JULY |
| 4 | → DAY = 4 | DAY = 4 |

## 2.3 Case Study: SAD–SAM

### AD HOC REPRESENTATION

SAD–SAM, Sentence Appraiser and Diagrammer-Semantic Analyzing Machine (Lindsay 1963), analyzed statements in English about kinship relations, and represented those relations in a tree structure. One of the primary assertions of this work also inspired its strongest criticism. Lindsay asserted that by representing kinship relations in a tree structure, many relationships that have not been explicitly asserted can nevertheless be found in the data structure. If the assertions "John is the son of Bill" and "Mary is the daughter of Bill" have been assimilated into the memory, the following structure has been built:

FAMILY UNIT 1
 HUSBAND: Bill
 WIFE: unknown
 OFFSPRING: John, Mary
 HUSBAND's PARENTS: unknown
 WIFE's PARENTS: unknown

The fact that Mary and John are siblings is now immediately available without its ever having been explicitly asserted (the system does not allow multiple marriages which would make the sibling deduction not always true). Lindsay suggested that this capability of an understander to know more than it has been told is an essential component of intelligent systems. SAD-SAM's ability to understand more than it had been told was based on a data structure that was analogous to the relationships it described. Later systems used more explicit deductive mechanisms in cases where a simple data structure analogy was not adequate.

## ANALYSIS

SAD-SAM could accept the vocabulary of Basic English (of course, many things can be said in Basic English that SAD-SAM could not understand). The analysis routines first got a syntactic parse of the sentence through a combination of bottom-up and top-down parsing. For example, there were no expectations at the beginning of the sentence. If the first word was "the," elements of a noun phrase were expected to follow. Some parsers still work this way.

After completion of the syntactic parse, the sentence was scanned for any of the eight kinship words that occur in the vocabulary. When a kinship word was found, the parse tree was examined for modifiers that included proper names such as "Jane's brother" or "the father of John." Forms of "be" were located to establish equivalence as in "John's father, Bill, is Mary's father." A list of elementary relationships was then collected from the sentence and used to augment the tree.

Lindsay defended his use of a memory structure designed specially for representing kinship with the argument that more general memory representations will pay for their generality in greater difficulty in retrieval and inference. This must be so since a more general representation allows the data elements to be related in many more ways than a specially designed representation. However, many of the relationships possible in a more general representation are of no interest for any one particular problem. Also, since we introspectively feel that we approach different problems in different ways, it may be that we use problem-specific information representations rather than the same structure for all problems.

## 2.4 Case Study: SYNTHEX

### PROTOSYNTHEX

SYNTHEX, SYNTHesis of complEX verbal behavior (Simmons 1965, 1966; Simmons et al. 1962), was a system designed for retrieval of facts from a database of English text. The text was the *Golden Book Encyclopedia*. Questions from children's quiz books were used to exercise the system (however, the performance of the prototype incarnation, PROTOSYNTHEX, was not described). An inverted index of the text was made of all the words other than prepositions, conjunctions, article adjectives and pronouns (they called these "function" words).

Each word in the index pointed to a list of all the locations in the text where the word occurred. The locations of word occurrences in the text were described by the volume, article, paragraph and sentence in which they occurred. It was simplified by combining lists of references to synonyms. Synonyms were either added manually to the system or found automatically. The automatic synonym procedures looked for words that had initial substrings that agreed. The substrings from where disagreement started were checked against a list of acceptable suffixes. If the suffixes were appropriate to synonyms, the candidate words were checked against a list of words that were exceptions to the suffix test. "-Ish" is a legal suffix as in "fool" and "foolish," but "finish" is not a synonym of "fin"; "finish" would have been stored as an exception. This process equates the meaning of such words as "farmer," "farmers," "farming," "farmlands," "farm" and "farms."

When a question was given to the system, its content words were identified and the question was given a brief syntactic analysis. The index was then searched for each of the content words in the question, and the resulting lists of references from each of the content words in the question were intersected to find the smallest units of text in which they occurred. A score was given to each find based on the frequencies of the content words. The highest scoring text fragments were then analyzed syntactically to eliminate such mismatches as "Boys fly kites" for the question "How do kites fly (content words are underlined). Human operator interaction was often required to resolve ambiguities. For the question,

> What do worms eat?

facts found in complete syntactic agreement with the question are,

> Worms eat grass
> Grass is eaten by worms

Partial agreement:

> Worms eat their way through the ground
> Horses with worms eat grain

No agreement:

> Birds eat worms.

SYNTHEX was designed to work on a large body of text with a large vocabulary, and do so with a small computer. The data was stored on magnetic tape. The syntactic analysis was primarily a computational task rather than memory look up. Parts of speech were identified by using either a 300-word vocabulary of function words, by inflectional endings (e.g., _____er → noun, _____ly → adverb), or by the context of the content words (a few words on each side of the content words). It also had a dictionary of about 1,500 context words denoting plurals, irregular verbs and words with irregular suffixes.

The problem with this approach to question answering is that it is based on words. When humans communicate, we use words as a vehicle, but the actual communication is based on the concepts described by the words we use. Since the description of a concept can be worded in many different ways, it is unreliable and incomplete to attempt to identify occurrences of the description of a concept in text by searching for words that commonly name the concept. This was recognized in the work on SYNTHEX, as it was elsewhere. It was reported that the use of synonyms, thesauri, and the syntactic structure surrounding content words really did not help much. What was needed was a dictionary that described words in terms of class membership, attributes, associations and related actions.

## PROTOSYNTHEX II

Instead of the full text database that was used for PROTOSYNTHEX, the second prototype of SYNTHEX, PROTOSYNTHEX II, was composed of simple assertions of relationships. Class memberships linked an object name with the name of a class it belonged to. "Aardvarks" was linked to the classes "mammal" and "animal." Attributes linked an object to its characteristics. An attribute of "grass" is "green." Associations linked an object with its component objects. "John" is then associated with "nose" and "wallet" since he has both (no distinction was mentioned between an integral component and ownership that these two associations require).

Not only was the database put into the form of assertions, but the questions for PROTOSYNTHEX II also had to be in the form of simple assertions. Techniques were studied for transforming complex English sentences into simple assertions (called kernel sentences), but much of the PROTOSYNTHEX II research was done using text and questions that were transformed by hand. The kernel sentence representation of the question, "What are the paths of rockets or missiles called?" is:

Paths are what?
Someone calls paths.
Paths are of rockets.
Paths are of missiles.

If similar assertions were found in the database, the sentences they were derived from may have constituted an appropriate answer to the question. If the assertions from the question were not matched to those in the text, rules of inference were used. For example, some links are transitive: if X is_a W and W is_a Y, then X is_a Y. Other inference rules that could be used were inverse relations (e.g., X likes Y implies Y pleases X because "likes" and "pleases" are inverse links) and what was called "weak implication" operators. These latter are an attempt to include knowledge that is shared by listener and speaker (in this case database and question asker) that may be important to understanding. Examples are:

A eats B → B is inside of A
A is_above B → B is_below A
A struck B → B received a blow

Natural language researchers are still grappling with the problems suggested by weak implications.

## 2.5 Case Study: STUDENT

### SOLVING ALGEBRA STORY PROBLEMS

STUDENT (Bobrow 1968) was a program designed to analyze and solve algebra story problems. It operated by transforming the story problems into a set of algebraic expressions. If these expressions could be solved as a set of simultaneous equations, they would be solved and the answers printed out. If they could not be solved, several alternative methods were applied in sequence.

STUDENT's first alternative method was based on a collection of useful facts such as conversions between units of measure and formulas (distance equals rate times time). These facts were expressed as equations. If any such facts were relevant to the problem, the equations representing the appropriate facts were appended to the list of equations from the problem analysis. The equations were stored in a dictionary under the key words that implied that they might be useful. (Notice that some equations could be retrieved from the dictionary that had little to do with the solution of the particular problem being solved.) If the simultaneous equations still could not be solved in spite of the new equations, the problem statement was rescanned for the presence of idiom. If one was found, a paraphrase for the idiom was substituted, the analysis repeated, and a solution for the resulting equations sought again. If again no solution was found, the sentence was scanned for still another idiom or possibly a different substitution for a previously identified idiom. If idiom substitution did not result in a solvable set of equations, STUDENT asked the user for help.

## LANGUAGE ANALYSIS

The language analysis part of STUDENT was apparently designed for conceptual completeness rather than linguistic completeness. The only statement Bobrow made about its capabilities refers to its conceptual completeness:

> . . . though most algebra story problems found in standard texts cannot be solved by STUDENT exactly as written, the author has usually been able to find some paraphrase of almost all such problems which is solvable by STUDENT. [P.183]

Bobrow made a claim about the possibilities of the technique in spite of the limitations his version had:

> I believe that on a larger computer one could use these techniques to construct a system of practical value which would communicate well with people in English over the limited range of material understood by the program. [P.184]

The language analysis in STUDENT was done by reducing complex sentences to simpler ones and transforming these sentences into simultaneous equations. The first stage in analysis makes mandatory substitutions of some words and phrases to put the vocabulary in canonical form; "2 times" for "twice," "percent" for "per cent." Then the words in the sentence that correspond to mathematical operators, verbs, question words and certain other classes important in the analysis are tagged. The next step is the most significant. The problem statement is compared with sets of recursive templates to identify meaningful constructions. Consider the following problem:

If the number of customers Tom gets is twice the square of 20 per cent of the number of advertisements he runs, and the number of advertisements he runs is 45 what is the number of customers Tom gets?

In canonical form with tags:

If the number (OF/OP) customers Tom (GETS/VERB) is 2 (TIMES/OP 1) the (SQUARE/OP 1) 20 (PERCENT / OP 2) (OF/OP) the number (OF/OP) advertisements (HE/PRO) runs, and the number (OF/OP) advertisements (HE/PRO) runs is 45, (WHAT/QWORD) is the number (OF/OP) customers Tom (GETS/VERB) (QMARK/DLM)

Two template patterns matched to reduce the problem statement to simpler sentences. The first is [IF X1, (?/QWORD) X2 ] which separated the sentence into two sentences: {X1} and {(?/QWORD) X2} (which means the question word followed by string matching X2). The second template matched on the X1. It was [X2, and X2 ] and separated the two clauses, making two new sentences. After these have been applied to the problem statement, the resulting simple sentences are:

The number (OF/OP) customers Tom (GETS/VERB) is 2 (TIMES/OP 1) the (SQUARE/OP 1) 20 (PERCENT/OP 2) (OF/OP) the number (OF/OP) advertisements (HE/PRO) runs (PERIOD/DLM)

The number (OF/OP) advertisements (HE/PRO) runs is 45 (PERIOD/DLM)

(WHAT/QWORD) is the number (OF/OP) customers Tom (GETS/VERB) (QMARK/DLM)

The next step was to search for matches to templates that indicate equality, such as [X1 IS X2] (where X2 cannot begin with "multiplied by," "divided by" or some other such phrase). Then the operator templates were applied in the order of their precedence, e.g., multiplication before addition. The templates applied to this problem were:

[P1 K (PERCENT/OF 2) (OF/OP) P2]
  → P1 (DIVIDE K 100) P2
[P1 TIMES P2]
  → (TIMES P1 P2)
[SQUARE P1]
  → (EXPT P1 2)
[OF] → TIMES*
[WHAT IS P1]
  → Solve for P1

*"OF" does not always transform to "times." The context is checked to see that some other special case is not indicated such as "NUMBER OF"

After the application of these templates the problem statement has become:

(EQUAL (NUMBER OF CUSTOMERS TOM (GETS/VERB))
  (TIMES 2
    (EXPT (TIMES (DIVIDE 20
              100)
         (NUMBER OF ADVERTISEMENTS
         (HE/PRO) RUNS))
    2)))
(EQUAL (NUMBER OF ADVERTISEMENTS (HE/PRO) RUNS)
  45)
(SOLVE-FOR (NUMBER OF CUSTOMERS TOM (GETS/
VERB)))

The strings such as "number of advertisements (HE/PRO) runs" and "number of customers Tom (GETS/VERB)" are now used as variable names. In this case, each reference to each of these two variables is worded identically. Additional processing would be required if, for instance, "number of advertisements Tom runs" was used once and "number of advertisements he runs" was used the other time. Pronoun reference was checked only if the equations were unsolvable without it. When it was checked, the preceding variable names were checked for similarity to the one containing the pronoun. If they were "similar," they are equated. Criteria for similarity were not cited, but it is easy to imagine what they might be.

## 2.6 Case Study: DEACON

### DOMAIN-INDEPENDENT LANGUAGE ANALYSIS

DEACON, Direct English Access and CONtrol (Craig et al. 1966), was a natural language system designed to start with an input sentence and successively rewrite phrases of it until either the sentence had been fully analyzed or no more rules could be applied and the analysis failed. The rewrite rules dealt only with structural categories rather than with the actual words of the sentence. The goal was to make the language analysis as independent of the vocabulary and content of the domain of discourse as possible. This would facilitate the transfer of DEACON's language analysis techniques from one domain to another.

The database that DEACON used was based on intersecting ring structures. There were two kinds of rings: referent rings and connective rings. There was a referent ring for each concept that could be recognized by the system. Each relationship between concepts was indicated by a connective ring. DEACON's domain of discourse included information about the locations, commanders, functions and movements of military units. In this domain, typical referent rings were the following:

BATTALION
638TH (i.e., the 638th BATTALION)
522nd
436th
COMMANDER
FORT LEWIS
JONATHAN PARKER
LOCATION
LT. COL.
RANK
TYPE
ENGINEER

A referent ring served to chain together all the relationships in which the referent was involved.

Connective rings were rings of unlabeled links that associated two or more referents. For example, to assert that the 638th was a battalion, a connective ring was built that connected the referent ring representing 638th and the referent ring representing BATTALION. The structure in Figure 2.1 was built to represent THE 638TH IS A BATTALION and THE COMMANDER OF THE 638TH IS PARKER.

This technique of representing relationships in unordered rings can cause problems due to the fact that the representation for THE 638TH IS A BATTALION is identical to that for THE BATTALION IS A 638TH. The representation itself does not distinguish between these interpretations. The ambiguity can only be resolved in the mind of the reader using his or her knowledge of what a battalion is and what 638th represents.

## REWRITE RULES

Analysis of input sentences was carried out by identifying a class for each word or phrase in the sentence, then applying rewrite rules. The classes were referent (R), verb (V), number (N), pronoun (X), function words (F), time (T), and sentence (S). For the sentence WHO IS COMMANDER OF THE 638TH BATTALION, the sentence with phrase classes is:

```
F        R      F  F  R       R     F
1. WHO IS COMMANDER OF THE 638TH BATTALION?
```

|   | *Rule* | *Result* |
|---|--------|----------|
| 2. | r1 + r2 → r1 | WHO IS COMMANDER OF THE 638TH? |
| 3. | THE + r1 → r1 | WHO IS COMMANDER OF 638TH? |
| 4. | r1 + OF + r2 → r3 | WHO IS JONATHAN PARKER? |
| 5. | WHO IS + r + ? → S | JONATHAN PARKER |

At each step, after a rule was identified as a candidate for application, whether the rule would actually be applied depended upon the database. For example, the application of the rule in line 2 requires that R1 and R2 be linked with a connective ring. The application of the rule in line 4 requires that R1 and R2 are on the same connective

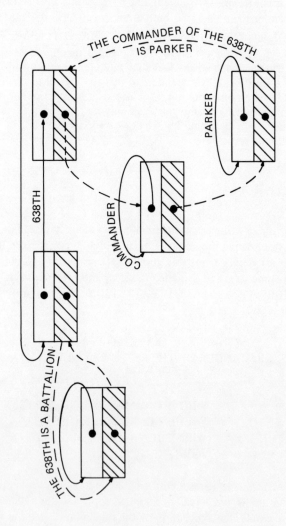

**Figure 2.1 THE COMMANDER OF THE 638TH IS PARKER.**

ring, and that there is a third referent on that ring. If there were more than one interpretation of the sentence at one time in the parsing (there usually would be), all candidate interpretations were developed in parallel. If the sentence were unambiguous (from DEACON's point of view), all but one interpretation would be dropped as ungrammatical before parsing was completed.

## VERB TABLES

In the example above, "is" was not considered a verb. Verbs that were recognized as such depicted events, the existence or change of a time-dependent relationship (connective ring). They were treated specially. When a nonverb rewrite rule pattern was found, it was applied immediately. When a verb was found, information about the event it depicts was collected in a verb table until the entire sentence had been analyzed. The last step in the analysis was to construct a database query based on the contents of the verb table. For example, the analysis of "HAS THE 638TH BATTALION ARRIVED AT FORT LEWIS SINCE 18000?" (times were represented as points on a time line like 18000) produces the following verb table:

*Arrived*

| | |
|---|---|
| SUBJECT | 638TH |
| ATTRIBUTE | LOCATION |
| ASPECT | BEGIN |
| VALUE | FORT LEWIS |
| TENSE | PAST |
| TIME 1 | 18000 |
| TIME 2 | 20500 (NOW) |

From this table a database query was built to find a BEGINNING LOCATION of the 638TH at FORT LEWIS between 18000 and 20500. This information is represented with a connective ring linking 638TH, LOCATION, FORT LEWIS and the BEGIN time. The BEGIN time must satisfy $18000 \leq$ BEGIN TIME $\leq 20500$.

DEACON's language analysis was based on rewrite rules that applied to word classes, not to the words themselves. A table lookup was required to identify the class of each word, but once that was done, the analysis process was domain independent. Consequently, the language analysis programs would have applied to other domains after no more than writing a dictionary.

## 2.7 Case Study: DOCTOR

The DOCTOR (Weizenbaum 1966, 1976) program, or ELIZA, as it was also called in the literature, has received a great deal of attention. DOCTOR can create an amusingly convincing illusion of intelligence. It acts like a psychiatrist analyzing the user. The user types in a sentence about personal problems and the DOCTOR responds in a patient, reassuring way. There is no attempt to understand the user, i.e., to model the concepts and the relationships between concepts that the user is describing. All of DOCTOR's responses are made on the basis of matching templates containing key words to the user's input. For example, the rule (____I REMEMBER____) will match any sentence in which "I remember" occurs. The components of the template that match a user's sentence are numbered so they can be referred to in the generated response:

(____I REMEMBER____)
  1 2    3     4

DOCTOR then generates a response such as (DO YOU OFTEN THINK OF 4) where the fourth component of the template is substituted for "4" in the response. If the user enters "I remember Christmas in New Hampshire," DOCTOR responds with, "DO YOU OFTEN THINK OF CHRISTMAS IN NEW HAMPSHIRE?" In order to keep the pronouns straight, "you" is substituted for "I" and "I" for "you" before the template matching is done. This means that the template above would actually have been written (____YOU REMEMBER____).

The templates are stored under key words. The (____YOU REMEMBER____) template is under "REMEMBER." Each key word can have several associated templates and each template can have several responses. The responses are selected in round robin fashion. The templates and responses under "REMEMBER" are shown below:

| *Key word* | *Templates* | *Responses* |
|---|---|---|
| REMEMBER | (____YOU REMEMBER____) | DO YOU OFTEN THINK OF 4 |
| | | DOES THINKING OF 4 BRING SOMETHING ELSE TO MIND? |
| | | WHY DO YOU REMEMBER 4 JUST NOW |
| | | WHAT IN THE PRESENT SITUATION REMINDS YOU OF 4 |
| | | WHAT IS THE CONNECTION BETWEEN ME AND 4 |
| | (____DO I REMEMBER____) | DID YOU THINK I WOULD FORGET 5 |
| | | WHY DO YOU THINK I SHOULD RECALL 5 NOW |
| | | WHAT ABOUT 5 YOU MEN- TIONED 5 |
| | (____) | NEWKEY |

The last template (_____) will match any sentence. If the other two fail to match, (_____) will match giving the response NEWKEY. NEWKEY is a message to DOCTOR to find a new key word and reprocess the sentence.

Table 2.1 shows a conversation the author had with a version of DOCTOR. There are several interesting features in this dialog. First, there was always some sort of response; DOCTOR is very robust in this regard. Next, it only processes a sentence up to the first comma or end of sentence punctuation. In question 2, the comma after "yes" truncated the sentence at that point.

DOCTOR does not limit its keys to words. Words can be classed into categories, and the occurrence of any word in the category triggers a template. An example of a category is in questions 3 and 4 where "mother" and "father" match the category "family."

Question 10 is one in which no key words are found. There are a number of possible responses if this is the case. The one given for this question is not one of the canned answers, but a response composed at the first reference to the family category, the one referring to the beatings, question 3. A similar sentence was prepared when question 5 contained a family word. It used the response form (BUT 2 3 4 5) producing BUT YOUR FATHER CALLS YOU NASTY NAMES, however this response was never needed.

The key words have priorities associated with them. Of all the key words identified in a sentence, the one with the highest priority is used. In question 12, key words YOU and YOUR precede PROB—LEMS in the sentence, but PROBLEMS has the highest priority so the templates attached to that word are used. The words with the highest priority in the version the author used are obscenities. Responses to sentences containing obscenities are: "Are such obscenities frequently on your mind," "You are being a bit childish," "Really now," "Dear me," and "I really shouldn't tolerate such language."

In question 13 the template contains a nonzero integer. An integer, N, indicates that it can match a string of exactly N words. The effect of the 1 in the question 13 template is to insure that the sentence does not end with "your."

Usually, when a question is matched to a template, the response is printed. In question 18 the template is marked PRELIMINARY. Its response is not printed immediately. The question is transformed according to the response rule, but then the transformed sentence is analyzed again.

There are a limited number of responses for each template. The template (____) under the key word "Problems" has four, for example. Question 25 was the fifth question to have "PROBLEMS" as its highest priority key word. Instead of repeating the first response, a tag, "NEWKEY," is returned instead of a response. When this is found, a key of lower priority is used to interpret the sentence.

DOCTOR does very little toward understanding an input in any sense of the word, but it does create a good illusion in this domain of discourse.

---

**Table 1**

A conversation with the DOCTOR. The "patient's" statements are written next to the utterance number. DOCTOR's internal form of the utterances, templates and responses, are indented. DOCTOR's responses are shown below that with the substitutions made.

---

(1) I have been very depressed lately
  YOU HAVE BEEN VERY DEPRESSED LATELY
  TEMPLATE: (____) [this template matches anything]
  RESPONSE: (YOU SAY 1)
You say you have been very depressed lately
(2) Yes, my mother beats me and my father calls me names
  yes
  TEMPLATE: (____)
  RESPONSE: YOU'RE BEING SOMEWHAT SHORT WITH ME
You're being somewhat short with me
(3) What about my mother beating me?
  WHAT ABOUT YOUR MOTHER BEATING YOU
  TEMPLATE: (____ YOUR ____ (CATEGORY FAMILY) ____)
  RESPONSE: TELL ME MORE ABOUT YOUR FAMILY
Tell me more about your family

(4)  My father calls me nasty names
        YOUR <u>FATHER</u> CALLS YOU NASTY NAMES
        TEMPLATE: (\_\_\_\_YOUR\_\_\_\_(CATEGORY FAMILY)
        \_\_\_\_)
        RESPONSE: WHO ELSE IN YOUR FAMILY 5
Who else in your family calls you nasty names
(5)  I think the dog would if he could
        YOU THINK THE DOG WOULD <u>IF</u> HE COULD
        TEMPLATE: (\_\_\_\_IF\_\_\_\_)
        RESPONSE: DO YOU THINK IT'S LIKELY THAT 3
Do you think its likely that he could
(6)  No, do you
        <u>NO</u>
        TEMPLATE: (\_\_\_\_)
        RESPONSE: YOU DON'T SEEM VERY TALKATIVE
          TODAY
You don't seen very talkative today
(7)  I guess what is really bothering me is that I don't have any money
        <u>YOU</u> GUESS WHAT IS REALLY BOTHERING YOU
        IS THAT YOU DON'T HAVE ANY MONEY
        TEMPLATE: (\_\_\_\_)
        RESPONSE: CAN YOU ELABORATE ON THAT
Can you elaborate on that
(8)  The problem is that I know psychiatrists are expensive and I may
not be able to pay you
        THE <u>PROBLEM</u> IS THAT YOU KNOW THAT
        PSYCHIATRISTS ARE EXPENSIVE AND YOU MAY NOT
        BE ABLE TO PAY I
        TEMPLATE: (\_\_\_\_)
        RESPONSE: PLEASE CONTINUE, THIS MAY BE
          INTERESTING
Please continue, this may be interesting
(9)  I thought you might think so
        <u>YOU</u> THOUGHT I MIGHT THINK SO
        TEMPLATE: (\_\_\_\_YOU\_\_\_\_I\_\_\_\_)
        RESPONSE: PERHAPS IN YOUR FANTASY WE 3 EACH
          OTHER
Perhaps in your fantasy we thought each other
(10) Right doc
        RIGHT DOC
        TEMPLATE: (\_\_\_\_)

RESPONSE: EARLIER YOU SAID YOUR MOTHER
BEATING YOU
Earlier you said your mother beating you
　　[made from question 3; template:
　　(EARLIER YOU SAID 2 3 4 5)]
(11)I JUST SAID THAT TO GET YOUR ATTENTION
　　YOU JUST SAID THAT TO GET MY ATTENTION
　　TEMPLATE: (＿＿＿)
　　RESPONSE: DO YOU SAY 1 FOR SOME SPECIAL
　　REASON
Do you say you just said that to get my attention for some special
　reason
(12)The one thing I can't stand is telling a shrink my problems and
having him fall asleep
　　THE ONE THING YOU CAN'T STAND IS TELLING A
　　SHRINK YOUR PROBLEMS AND HAVING HIM FALL
　　ASLEEP
　　TEMPLATE: (＿＿＿)
　　RESPONSE: HAVE YOU ANY OTHER PROBLEMS YOU
　　WISH TO DISCUSS
Have you any other problems you wish to discuss
(13)Let's get back to my job
　　LET'S GET BACK TO YOUR JOB
　　TEMPLATE: (＿＿ YOUR 1 ＿＿)
　　RESPONSE: YOUR 3 4
Your job
(14)Yes I need the money but I am not enthusiastic about working
　　YES YOU NEED THE MONEY BUT YOU ARE NOT
　　ENTHUSIASTIC ABOUT
　　WORKING
　　TEMPLATE: (＿＿＿)
　　RESPONSE: YOU SEEM QUITE POSITIVE
You seem quite positive
(15)Not really
　　NOT REALLY
　　TEMPLATE: (＿＿＿)
　　RESPONSE: I AM NOT SURE I UNDERSTAND YOU
　　FULLY
I am not sure I understand you fully
(16)I am uncertain as to how I can get money without the problems
of having a job

YOU ARE UNCERTAIN AS TO HOW YOU CAN GET
MONEY WITHOUT THE
<u>PROBLEMS</u> OF HAVING A JOB
TEMPLATE: (_____)
RESPONSE: PERHAPS YOU'D RATHER CHANGE THE
SUBJECT

Perhaps you'd rather change the subject

(17) What if my mother had been beating me, what would you say then

WHAT <u>IF</u> YOUR MOTHER HAD BEEN BEATING YOU
TEMPLATE: ((_____ IF _____ –HAD_____) PRELIMINARY)
RESPONSE: (1 2 3 MIGHT HAVE 5)
WHAT <u>IF</u> YOUR MOTHER MIGHT HAVE BEEN
BEATING YOU
TEMPLATE: (_____ IF _____)
RESPONSE: DO YOU WISH THAT 3

Do you wish that your mother might have been beating you

(18) Not at all

<u>NOT</u> AT ALL
TEMPLATE: (_____)
RESPONSE: ARE YOU JUST SAYING "NO" TO BE
NEGATIVE

Are you just saying "no" to be negative

(19) I thought it might just be more interesting for you if I had a
juicier problem

YOU THOUGHT IT JUST MIGHT BE MORE
INTERESTING FOR I IF YOU
HAD A JUICIER <u>PROBLEM</u>
TEMPLATE: (_____)
RESPONSE: YOU SEEM A BIT UNEASY

You seem a bit uneasy

(20) Why do you say that

<u>WHY</u> DO YOU SAY THAT
TEMPLATE: (_____)
RESPONSE: WHY INDEED

Why indeed

(21) Doctor are you sure you're qualified for all this

DOCTOR <u>ARE</u> I SURE I ARE QUALIFIED FOR ALL
THIS
TEMPLATE (___ARE I_____)
RESPONSE: WHY ARE YOU INTERESTED IN WHETHER
I AM 4 OR NOT

Why are you interested in whether I am qualified for all this or not
(22)For one thing your grammar is not too great
    FOR ONE THING MY GRAMMAR IS NOT TOO GREAT
    TEMPLATE: (____ MY ____)
    RESPONSE:
    WHY ARE YOU CONCERNED OVER MY 3
Why are you concerned over my grammar is not too great
(23)Frankly it makes you sound a little ignorant
    FRANKLY IT MAKES I SOUND A LITTLE IGNORANT
    TEMPLATE: (____ I 1 ____)
    RESPONSE: WE WERE DISCUSSING YOU NOT ME
We were discussing you not me
(24)But my problems have not been solved
    BUT YOUR PROBLEMS HAVE NOT BEEN SOLVED
    TEMPLATE: (____)
    RESPONSE: NEWKEY
    TEMPLATE: (____ YOUR 1 ____)
    RESPONSE: WHY DO YOU SAY 3 4
Why do you say your problems have not been solved
(25)Because whenever I mention my money situation you change
the subject
    BECAUSE WHENEVER YOU MENTION YOUR MONEY
    SITUATION I CHANGE
    THE SUBJECT
    TEMPLATE: (____ YOUR 1 ____)
    RESPONSE: DOES THAT SUGGEST ANYTHING ELSE
        WHICH BELONGS TO YOU
Does that suggest anything else that belongs to you

## References and Further Reading

Bar-Hillel, Y. "The Present Status of Automatic Translation of Languages." In *Advances in Computers*, vol. 1, edited by F.L. Alt, A.D. Booth and R.E. Meagher. New York: Academic Press, 1960.

Bobrow, D.G. "Natural Language Input for a Computer Problem-Solving System." In *Semantic Information Processing*, edited by M. Minsky. Cambridge, Mass.: MIT Press, 1968.

Craig, J.A.; Berenner, S.C.; Carney, H.C.; and Longyear, C.R. "DEACON: Direct English Access and Control." In *Proceedings of the Fall Joint Computer Conference.* Montvale, N.J.: AFIPS Press, 1966.

Green, B.F.; Wolf, A.K.; Chomsky, C.; and Laughery, K. "Baseball: An Automatic Question Answerer." In *Computers and Thought*, edited by Feigenbaum, E.A. and J. Feldman. New York: McGraw-Hill, 1963.

Josselson, H.H. "Automatic Translation of Languages Since 1960: A Linguist's View." In *Advances in Computers*, vol. 11, edited by F.L. Alt, M. Rubinoff and M.C. Yovitts. New York: Academic Press, 1971.

Lindsay, R.K. "In Defense of Ad Hoc Systems." In *Computer Models of Thought and Language*, edited by R.C. Schank and K.M. Colby. San Francisco: W.H. Freeman and Co., 1973.

Lindsay, R.K. "Inferential Memory as the Basis of Machines Which Understand Natural Language." In *Computers and Thought*, edited by E.A. Feigenbaum and J. Feldman. New York: McGraw-Hill, 1963.

Simmons, R.F. "Answering English Questions by Computer: A Survey." CACM 8 (January 1965): 53-70.

_____. "Storage and Retrieval of Aspects of Meaning in Directed Graph Structures." CACM 9 (March 1966): 211-15.

_____; Burger, J.F.; and Long, B.E. "An Approach Toward Answering Questions from Text." In *Proceedings of the Fall Joint Computer Conference.* Montvale, N.J.: AFIPS Press, 1966.

_____; Klein, S.; and McConlogue, K. "Toward the Syntheses of Human Language Behavior." *Behavioral Science* 7 (July 1962): 402-07.

_____; and McConlogue, K. "Maximum-Depth Indexing for Computer Retrieval of English Language Data." *American Documentation* 14 (January 1963): 68-73.

Weizenbaum, J. *Computer Power and Human Reason.* San Francisco: W.H. Freeman, 1976.

_____. "ELIZA—A Computer Program for the Study of Natural Language Communication Between Man and Machines." CACM 9 (January 1966): 36-45.

# 3. Syntax

## 3.1 Structural Constraints in English

Words cannot be arranged in an arbitrary order in a sentence and still make sense. In English, we cannot say

"Thrilling a is subject grammar."

But we can say

"Grammar is a thrilling subject."

It does not matter whether the speaker or the listener believes the statement, but there is something about the order of the words in English that makes one sentence acceptable and the other not. No one would agree that

"Every cow in Wisconsin takes ballet lessons on Tuesday nights."

But we would agree that that is a proper way to say it. We can even agree on the right way to say something that makes no sense:

The wet happiness that whistled a bulldozer glowed with a large hue.

Nonsensical as that sentence is, it is more nearly correct than

49

The glowed wet which happiness a whistled a with hue bulldozer large.

Finally, there is even a correct way to use nonsense words, as can be seen in Lewis Carroll's "Jabberwocky":

'Twas brillig and the slithy toves
Did gyre and gimble in the wabe

What makes these lines more satisfying than the following?

And slithy the toves brilling in And gyre gimble wabe the did.

Syntax is the description of the ways in which words must be ordered to make structurally acceptable sentences in a language. From these examples, it is clear that there is a syntax—a system of word ordering—for sentences in English. In fact, every natural language has a syntax.

There could be many ways to describe the syntax of a language. One of the most durable is the one we all learned in school. Words are grouped into classes of nouns, verbs, adjectives, adverbs, and so on. Rules for the proper construction of noun phrases, verb phrases, sentences, and other structures are based on these classes. An acceptable noun phrase, for example, can be composed of an article adjective, any number of adjectives, a noun, and perhaps some prepositional phrases. A prepositional phrase is a preposition followed by its object, a noun phrase. The rules for these two structures are shown below in a notation more familiar to the computing community than to high school English teachers:

⟨NP⟩::=⟨ART⟩⟨ADJ⟩ * ⟨N⟩⟨PP⟩
⟨PP⟩::=⟨PREP⟩⟨NP⟩
⟨ART⟩::=a | an | the
⟨ADJ⟩::=large | green | red | small . . .
⟨N⟩::=house | idea | grasshoppers . . .
⟨PREP⟩::=of | in | against | on

We know how familiar words can be used. Each of us reading the sentence about the wet happiness knows that, for instance, the word "wet" can be used as an adjective and "happiness" can be used as a noun. We recognized the grammatical sentence because the word classes were arranged according to the rules of syntax.

The "Jabberwocky" example illustrates two features of syntax. First, there are two kinds of classes of words, open classes and closed classes. Nouns and verbs are open classes. They can have any number of members; new nouns and verbs can be defined whenever they are needed. Prepositions, article adjectives and auxiliary verbs are closed classes. Usually there are no new words being defined to be included as members of the closed classes. The closed-class words are learned early in life, are used frequently, and when reading "Jabberwocky" we are quite confident that none of the unknown words are going to be defined as closed-class words.

Second, "Jabberwocky" illustrates the close connection between the inflections that a word can have and its syntactic class. Morphology, the study of variations in word forms, is closely linked to syntax. If "tove" describes one object, then to describe a group of them the morphological rule is to add an "s," making "toves." If the toves are covered with things called "sliths," we can indicate that by adding a "y" to "slith," making the adjective "slithy." (In more familiar terms, a trail paved with many rocks is a "rocky trail.") The endings of the words in "Jabberwocky" give clues as to which classes the words belong. These clues, combined with the clues from closed-class words, provide strong evidence as to the class of each word in the poem. The sequence of word classes from the closed-class words and the presumed classes of the unknown words allow comparison of syntax rules to the poem's structure. The rules agree with the structure of "Jabberwocky," but do not agree with the scrambled sequence of the same words.

These examples have highlighted four kinds of knowledge used in understanding and generating language. One is syntax, which will be discussed more thoroughly later in this chapter. Another is morphology, concerned with the forms of words. A third is pragmatic knowledge which deals with the way we see the world. It is this knowledge, such as general knowledge about cows and ballet lessons, that prevents us from believing that Wisconsin cows take ballet lessons. A fourth kind of knowledge is semantics, or the ways in which words are related to concepts. Semantics, for example, helps us select word senses (e.g., the difference in the meaning of "green" in "green

Chevy" and a "green tinhorn who just arrived in Tombstone from St. Louis"). Semantics also includes such generalizations as only physical objects can get wet, only people and birds can whistle, only a form of music can be whistled and the only way to describe a hue is by its visual attributes. These generalizations might alternatively be considered to be pragmatic information. The division between semantics and pragmatics is not always distinct, but a matter for interpretation. As we shall see when discussing semantic grammars, the divisions between syntax, semantics and pragmatics can be blurred even more. For the purpose of making computer programs that handle English, we are not so interested in defining the differences between these classes as we are in using the knowledge from them.

There are numerous different conventions for representing the syntactic structure of a sentence, many of which have been used in syntactic analysis programs in natural language processors. By and large, the conventions by which a natural language program was originally described have been retained in the summaries presented in this book. It is hoped the minor variations between conventions will not be confusing.

## 3.2 Transition Networks

### ACCEPTANCE OF GRAMMATICAL SENTENCES

A parser is a formalism (usually embodied in a program) which can determine whether a sentence conforms to the constraints of the syntax of a language, and also can build a representation of the syntactic structure. A simple parser can be modeled after the transition network formalism. The network in Figure 3.1 will accept sentences with intransitive verbs (i.e., verbs that do not require objects). The e indicates that there are no words left in the sentence. If that arc is taken, the sentence has been accepted by the grammar that the network represents, i.e., it conforms to the constraints of the language. If there is more than one arc leaving a node, the arcs are ordered and checked sequentially. This network accepts the sentence "Blackbeard slashed." Parsing begins at node S. The class of the first word,

"Blackbeard," is compared with the first arc, ARTICLE, and does not match. The second arc, however, matches any class and JUMPs to node S/A. By convention, transition arcs that match a word class consume a word when they are taken. The JUMP arc is different in that it does not consume a word in the transition. Therefore, we are now at node S/A and still trying to match the word "Blackbeard." "Blackbeard" matches NOUN, and the transition is taken to node S/N. "Blackbeard" is consumed, so now "slashed" is checked. Since it matches the class VERB, the transition to S/V is taken and "slashed" is consumed. All the words in the sentence have been consumed, so the empty sentence condition of the exit arc is met, indicating the successful acceptance of the sentence. The sentence "The Mongols fought" is accepted by taking the arcs, JUMP, NOUN, VERB, e.

Discovering whether a sentence is accepted by a transition network is only half the task. The other half is building a representation of the structure of the sentence. This is done by allowing arc transitions to cause side effects. For example, the side effect for the NOUN arc from S/A to S/N would be to designate the word being consumed on that arc transition as the subject of the sentence. The word consumed on the VERB transition is the verb of the sentence. More will be said on structure building after we have developed a network for a more complex grammar.

When we add transitive verbs that take a direct object (but not an indirect object), we see some redundancy. In Figure 3.2 the subject (from node S to S/N) and the object (from S/V to S/NO) have the same structure: they are noun phrases. Considerable clarity and simplicity can be gained from centralizing this regularity by making what is essentially a subroutine call to a noun phrase network. We can devise a network for accepting noun phrases and use it whenever a

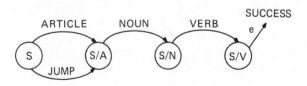

**Figure 3.1 Transition network for sentences with intransitive verbs**

noun phrase is required. The result is shown in Figure 3.3. PUSH NP means that the test for the arc involves comparing the sentence with the subnetwork NP. If NP identifies the words of a noun phrase, the POP arc is taken, which returns control from the NP subnetwork to the network that made the PUSH. The addition of subnetworks increases significantly the theoretical power of the grammar-accepting formalism.

In the parlance of formal languages, adding the ability to PUSH to subnets increases the power of the system from accepting regular grammars to accepting context-free grammars. One advantage of PUSHes and POPs to the programmer of language understanders is that the grammar is much easier to write and understand. If we now wish to expand the definition of a noun phrase from the simple one in Figure 3.3 to the more sophisticated version mentioned above,

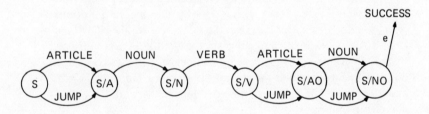

**Figure 3.2 Transition network for sentences with transitive verbs**

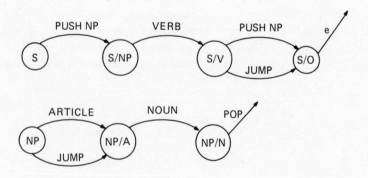

**Figure 3.3 Recursive transition network with noun phrase subnet**

the changes are all centralized in the NP net, not scattered throughout one enormous network and repeated dozens of times wherever noun phrases are needed. The enormous advantage of this ability to PUSH to a subnetwork is in the way it simplifies the design of the grammar. Figure 3.4 shows a sentence network with a verb phrase net and an expanded noun phrase net.

The grammar represented by the network here is still very simple. It accepts sentences with intransitive or transitive verbs. It accepts moderately elaborate noun phrases. It would not, however, accept such sentences as the following:

Aggrippina *cleverly* poisoned Emperor Claudias. (adverb)

The *third* wave of plague subsided. (ordinal)

*What caused it*? (question)

The Black Plague *had* decimated the population. (auxiliary verb)

The rebellion *was smashed*. (passive construction)

Fire *and* brimstone rained *from the heavens*. (conjunction, adverbial prepositional phrase)

Ivan, *who had been cruel when a boy*, became the Czar. (subordinate clause)

The peace cost *more than* the war. (comparative)

This is by no means all the sentence types that cannot be accepted. It does show, however, that a set of simple sentences can have a broad range of syntactic structures. Before describing how more of these structures can be accepted by transition networks, it is time to examine the construction of the syntactic structures in sentences.


## SYNTACTIC STRUCTURES


There has been no single standard way of representing the syntactic structure of sentences in natural language understanding programs.

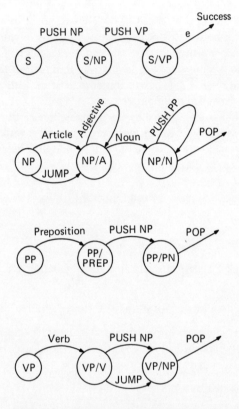

**Figure 3.4 Recursive transition network**

Some programs do not even generate syntactic structures. The structures described here were chosen because they are fairly typical of the kind of structures that are used frequently. Unfortunately, the nomenclature describing these structures is not standardized. One can get quite confused going from one text to another because the same terms are often applied with different meanings.

### Phonological Structure

Sentence structure is often viewed at three or more levels. The first—the phonological level—is the level that is actually written or spoken. The sentence structure reflects the associations between words and word groups as they appear in the sentence. Figure 3.5 shows the phonological structure of the sentence "The Mongols devastated the irrigation systems in Persia."

The phonological structure of a sentence is similar to a sentence "diagram" that is often taught in school; see Figure 3.6. However, phonological structure has the advantage that structural units such as sentence, noun phrase, noun, determiner and so on are labeled. Phonological structures are sometimes the target structures of the syntactic components of natural language understanding programs.

Performing syntactic analysis in natural language processing makes the relationships of words and phrases explicit. Another potential advantage of syntactic analysis is to put the sentence into a standard form that other analysis programs can operate on. One way

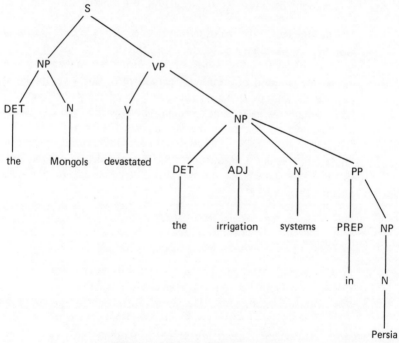

**Figure 3.5 Phonological structure**

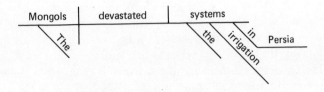

**Figure 3.6 Sentence diagram**

of standardizing the form is in the leaves of the tree structure. The following sentences would all have the same phonological structure except for the leaves:

The Mongols devastated the irrigation systems in Persia.

The Mongol devastates the irrigation systems in Persia.

The Mongols devastated the irrigation system in Persia.

The differences in the words in these sentences are in their forms, or morphology. A more nearly standard structure can be built if the leaves of the syntax tree consist of *morphemes* rather than words. A morpheme is a unit of meaning, where a word may be composed of more than one morpheme. The words "system" and "systems" both contain the morpheme "system," but the presence or absence of the suffix "s" indicates the morphemes "PLURAL" and "SINGULAR," respectively. "Devastated" is composed of the morpheme "devastate," and the morpheme "PAST" is indicated by the "ed" suffix. "Devastates" has the morpheme "devastate" and the morpheme "PRESENT."

*Surface Structure*

A tree with morpheme leaves is called a surface structure tree (phonological structures are sometimes called surface structures, too). The surface structure of "The Mongols devastated the irrigation systems in Persia" is shown in Figure 3.7. The sentence (S) node has three descendants: noun phrase (NP), auxiliary (AUX) and verb phrase (VP). The noun phrase and verb phrase are familiar, but the auxiliary is new.

The auxiliary always contains the tense of the main verb and may also contain the modals, perfect and progressive. The tense of the auxiliary depicts whether the action of the main verb is in past or present time. Future time is not indicated by the main verb, but by the modal "will." Modals are auxiliary verbs used to express the conditional validity of the proposition expressed in the sentence. If the verb is in present tense, the modals "can," "may," "must," "shall" and "will" can be used. If the verb expresses past tense, the modals "could," "might," "should," and "would" can be used. The modals occur in front of the perfect. The perfect is formed from the helping verb "have" followed by a verb in the past participle form (i.e., usually with an "en" ending). The tense is determined by the tense of "have." For example:

Past perfect: The Mongols *had beaten* their foes.

Present perfect: The Mongols *have beaten* their foes.

The perfect gives English the capability of expressing complex time relationships. "The Mongols beat their foes" indicates that it occurred in the past. "The Mongols had beaten their foes" indicates two times in the past: the time being referred to, and a time prior to that when they beat their foes.

The last element of the auxiliary is the progressive. It is formed from a form of the helping verb "be" with the main verb having the present participle marker (i.e., an "ing" ending). Use of the progressive usually suggests a description of an action rather than the action itself:

Action: The Mongols rode west.

Description: The Mongols were riding west.

In the progressive, as with the perfect, the tense is indicated by the auxiliary verb rather than by the main verb.

It was mentioned that one of the reasons for using the surface structure of the sentence rather than the phonological structure is that the leaves of the surface structure tree are in a more convenient form;

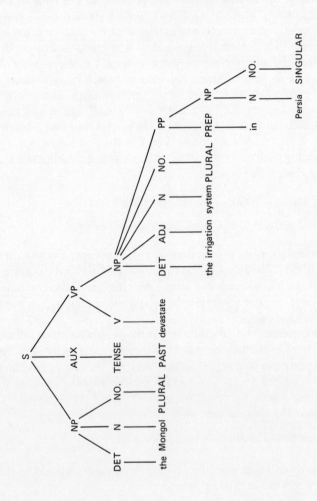

**Figure 3.7 Surface structure**

they are morphemes rather than words. With the description of surface structure we also introduced the concept of a subtree for the auxiliary, which centralizes time and conditional validity in one structure.

### Underlying Structure

Still more regularity could be found if the surface structure were transformed to another structure variously called the underlying structure, deep structure or conceptual structure. Since deep structure and conceptual structure have been used to refer to other things, we shall use the term underlying structure. The fundamental differences between surface structure and underlying structure are the word order and the insertion or deletion of morphemes. The sentences,

The thatched roofs were infested by rats.

Rats infested the thatched roofs.

are, respectively, the passive and active expressions of the same proposition. The focus of the two sentences is different: the first is about roofs, the second about rats. Their surface structures would be different, but their underlying structures would be identical.

An example of the insertion of an "understood" word between the surface structure and underlying structure can be seen in the following:

Hoppalong waved (his hand) goodbye.

The thatched roofs were infested (by something).

The phrases in parentheses represent information that is understood and that would appear in the underlying structure but not in the surface structure.

### Building Syntactic Structures

Recall that the arcs of transition network grammars each have some condition that must be met before the arc can be traversed (e.g., next word is a noun, next group of words is a prepositional phrase, etc.). Arcs can also have procedures attached to them for structure building. A set of registers or variables local to each subnet hold the structure fragments as they are being collected and assembled. When a subnet is popped, meaning that it has been completed successfully, a procedure attached to the POP arc assembles the fragments into a larger structure that is passed up to the calling network; see Figure 3.8.

The arcs have been numbered for easy reference. The following registers are used for the noun phrase net:

DETERMINER

ADJECTIVE

NOUN

NUMBER

POST-NOMINAL

The structure-building procedures attached to each arc are as follows:

1. Set register DETERMINER to current word.

2. Set register DETERMINER to NIL.

3. Add current word to the end of the list on register ADJECTIVE.

4. Set register NOUN to root of current word; set register NUMBER to number of current word (singular or plural).

5. Add popped structure to the end of the list on register POST-NOMINAL.

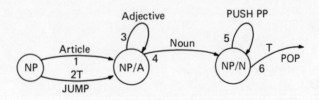

**Figure 3.8 Noun phrase subnet**

6. Build structure from registers.

The output of the function attached to arc 6 should return a structure like the one in Figure 3.9 with the leaves and subtrees filled in appropriately.

Consider the parsing of the noun phrase below:

"the mean hulking Viking with the bloody axe"

"The" satisfies the ARTICLE condition on arc 1, the DETERMINER register is set to "the," and "the" is consumed. The ADJECTIVE condition on arc 3 is satisfied by "mean," so the ADJECTIVE register is set to "mean" and "mean" is consumed. Next, arc 3 is tested again and taken with "hulking," and the ADJECTIVE register is set to the list "mean hulking." Arc 3 is tested again against "Viking" and fails. Arc 4 is then tested against "Viking" and succeeds. The dictionary is consulted to determine whether "Viking" is singular or plural (or this may be done by morphological routines looking for a suffix). NOUN is set to "Viking" and NUMBER to SINGULAR. Next, push to the prepositional phrase from arc 5. It returns successfully, and POST-NOMINAL is set to the structure shown in Figure 3.10. (Notice that in order to parse the prepositional phrase, a recursive call was made to the noun phrase subnet. This is the reason that the registers must be local to the networks.) Another push is made on arc 5, but it fails to find another prepositional phrase. Arc 6 is tested and since its condition is always satisfied, it is taken. In taking it, the structure in Figure 3.11 is build and returned to the network that pushed to the noun phrase.

## AUGMENTED TRANSITION NETWORKS

Two additions to transition network grammars enable them to perform word order changes and insertions and deletions. These are the use of registers in recognition (in addition to the ones used for structure building), and the addition of arbitrary conditions on the arcs. The use of registers is extended to enable storing condition flags and to permit holding temporary structures in global storage

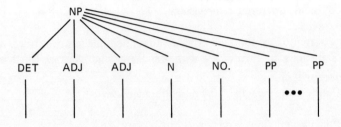

Figure 3.9 Structure built by noun phrase parser

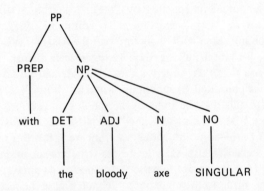

Figure 3.10 Post-nominal structure

to facilitate their relocation in the underlying structure. The addition of arbitrary conditions on the arcs extends the condition checking from being merely dependent on the current state and the next word or phrase in the sentence. A transition network parser with these extensions is called an augmented transition network or ATN.

The extended use of registers can be illustrated with a passive sentence:

The thatched roofs were infested by rats.

When parsing begins, the first noun phrase is assumed to be the subject of an active sentence. However, when "were infested" is

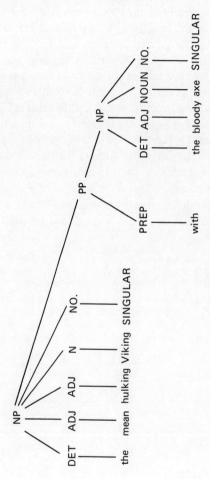

**Figure 3.11 Noun phrase structure**

encountered, the sentence is identified as passive, and the noun phrase "the thatched roofs" is taken from the local subject register and put into a global holding register. A global flag is set indicating a passive sentence. In passive sentences, the preposition "by" often indicates the location of the subject of the underlying structure. When "by" is encountered, the arc condition, in addition to testing for the word "by," checks the passive sentence flag (with the arbitrary condition extension). The test shows that the sentence is in fact passive, so the noun phrase following the "by" is taken as the subject and the noun phrase in the hold register is taken to be the object. The resulting underlying structure would look like that in Figure 3.12.

Still more regularity may be had if every proposition in this sentence were represented separately. There is an implied proposition in this sentence that the roofs referred to were thatched. If one were to choose this form of representation, the ADJ substructure would be replaced by a proposition.

ATN parsers operate top down, making implicit expectations of what will be found next in the sentence, based on what has been

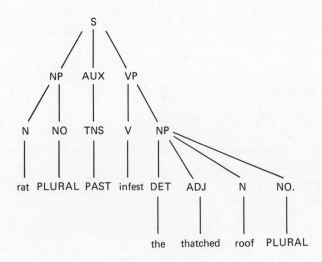

Figure 3.12 Underlying structure

found. Each arc represents an expectation. If an arc is followed, and later proves not to lead to a successful parse of the sentence, the ATN parser backs up to the last choice point and tries an alternative choice. ATN grammars can be implemented so that the most probable (or least expensive) choices are considered first, thus minimizing backup. This is called heuristic parsing. There are, however, some constructions that can cause a lot of backup. Consider, for example, the case of the conjunction "and." When an "and" is encountered, the structure to the right of the "and" will match one of the structures to the left of it. Consider the following sentences:

1. We exterminated black rats with infected <u>fleas</u> and <u>lice</u>.

2. We exterminated black rats with <u>infected fleas</u> and <u>healthy lice</u>.

4. We exterminated <u>black rats with infected fleas and huge roaches</u>.

5. We <u>exterminated black rats with infected fleas</u> and <u>sprayed for roaches</u>.

6. <u>We exterminated black rats with infected fleas</u> and <u>we sprayed for roaches</u>.

With all the possible structures to connect, any top-down method of conjunction parsing is bound to result in a significant amount of backtracking.

One of the most distressing aspects of backup is that certain phrases may be parsed over and over again, each time yielding the same structure and repeatedly being rejected because the larger structure that it is embedded in does not meet the parser's expectations. One way to circumvent this is to mark phrases that are known to be parsed correctly. They are called well-formed substrings. If the parser must backtrack, it will not do so into subnets that would reparse the well-formed substrings. They are accepted in their entirety.

Two other techniques for controlling backtracking in ATNs are the use of weights on arcs and splitting the parsing into parallel tasks. Weights on arcs can be manipulated by the attached procedural component on the arcs. The decision of which arc should be followed next depends on the relative weights of the alternatives. Splitting the parse into parallel tasks mixes a depth-first search technique, which is the usual method for ATNs, with breadth-first searching. It is not clear that any of the techniques mentioned here would justify themselves with respect to implementation costs and operating resource requirements.

### 3.3 Case Study: The LUNAR ATN Parser

#### ARC TYPES

The parser described above is, for the most part, the one described by Woods (1970), who first described ATNs. Other recursive transition network parsers have been built, but versions of the Woods ATN have been applied widely. The application which brought the most attention to ATNs was LUNAR, a natural language application designed to answer questions using a database on the Apollo lunar geology samples. The expressive power of ATN arcs has been improved by Finin (Finin and Hadden 1977), and the arc types in his version are shown below:

(CAT ⟨CATEGORY NAME⟩ ⟨TEST⟩ ⟨ACTION⟩* ⟨DESTINATION⟩)

(WRD ⟨WORD(s)⟩ ⟨TEST⟩ ⟨ACTION⟩* ⟨DESTINATION⟩)

(PHRASE ⟨PHRASE(s)⟩ ⟨TEST⟩ ⟨ACTION⟩* ⟨DESTINATION⟩)

(ROOT ⟨ROOT(s)⟩ ⟨TEST⟩ ⟨ACTION⟩* ⟨DESTINATION⟩)

(PUSH ⟨STATE NAME⟩ ⟨TEST⟩ ⟨ACTION⟩* ⟨DESTINATION⟩)

(POP ⟨VALUE⟩ ⟨TEST⟩ ⟨ACTION⟩*)

(POP! ⟨VALUE⟩ ⟨TEST⟩ ⟨ACTION⟩*)

(TO ⟨STATE⟩ ⟨TEST⟩ ⟨ACTION⟩*)

(JUMP ⟨STATE⟩ ⟨TEST⟩ ⟨ACTION⟩*)

(VIR ⟨CAT⟩ ⟨TEST⟩ ⟨ACTIONS⟩* ⟨DESTINATION⟩)

(TST ⟨LABEL⟩ ⟨TEST⟩ ⟨ACTIONS⟩* ⟨DESTINATION⟩)

(FAIL ⟨WHERE⟩ ⟨TEST⟩ ⟨ACTIONS⟩*)

(DO ⟨LABEL⟩ ⟨TEST⟩ ⟨ACTION⟩*)

(AND ⟨ARC⟩*)

DESTINATIONS:

(TO ⟨STATE⟩)

(JUMP ⟨STATE⟩)

CAT is used frequently in syntactic parsing. The dictionary entry of the first word on the input string is checked for the presence of ⟨CATEGORY NAME⟩, such as noun, verb, etc. If the word has that category, then ⟨TEST⟩ is performed. If ⟨TEST⟩, the arbitrary predicate slot, is satisfied, the ⟨ACTION⟩ entries are performed. These are usually register-setting actions, but may be any function. Last, the ⟨DESTINATION⟩ part is executed, transferring control to the appropriate node. There are two forms that the ⟨DESTINATION⟩ may take—TO and JUMP. With TO, the current first word in the input string is consumed, i.e., removed from the string. With JUMP, the word is not consumed. If backtracking occurs, words that have been consumed are restored.

The WRD arc checks the current first word in the input string against ⟨WORD(s)⟩.

PHRASE compares its phrase or phrases against the input string.

ROOT checks the root form of the current word against the ⟨ROOT(s)⟩ possibilities. Morphology routines are included for regularly inflected words, but irregular ones are entered separately in the dictionary.

PUSH will execute the subnetwork starting at ⟨STATE NAME⟩ if ⟨TEST⟩ is satisfied. If the subnetwork parses successfully, the ⟨ACTION⟩s are taken and control is transferred to ⟨DESTINATION⟩.

POP returns from a subnetwork with ⟨VALUE⟩, usually the structural representation of the input phrase it parsed.

POP! is the same as POP except when the ATN is backtracking; a subnet that has been POP!ed cannot be reentered. This is equivalent to treating the phrase parsed by the subnet as a well-formed substring.

The TO and JUMP arcs have the same effect as the TO and JUMP DESTINATIONs.

The VIR (virtual) arc is used in conjunction with the HOLD list. If a component of category ⟨CAT⟩ is on the HOLD list and the ⟨TEST⟩ condition is satisfied, the arc will be taken. As mentioned above, the HOLD list and accompanying VIR arc are useful for handling components that are parsed "out of order" such as the objects of passive sentences.

TST does not require a test of the input word. ⟨LABEL⟩ is used simply to name the test arc.

FAIL is used to control backtracking. If ⟨TEST⟩ is satisfied, the actions are executed and control returns to the node ⟨WHERE⟩, restoring all registers and the input string to the values they had at that point.

The DO arc is like the TST arc, except it has no destination. A DO is used for its side effects, such as initializing registers.

The AND arc has a somewhat different syntax than the other arc types. Each argument of the AND arc is another ATN arc. The argument arcs are evaluated left to right until one returns a nil value or they have all been evaluated. Only the final argument arc should have a destination. The AND arc is useful for collapsing several nonbranching states into one, making it more readable.

An examination of the arc types shows that the ATN formalism is not limited to parsing based on the grammatical word categories (noun, verb, etc.). Dictionary entries may be made with any sort of word categories. Semantic grammars, which may make no use of the traditional grammatical word categories, have been implemented successfully using ATNs. Semantic grammars are described in Chapter 6.

## SPEED

One of the early objections to ATNs was that since they ran interpretively, they were too slow for real-time natural language processing. A technique has been developed for compiling ATNs which speeds them up by about a factor of 10. The ATN compiler first rewrites the ATN network as LISP functions with the tests and actions set in conditional statements. Each subnetwork is converted to a separate LISP function. These LISP functions representing the ATN are then compiled by a LISP compiler.

## DIAGRAM OF THE LUNAR GRAMMAR

A transition network diagram representing the ATN syntactic grammar used in LUNAR (Woods, Kaplan and Nash-Webber 1972) is shown in Figure 3.13. The initial node of the top level network is the S/ node. The ambitious reader may try to parse the following sentences by hand with the grammar. The diagram gives the flavor of the grammar, but the code for it in all its detail can be found in the above report.

1) Samples with silicon.
2) Give me all the lunar samples with magnetite.
3) Which samples are breccias?
4) What is the average concentration of olivine in breccias?
5) How many rocks have greater than 50 ppm nickel?
6) Of the type A rocks which is the oldest?

In addition to illustrating ATNs, this grammar diagram demonstrates the utility of a computer model for representing a complex theory of language.

Unless the order of the arcs is indicated explicitly by numbers on the arcs, they are ordered clockwise from the top of the state. The symbol & on an arc indicates that there is a condition associated with the arc that is not included in the diagram. The function GETR takes a register as an argument, and returns its value; NULLR checks whether a register is null. The MEM arc is equivalent to the WRD arc described above.

### 3.4 Bottom-Up Parsing

Top-down parsers, such as those designed with the ATN formalism, have two advantages. They are easy to write, and they can be ordered heuristically so that if only one parse of a sentence is desired the ordering of arcs can allow the parse to be found with minimum searching.

They also have several disadvantages. First, when backtracking, a lower level constituent may be parsed repeatedly, always yielding the same result. Second, the boundaries of the input sentence must be delineated. Top-down parsers only register success when the end of the sentence has been reached; sentence boundaries may not be delineated clearly in such applications as connected discourse. Third, if a sentence cannot be parsed, a top-down approach with backtracking provides little help as to where the problem lies in the sentence. Fourth, if a component in the middle of the sentence cannot be parsed, the parser is of no help in determining the structure of the remainder of the sentence. Constituents to the right of the unparsable component are never reached.

An alternative to top-down parsing is bottom-up parsing. Bottom-up parsing, sometimes called data-driven parsing, works by attempting to build any structures it can from the input string. Bottom-up parsers typically work by starting at the left end of the input string and advancing a pointer in steps past one word at a time. At each step, the bottom-up parser builds all the structures possible on the string to the left of the pointer. Since there are no expectations as there are in top-down parsing, a bottom-up parser could build a number of lower level structures that will never contribute to the overall parse of the sentence. However, this can be an asset for input strings that are not clearly delineated sentences or that contain unknown words or ungrammatical constructions.

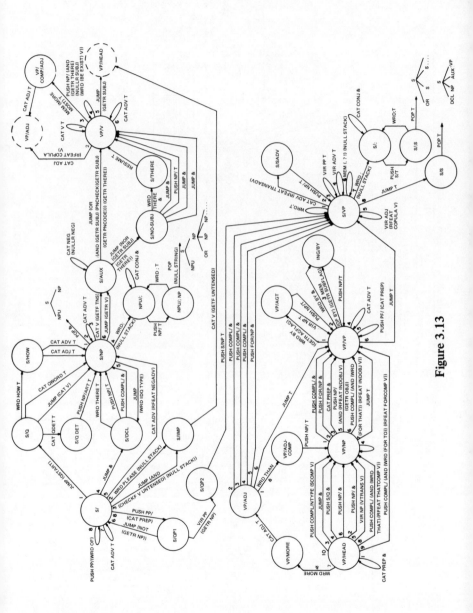

**Figure 3.13**

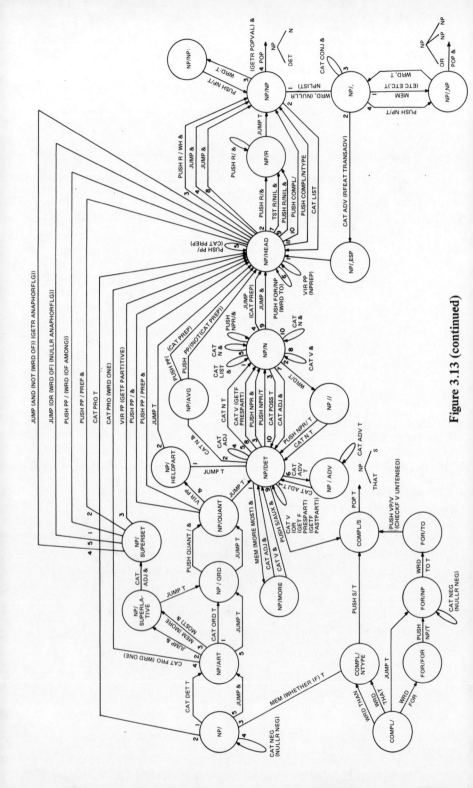

**Figure 3.13 (continued)**

## CASE STUDY: THE CHART PARSER

A system for implementing bottom-up parsers was written by Kay (1967, 1973). It works by moving a pointer over one word at a time in the sentence (it happened to go right to left in the original implementation). When the pointer is advanced, grammatical rewrite rules are applied to the string. If the application of rules results in a potential conflict as to what the resulting string should look like, all the possible versions are produced. At each level, all the versions of the previous level are considered independently.

Rewrite rules:
  (DET) ADJ* N PP* → NP
  PREP NP → PP
  V (NP) PP* → VP
  NP VP → S
Sentence:
  Plows changed life in Europe.
   N,V    V,ADJ  N  PREP  N

**Figure 3.14 Simple Grammar**

When the rewrite rules of the simple grammar given in Figure 3.14 are applied to the sentence, two versions are written when the pointer is between "plows" and "changed," twelve when it is between "life" and "in" and 22 when the whole string is considered. A top-down parser would not have made the mistakes of considering "plows" as a verb or "changed" as an adjective because of their placement in the sentence. A top-down parser using the same grammar would only produce eight versions of the sentence. However, if the word "changed" were garbled, a top-down parser would only identify that "plows" is a noun phrase. A bottom-up parser would identify "plows" as a noun phrase (and as a verb) and identify "in Europe" as a prepositional phrase and "life in Europe" as a noun phrase. This additional information could be very helpful in identifying why the sentence did not parse completely.

A bottom-up parser may have to carry along several versions of the same phrase in the course of parsing. If a new sentence must be written for each version of each phrase, the number of combinations

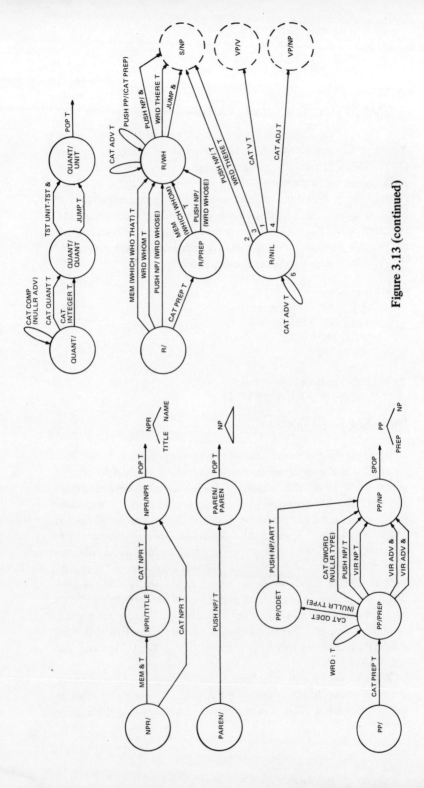

**Figure 3.13 (continued)**

for long sentences grows out of hand quickly. In response to this, Kay developed the chart. The chart is a data structure which represents the parses of various phrases of a sentence. It consists of nodes and arcs. The nodes represent points in the sentence between words, and the arcs represent parses of phrases. The chart for the sentence in Figure 3.14 is shown in Figure 3.15.

The chart is useful for other levels of analysis as well as syntax. The sentence in Figure 3.16 has two parses of the prepositional phrase, one of which will be eliminated on semantic grounds. The semantic interpretation program can refer to the chart just as the syntax programs can.

### 3.5 Combining Top-Down and Bottom-Up Parsing

CASE STUDY: LINGOL

The parsing scheme for LINGOL, LINGuistics Oriented Language (Pratt 1973, 1975), is interesting in that it combines two general-purpose context-free parsing algorithms. The bottom-up component operates on the input sentence, proposing possible production rules that may be relevant. One of the problems of bottom-up parsers, as discussed above, is that many constructions may be proposed that could never contribute to the parse of any entire sentence. A top-down parsing method will only consider the production rules that could contribute to the parse of the entire sentence. A top-down method may, however, consider some productions that could never contribute to the parse of the particular input sentence. Consider the simple grammar and sentence below:

(a) S → NP VP
(b) S → Wh VP
(c) S → VP
(d) NP → N
(e) NP → ADJ N
(f) VP → V NP

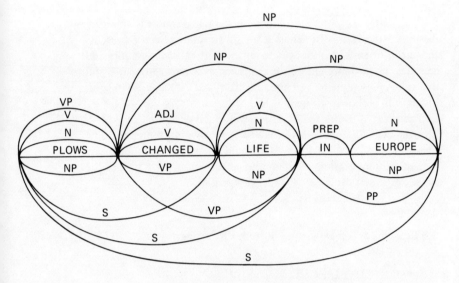

**Figure 3.15 Syntactic chart**

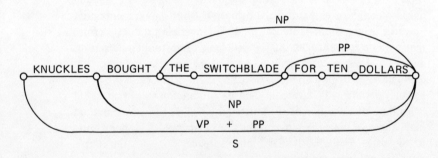

**Figure 3.16 Prepositional phrase attachment**

(1) Capable generals command vast armies

A bottom-up parser would interpret "command" as both a noun and a verb. However, with the grammar given, a top-down parser would have identified the noun phrase "capable generals" and been searching for a verb at that point in the sentence. But when the top-down parser was beginning the parse of the sentence, it was prepared to test it for a noun phrase, a Wh-word (e.g., what, who, where) or a verb phrase. The bottom-up parser would have unambiguously identified "capable" as an adjective, part of a noun phrase, and never considered the alternatives.

LINGOL combines a modified version of a context-free bottom-up parser, the Cocke-Younger-Kasami algorithm, with parsing goals from a context-free top-down parser, the Earley algorithm. The parser scans the input sentence from left to right, advancing a pointer by one word at a time. The function of the bottom-up component is to find all possible grammar rules that apply to the part of the input sentence that is to the left of the pointer. The top-down component, called the *oracle*, is then consulted. If any of the nonterminals produced by the bottom-up component could not contribute to a parse of an entire sentence, they are not approved by the oracle.

The oracle works by setting goals based on what has been parsed. A different set of goals is maintained for each starting position in the input sentence. When parsing starts, only one goal is present, the sentence nonterminal starting in position 0 (the point to the left of the first word). The operation can most easily be understood by stepping through an example.

Parsing begins by advancing the pointer from 0 to 1. The bottom-up component finds all the possible parses to the left of the pointer, which in this case is simply ADJ. The oracle is consulted to see if it has foreseen such a nonterminal starting at position 0. The oracle consults its goals for position 0, finding S. If a series of productions can be found such that ADJ is a left constituent of S, the oracle will approve. Rules A and E satisfy the S → ADJ X condition, so it is accepted. Now the oracle adds all the elements X to its list of goals starting at the pointer position. The table and goals are shown in Figure 3.17.

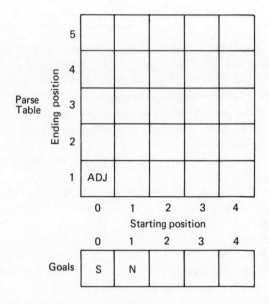

**Figure 3.17**

The pointer is now moved to 2. The bottom-up component identifies an N starting at 1 and an NP starting at 0. The oracle was expecting the N, and NP is approved after considering production A. The use of production A inspires the goal VP starting at position 2. The pointer is advanced to include "command" which the bottom-up component identifies as both a V and N at 2. The oracle has only the goal VP starting at 2. Because of rule F the V is accepted and an NP goal is established at starting position 3. The N is rejected. The table is shown in Figure 3.18.

The pointer is then advanced to 4 and "vast" is identified as an ADJ starting at 3. The oracle finds the goal for 3, NP, and ADJ can be accounted for with rule E. An N goal is set for position 4. The pointer is advanced to 5, "armies" is parsed to an N starting at 4. The ADJ N becomes an NP starting at 3, the V NP becomes a VP starting at 2. The NP VP becomes an S starting at 0. These non-terminals are given to the oracle for approval. Each is approved, the parse is complete and Figure 3.19 shows the final table.

With a more complex grammar, more goals would have been set for each position. With a more complex sentence, more nonterminals would have been rejected by the oracle, emphasizing its importance. Also note that the oracle does not need to perform an actual top-down analysis. It must only find rules A → ... → B given A and B.

What has been described to this point will only accept sentences in context-free languages, but its power can be extended through attaching arbitrary procedures (critics) to the production rules. Another procedure is attached to each rule for generating a structural representation of the sentence.

The parser in LINGOL combines a top-down algorithm with a bottom-up algorithm, but it does not retain all that is good about each method. Since the oracle has the power to approve and disapprove, the parsing is still sensitive to the sentence beginning to the right of position 0. If a sentence is embedded at some arbitrary position in a string of words, as may happen with speech understanding, the sentence cannot be found as it could with a bottom-up

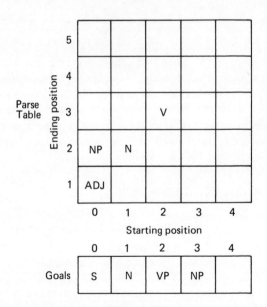

**Figure 3.18**

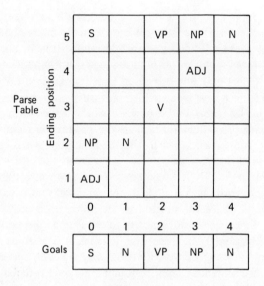

**Figure 3.19**

method. Similarly, if the string does not parse to a sentence, say, due to an unknown word, the parser cannot give as much information about the structures surrounding the unknown word. Furthermore, unlike an ATN, the parser cannot be guided by heuristics to find one most probable parse first. All parses are developed simultaneously. The ATN is, however, in danger of backtracking if the most probable parse is not the correct parse of a particular sentence. There is no backtracking in the LINGOL parser.

## CASE STUDY: READER IN PSI

Reader (Ginsparg 1978) is the parser written for the PSI (Green and Barstow 1977) automatic programming project. The PSI project has produced some very impressive demonstration examples. The example in Figure 3.20 illustrates several interesting facets. First, PSI has a knowledge of programming. Question 4 was prompted by the program requiring the structure of data structures to be made explicit, and recognizing that the dialog to that point had not made it explicit. Question 12 shows that the program requires a loop to have an exit condition.

Second, the program allows for rather sophisticated references to objects (more will be said about the general problem of reference in the next chapter). Notice that the user uses pronouns and definite noun phrases. In the answer to question 3, "the guess" refers to the printed result of the match mentioned earlier. Third, user responses vary from the short sentence fragment answer to question 6 to the long explanation in answer 11.

This description will concentrate primarily on the structure of the parser, a program called Reader. Reader's task is to find a parse for the sentence that identifies the main verb, subject, object and indirect object. Any modifiers are attached to the words they modify, and embedded clauses are structured like main clauses, around the verb. Semantic information is used while attaching constituents to one another, so when the parser has completed the parse, the resulting structure is not only syntactically correct, but it makes sense semantically as well (e.g., prepositional phrases are attached to words that they could sensibly modify).

1. WHAT IS THE NAME OF THE PROGRAM YOU WISH TO WRITE?
   Arch.

2. DOES ARCH HAVE A SPECIAL PROGRAM TYPE?
   Theory formation.

3. DESCRIBE ARCH.
   The program is a loop. On each iteration, it reads in a trial-item, matches the input to the internal concept model, and prints the result of the match. The user must then inform the program whether or not the guess is correct, and the program modifies its model of the concept accordingly.

4. WHAT IS THE STRUCTURE OF THE TRIAL-ITEM?
   A trial-item is a set of relations.

5. WHAT IS THE STRUCTURE OF THE MODEL?
   The model is a set of relations, each marked "necessary" or "possible."

6. WHAT IS THE STRUCTURE OF THE RESPONSE?
   "Correct" or "wrong."

7. WHAT IS THE STRUCTURE OF THE RELATIONS IN THE TRIAL-ITEM?
   A relation is a property name and a list of atoms.

8. WHAT IS THE INITIAL VALUE OF THE MODEL?
   Nil.

9. PLEASE DEFINE WHAT IT MEANS FOR A SCENE TO MATCH A CONCEPT.
   A trial-item matches the model if all the relations in the model that are marked "necessary" are elements of the trial-item.

10. WHAT IS THE FORMAT OF THE PRINT?
    Type "the trial-item matches" if the trial-item matched, and "the trial-item does not match" if it did not.

11. DESCRIBE MODIFYING THE MODEL.
    If the trial-item matched and the user said the guess was correct, then every relation in the trial-item which is not in the model should be put in the model and marked "possible." If the trial-item matched and the user said "wrong," then change the marking of a relation marked "possible" which is in the model and not in the trial-item to "necessary." If the trial-item did not match, and the user said "correct," then do nothing. If the trial-item did not match, and the user said "wrong," then re-mark each relation in the model marked "necessary" that is not in the trial-item "possible."

12. WHAT IS THE EXIT TEST OF THE LOOP?
    Stop when the user types "quit" instead of a trial-item.

13. ARE WE FINISHED?
    Yes.

```
ARCH
  A1←PHI
  LOOP1:
  PRINT ("Ready for the TRIAL-ITEM")
  A2←READ ()
  If EQUAL (A2 "quit")
    Then go EXIT1
  A4←MATCH (A2 A1)
  Cases: If A4
```

Then PRINT ("the trial-item matches")
else If NOT (A4)

Then PRINT ("the trial-item does not match")
A5←READ ()
Cases: If AND (A4 EQUAL (A5 "correct"))
      Then A11←The set of all A10 in A2 such that:
             NOT (MEMBER (A10 A1)
        For all A10 in A11 do:
            A1←INSERT (A10 A1)
            MAP (A3 A10 "possible")
else If AND (A4 EQUAL (A5 "wrong"))
      Then A7←The set of any 1 A6 in A1 such that:
             AND (NOT (MEMBER (A6 A2))
                EQUAL (1MAP (A3 A6)
                "possible"))
        For all A6 in A7 do:
            MAP (A3 A6 "necessary")
  else IF AND (NOT (A4)
            EQUAL (A5 "correct"))
      Then NIL
  else IF AND (NOT (A4)
            EQUAL (A5 "wrong"))
      Then A9←The set of all A8 in A1 such that:
             AND (EQUAL (1MAP (A3 A8)
                      "necessary")
                NOT MEMBER (A8 A2)))
        For all A8 in A9 do:
            MAP (A3 A8 "possible")
  Goto LOOP1
  EXIT 1:
MATCH (B1 B2)
  FORALL (B3) IMPLIES (AND (EQUAL (1MAP (A3 B3)
                          "necessary")
                MEMBER (B3 B2))
                MEMBER (B3 B1))

A5 is either a string whose value is "wrong" or a string whose value is "correct."

A4 is either TRUE or FALSE. B3 is a variable bound to A12.

A3 is a mapping from the elements of A1 to either a string whose value is "possible" or a string whose value is "necessary."

B2 is a variable bound to A1. B1 is a variable bound to A2.

A2 is either a set whose generic element is a record whose fields are PROPERTY: a primitive name and ATOM-LIST: a list whose generic element is a primitive or a string whose value is "quit."
A1 is a set whose generic element is a record whose fields are PROPERTY: a primitive name and ATOM-LIST: a list whose generic element is a primitive with assertions:
EXISTS (B4) EQUAL (1MAP (A3 B4) A13)
A13 is either a string whose value is "possible" or a string whose value is "necessary."
B4 is a variable bound to A12. A12 is the generic element of A1.

**Figure 3.20**
**An example from PSI**
(Reprinted with permission of the author from *Natural Language Processing in an Automatic Programming Domain* by Jerrold Ginsparg)

Reader uses a fairly simple parsing formalism. It consists of a stack, a modifier list and two message slots. The stack is used to store partial structures. The structures are not combined into a single structure until the state of the parse forces the combination. Forcing conditions will be discussed in a moment. The modifier list holds words until a structure can be built that uses them. The main use for the modifier list is to hold prenominal modifiers (i.e., the determiner, adjectives and their adverbs). When the head noun of a noun phrase is identified, the words are removed from the modifier list and attached to the head noun. The noun phrase structure is then pushed on the stack. One of the two messages is a single atom description about the structure on the top of the stack, like NOUN or VERB. The other message is a list of features describing the contents of the entire sentence. It designates features such as interrogative or declarative and the characteristics of the verb.

The grammar is written as a set of programs, one program for each of the following word classes: VERB, PREPOSITION, NOUN, MODIFIER, ARTICLE, CONJUNCTION and PUNCTUATION. The words in the sentence are processed one at a time in a left to right scan. The appropriate word class program is executed to process each word.

Executing a program for each word in the sentence is a bottom-up parsing strategy. However, examining the contents of the stack for expected structures is a top-down strategy. The two are combined in Reader.

The bottom-up strategy in Reader avoids the proliferation of partial parses, but retains the robustness of bottom-up parsing. The main function of the parsing program is merely to bracket phrases and clauses that are used as functional units and push them on the stack. Attaching units such as noun phrases to a subject slot of a verb or prepositional phrases and relative clauses to the words they modify is done primarily by another process, called "collapsing" the stack.

In cases where more than one parse is possible, Reader can develop alternatives in parallel. It usually needs to develop only one parse at a time, however. This is because decisions other than bracketing are deferred as long as possible. When they are made, they use both syntactic and semantic constraints.

Phrases are bracketed and pushed on the stack until one of two conditions arises: Either the end of the sentence is reached or a word must be attached to a structure on the stack that is not at the top. For example, consider the parse of "The woman from the city bank gave the man his change." The parse starts by pushing an empty structure for the clause on the stack. The noun phrase "the woman" is put into this structure. It will be determined later whether "the woman" functions as a subject or object of the verb. Next, the preposition "from" causes a new structure for a prepositional phrase to be pushed. The noun phrase "the city bank" is identified and put in the object slot of the prepositional phrase structure. Figure 3.21 shows the current state of the stack.

At this point the verb "gave" is read, but the structure at the top of the stack cannot accept a verb. The CLAUSE structure can, however, so the stack must be collapsed to bring the CLAUSE structure to the top. The prepositional phrase is popped and attached to the noun phrase "the woman." This brings the CLAUSE to the top, and "gave" is put into the VERB slot. Next, the noun phrases "the man" and "his change" are each parsed and put in noun phrase slots in the CLAUSE structure. The resulting structure is then processed to

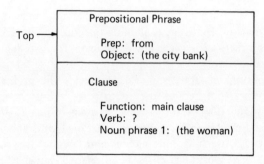

Figure 3.21 The reader stack after parsing "The woman from the city bank"

identify the subject, object and indirect object. If more than one interpretation is possible, the syntactic and semantic likelihoods of the structures are measured. The semantic measure checks the appropriateness of verb modifiers and verb surface cases (subject, object, indirect object) and the appropriateness of noun modifiers. Possible ratings are Perfect, Acceptable and Unacceptable. The syntactic measure is an accumulation of demerits based on unlikely structures. The structure that measures best semantically is chosen. If there is a tie for the best semantic measure, the tie is broken by choosing the one with the best syntactic measure.

1) The hostess served us drinks.

Many words can function as more than one part of speech. "Drinks," for instance, can be either a verb or a noun. When one of the programs begins executing for "drinks" in sentence 1, say, VERB, it examines the contents of the stack for a possible slot that can accept its part of speech. There is no verb slot available on the stack when the parser reaches "drinks." The only available verb slot has been filled by "served." Then the other program, NOUN, begins executing and finds a slot for a noun. The verb has a slot for a direct object noun phrase; "drinks" is put in there.

Another feature of the word class programs is that they are not restricted in any way. They can, for instance, look ahead to words to the right of the current word in the sentence. Also, the structure that has been pushed on the top of the stack may be altered. The phrase "the baseball" would cause a noun phrase to be pushed on the stack. If the next word were "bats," the noun phrase could be changed to show that "bats" is the head noun and "baseball" is a modifying noun.

## 3.6 Computational Linguistic Models of Syntax

### CASE STUDY: TQA

TQA, Transformational Question Answerer (Petrick 1973; Plath 1976; Damerau 1977), is a natural language question-answering program that is primarily interesting because of its syntactic parser. The parser is an attempt to implement a version of transformational grammar directly, i.e., not embedded in another formalism such as an ATN.

There are many versions of transformational grammar, but they all share some fundamental similarities. A transformational grammar consists of three components: a dictionary, a phrase structure grammar and a set of transformations. Transformational grammar was developed by linguists whose attention for the most part was focused on generating grammatical sentences in a language. The goal of a language analysis program is recognizing grammatical sentences and representing them in a canonical structure (the underlying structure). Our attention to transformational grammar will be focused on recognition rather than generation.

A transformational grammar analysis performs at least two distinct analysis phases on sentences. The first applies the phrase structure grammar to the sentence to identify its surface structure. The phrase structure grammar is composed of context-free rules and its purpose is to bracket phrases and establish the dependency relationships between phrases (e.g., which word does a particular prepositional phrase modify, what noun phrase is the object of the verb). The phrase structure grammar results in a surface structure parse tree.

The second phase applies an ordered list of transformational rules to the parse tree. These rules transform the tree into a canonical form.

In canonical form, all "understood" morphemes are inserted into the tree. The phrases in parentheses in example 1 are normally deleted as understood:

1) Is IBM's headquarters (located) in Armonk?
   How much (money) did GM gross in 1967?
   How (high) did Exxon rank in 1971 sales?
   List the companies (that are) (located) in Michigan.

In canonical form, clauses are in subject-verb-object form, regardless of the order  in which these components appeared in the surface structure. The surface structure of questions and passive sentences would thus need to be transformed. Their canonical form also requires that all propositions implied by clauses and modifiers be represented explicitly (e.g.,  "the green car" implies the proposition, "the car is green").

TQA begins its analysis with a lexical scan. The words of the sentence are replaced with tree fragments indicating word categories and compound words (e.g., both "automobile" and "car" become "auto"), and the trees are marked with features such as human, singular or plural.

The parser takes the list of tree fragments as input and performs three stages of analysis: string transformations, phrase structure parsing and transformational analysis. The string transformations are represented in an ordered list of rules that apply to local segments of the sentence. They select the intended meaning of ambiguous words and phrases and identify some idioms. String transformations avoid unnecessary ambiguities in the phrase structure parsing.

The phrase structure parser is then applied to produce a surface structure parse. The final stage is the application of an ordered set of transformations. The transformations are represented in the form of pattern-action rules. Both the pattern part and action part are tree fragments. If the pattern part of a transformational rule matches some fragment of the current state of the sentence tree, the tree is transformed into a new configuration by the action part. After syntactic analysis, TQA performs semantic interpretation and produces a database query to answer the question.

The first incarnation of this program operated on a database holding information on Fortune 500 corporations. One problem with a "toy" application such as this was that there were no users who were particularly interested in querying the database. As a result, a later version interfaced to the land use database of the municipality of White Plains, New York. City employees were given access to the system and encouraged to use it as frequently as they could. Researchers recorded all transactions. At the time of this writing, the experiment is still under way. This application is very interesting for natural language processing because it is the first time that the performance of a natural language program is being studied on a long-term basis, in use by users who have a real interest in the data.

## CASE STUDY: PARSIFAL

PARSIFAL (Marcus 1978a, 1978b) is designed to be able to parse the sentences that people can easily parse. PARSIFAL will fail on the sentences that human listeners stumble over, like the garden path sentence below:

2) The cotton clothing is made of grows in Mississippi.

This characteristic of modeling human language understanding makes PARSIFAL interesting as a tool for linguistics. It does not appear to be particularly attractive in its limited form for the near future for engineering natural language analysis programs.

### Deterministic Parsing

PARSIFAL is designed around the belief that language understanding is primarily deterministic. This means that language can be parsed left to right without backtracking or parallel computation. The deterministic hypothesis makes PARSIFAL significantly different from other formalisms. ATNs make extensive use of backtracking; bottom-up parsers make extensive use of parallelism in the form of keeping several candidate parses or partial parses active simultaneously. PARSIFAL builds syntactic structures only when it has decided that they are the correct structures for the sentence. It never builds a piece of syntactic structure that will not eventually be used in the final structure. It never destroys any structure that it has built.

On the other hand, PARSIFAL cannot parse the range of sentences that other formalisms can. It is important to realize, however, that there are many sentences in which an ATN would backtrack which PARSIFAL could parse. Backtracking in grammar implemented ATNs is not limited to garden path sentences, but it occurs very frequently. The same is true for parallel analysis of alternative parses in bottom-up parsers.

The justification for nondeterminism (whether embodied in backtracking or parallelism) is that it allows the grammar to make decisions based on very limited data. An ATN, for example, usually uses two kinds of information: what has been parsed so far (represented by the current state) and what the next word or phrase is (of course, using the arbitrary condition part of the arcs, ATN grammars could be written to use any information for parsing). When an ATN parses sentences 3 and 4, it must be in the same state when the word "riding" is reached in both sentences:

3) Were the men riding across the field?
4) Were the men riding across the field Mongols?

Since it decides what do to next based on its current state and the next word, it will make the same decision in both sentences. Let us say it decides that "riding" is the main verb of the sentence as it is in sentence 3. When the word "Mongols" is reached in sentence 4, the ATN backtracks. To parse sentence 4 correctly, the interpretation of "riding" as the main verb of the sentence must be changed. If "riding" is interpreted as the verb of a relative clause, "(who were) riding across the field," then the main clause can be properly interpreted as "were the men Mongols?" Sentence 4 causes backtracking because of a missing relative pronoun. Other structures notorious for causing backtracking are conjunctions (sentences 5 and 6 below) and noun-noun modification, like the "cotton clothing" in example 1 (example 1 also has a missing relative pronoun).

5) I fixed the brakes and the steering wheel.
6) I fixed the brakes and the steering wheel broke.

A parser could trade the overhead of backtracking for the overhead of lookahead. When a questionable construction is being analyzed, the assignment of its structure could be deferred. Deferring the structure assignment allows the parser to gather more information before assigning a structure. Lookahead would serve the same function as backtracking: it would lead the parser to an appropriate parse. With lookahead, however, no structures would be built until the parser was confident that they were appropriate.

PARSIFAL uses lookahead, but it is restricted lookahead. If the parser were allowed to look arbitrarily far ahead, it would be as non-deterministic as an ATN. The nondeterminism would just be hidden in the lookahead routines. The lookahead in PARSIFAL is limited to three "constituents," which will be explained in a moment. But first, the parsing formalism will be described.

### The PARSIFAL Formalism

The PARSIFAL parsing formalism is quite simple. It consists of a stack, a constituent buffer and a grammar composed of packets of pattern/action rules (Figure 3.22). The rule packets are activated and deactivated throughout the course of the parse. The constituent buffer is composed of three cells, each of which can hold a constituent. A constituent is a structure whose descendants are known but which is in search of a parent node. A constituent may be as small as a word, or as large as a relative clause, but there can be only one constituent per cell. The stack holds structural nodes that are in search of descendants, e.g., a sentence node waiting for its verb phrase, or a noun phrase node waiting for a head noun. Along with each node on the stack is the set of rule packets that were active when the node was put on the stack. The packets associated with the node at the top of the stack are active. The rules associated with the nodes deeper in the stack are inactive, but will become active when their node rises to the top of the stack.

If a rule is in an active packet, its pattern is compared with the constituents in the constituent buffer and the top of the stack. If the pattern matches, then the action part of the rule is performed. Rule actions can create new nodes and push them on the stack, remove constituents from the buffer and attach them to the node at the top of the stack or pop the node off the top of the stack and put it in the constituent buffer.

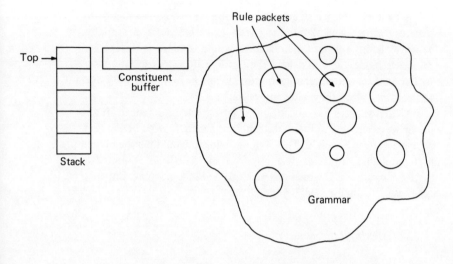

**Figure 3.22 The PARSIFAL formalism**

*An Example*

We can illustrate the operation of PARSIFAL by tracing the parse of an example sentence. The sentence is shown in Figure 3.23 along with the parse that PARSIFAL is implemented to produce. The grammar implemented in the demonstration version of PARSIFAL is trace theory, a brand of transformational grammar. The aspect of trace theory revealed in this example is embodied in the [trace] leaf of the tree. The theory suggests that when the sentence was being generated it was originally in the form, "John did see who." This sentence was transformed to, "Who did John see," but a trace was left behind in the original position of "who." The significance of the trace is not seen in this sentence, and a discussion of the merits of trace theory is beyond the scope of this book. Our interest is in discussing the parsing formalism.

When parsing begins, the stack and constituent buffer are empty. An initial set of parsing rules is active. One of these fires and "who" is brought into the buffer. Currently active rule packets are designed to parse constituents of a sentence. "Who" is seen as the first word of a noun phrase, so an NP node is pushed onto the stack, and noun phrase parsing rule packets are activated. The rule packets for parsing sentence constituents are deactivated. Figure 3.24 illustrates the current state.

The pronoun "who" is attached to the noun phrase. The NP node is popped off the stack and dropped into the buffer. The sentence parsing rules attached to S become active again. "Did" is brought into the buffer. The current state is shown in Figure 3.25.

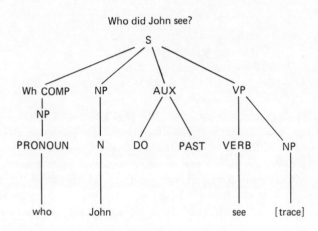

**Figure 3.23 Target structure**

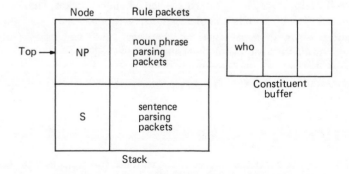

**Figure 3.24**

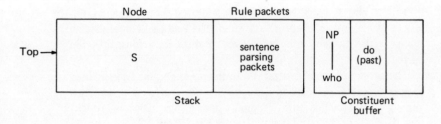

**Figure 3.25**

A rule with pattern part

BUFFER: [Wh-word] [verb]
STACKTOP: – –

matches the current state. This rule labels the sentence as a wh-question, and the NP as a WhComplement. The WhComplement is removed from the buffer and attached to the S node on the top of the stack. A rule packet that parses sentence subjects is activated along with a packet for parsing wh-questions. Another word, "John," is brought into the buffer. "John" is recognized as a proper name, so an NP node is built with "John" attached to it, and pushed on the stack. A rule packet that specializes in building names is activated. The rules in this packet would match on a full name like "John Wesley Harding." The next word, "see," is brought into the buffer, but it does not match any rules in the name-building packet. The noun phrase "John" is thus complete, and it is dropped back into the buffer where it came from, i.e., between "did" and "see" (the mechanism for keeping track of this location will not be discussed here). The current configuration is shown in Figure 3.26.

A subject parsing rule that matches the pattern

BUFFER: [auxverb] [NP]
STACKTOP: – –

identifies the NP as the subject of the sentence and attaches it to the S node. The subject parsing rule packet is deactivated, and a packet

that recognizes the beginning of an auxiliary verb is activated. A rule
in this packet fires, creating a node for the auxiliary, and pushes it on
the stack. An auxiliary parsing packet is activated. The current state
is shown in Figure 3.27.

Next, the rule pattern below matches the buffer and adds "DO"
to the AUX node on the top of the stack:

BUFFER: [DO] [TENSELESS verb]
STACKTOP: – –

None of the other rules that build the auxiliary are triggered, so the
AUX is taken to be complete. This is done using priorities attached
to rules. All of the actual auxiliary building rules have a high priority.
Since none of them were triggered, a low priority dummy rule in the
auxiliary building packet that would trigger on any buffer contents is
activated. The activation of this rule indicates that the auxiliary
building is complete. The AUX node is popped and dropped back
into the buffer. A rule then fires that attaches the AUX node to the
S node. The auxiliary packet is deactivated and the main verb packet
is activated. Figure 3.28 shows the current state.

A rule now matches the verb "see," which pushes a VP node onto
the stack, attaches a VERB node to that, and "see" is attached to the
VERB node. The verb phrase parsing packet is deactivated, and a
packet for identifying the phrases is activated.

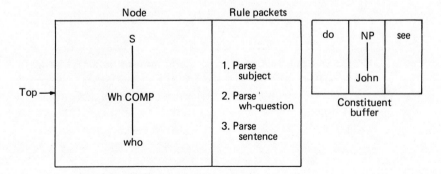

**Figure 3.26**

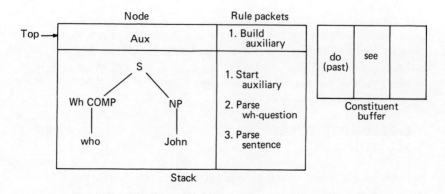

**Figure 3.27**

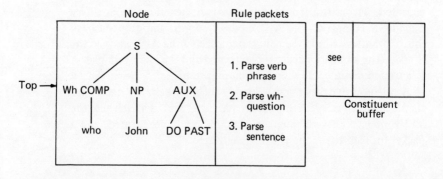

**Figure 3.28**

The end punctuation "?" is brought into the buffer. This triggers a rule that identifies this as the appropriate location for the [trace] of "who." A noun phrase with a [trace] is created and attached to the VP node on the top of the stack. The VP is complete, so it is popped and attached to the S node, which completes the parse.

# References and Further Reading

Bratley, P. and Dakin, D.J. "A Limited Dictionary for Syntactic Analysis." In *Machine Intelligence* 2, edited by E. Dale and D. Michie. New York: American Elsevier, 1968.

Damerau, F. "Advantages of a Transformational Grammar for Question Answering." In *Proceedings of the International Joint Conference on Artificial Intelligence*. Cambridge, Mass.: MIT, 1977.

_____. "The Derivation of Answers from Logical Forms in a Question Answering System." Research Report RC 6859 (29411). Yorktown Heights, N.Y.: IBM, Sept. 1977.

Finin, T. and Hadden, G. "Augmenting ATNs." In *Proceedings of the International Joint Conference on Artificial Intelligence*. Cambridge, Mass.: MIT, 1977.

Ginsparg, J.M. "Natural Language Processing in an Automatic Programming Domain." Ph.D. thesis, Stanford University, Memo AIM-316, Computer Science Department Report STAN-cs-78-671, June 1978.

Green, C. and Barstow, D. "A Hypothetical Dialogue Exhibiting a Knowledge Base for a Program-Understanding System." In *Machine Intelligence*, edited by E.W. Elcock and D. Michie. New York: Holsted Press, 1977.

Kaplan, R.M. "Augmented Transition Networks as Psychological Models of Sentence Comprehension." *Artificial Intelligence* 3 (1972): 77-100.

_____. "A General Syntactic Processor." In *Natural Language Processing*, edited by R. Rustin. New York: Algorithmics Press, 1973.

Kay, Martin. "Experiments with a Powerful Parser." Report RM-5452-PR. California: The Rand Corporation, 1967.

Kay, Martin. "The Mind System." In *Natural Language Processing*, edited by R. Rustin. New York: Algorithmics Press, 1973.

Kuno, S. and Oettinger, A.G. "Syntactic Structure and Ambiguity of English." In *Proceedings—Fall Joint Computer Conference*. Montvale, N.J.: AFIPS Press, 1963.

Marcus, M. "A Computational Account of Some Constraints on Language." In *Theoretical Issues in Natural Language Processing* 2. Urbana, Ill.: University of Illinois, 1978a.

Marcus, M.P. "A Theory of Syntactic Recognition for Natural Languages." Ph.D. Thesis, MIT, Feb. 1978b.

Petrick, S.R. "Transformational Analysis." In *Natural Language Processing*, edited by R. Rustin. New York: Algorithmics Press, 1973.

Plath, W.J. "REQUEST: A Natural Language Question-Answering System." *IBM Journal of Research and Development* (July 1976):326-35.

Pratt, V.R. "LINGOL—A Progress Report." In *Proceedings of the 4th International Joint Conference on Artificial Intelligence*. Cambridge, Mass.: MIT, 1975.

_____. "A Linguistics Oriented Programming Language." In *Proceedings of the 3rd International Joint Conference on Artificial Intelligence*. Stanford, Calif.: Stanford University, 1973.

Robinson, J.J. "An Inverse Transformational Lexicon." In *Natural Language Processing*, edited by R. Rustin. New York: Algorithmics Press, 1973.

Wilks, Y. "Parsing English I." In *Computational Semantics*, edited by E. Charniak and Y. Wilks. New York: North Holland Publishing Company, 1978.

Woods, W.A. "An Experimental Parsing System for Transition Network Grammars." In *Natural Language Processing*, edited by R. Rustin. New York: Algorithmics Press, 1973.

_____. "Syntax, Semantics, and Speech." In *Speech Recognition*, edited by Reddy R. New York: Academic Press, 1975.

_____. "Transition Network Grammars for Natural Language Analysis." CACM 13 (October 1970):591-606.

Woods, W.A.; Kaplan, R.M.; Nash-Webber, B. "The Lunar Sciences Natural Language System: Final Report." NTIS N72-28984, 1972.

Zwicky, A.M.; Friedman, J.; Hall, B.C.; and Walker D.E., "The MITRE Syntactic Analysis Procedure for Transformational Grammars." Bedford, Mass.: The MITRE Corp., 1965.

# 4. Semantics

The role of semantics in language analysis is to relate symbols to concepts. The effect of semantic processing should be to establish in the hearer the meaning of what is heard. In simple cases, such as highly restricted domains of discourse, semantic processing may not be very complex. In the normal use of language, however, semantics demands a great deal of computation. In fact, the semantics that language users deal with so effortlessly, significantly outstrips the capabilities of any computer-based language analysis devised so far.

A widely accepted view of language is that it is used to manipulate elaborate memory structures in the minds of the individuals involved. In Figure 4.1, Lefty has a detailed conceptual structure describing an event in which he was involved. He has selected a few of the details, encoded them into language, and transmitted them to his colleague, Knuckles. The task imposed on Knuckles' semantic analyzer is to identify the kind of events that are being talked about and the objects that play various roles in the event. As Knuckles analyzes the utterance he hears, he builds a representation in his own mind that duplicates Lefty's. The word *bought*, in this context, indicates that Lefty is talking about a Commercial Transaction event. Knuckles already has a general description of a Commercial Transaction, which he uses to represent events of buying, selling, barter, and so on. He then analyzes the other components in the sentence to establish the roles they play in the Commercial Transaction event.

Notice that Lefty "knows" (that is, he has represented in his memory) that the transaction involved a particular store and a

CommercialTransaction

Buyer: Me
Seller: COMMERCIALESTAB007
Payment: $39.95

CommercialTransaction

Buyer: PERSON993 (Lefty)
Object: FIREARM047
Seller: ?
Payment: ?

I bought
a heater

Lefty

Knuckles

**Figure 4.1**

particular gun. They have unique labels—COMMERCIALESTAB007 and FIREARM001, for convenience. This way, he doesn't confuse the store where he got the gun with the concept of stores in general or with COMMERCIALESTAB095, where he shopped for weapons but they charged too much. Likewise, FIREARM001 is the particular gun that Lefty bought. It is not confused with FIREARM137, FIREARM884, and FIREARM466, each of which Lefty considered buying. Furthermore, Lefty has an elaborate description of all the objects that were mentioned here. The names COMMERCIAL-ESTAB007, FIREARM884, and FIREARM001 are merely references to those descriptions.

When Knuckles hears Lefty's statement, his semantic analysis of it results in a structure similar to Lefty's. Knuckles has also depicted the gun as a particular object—FIREARM047. Knuckles, of course, doesn't know as much about his concept, FIREARM047, as Lefty knows about the concept FIREARM001. One would not be surprised if the ensuing conversation centered on helping Knuckles attach the same kind of details to the concept FIREARM047 as Lefty attached to his concept, FIREARM001.

One of the difficulties that Knuckles' semantic analysis must deal with is that of selecting the appropriate meanings of the words in the utterance. Knowing Lefty, Knuckles selects the firearm sense of "heater" rather than the heat-emitting appliance sense. If Lefty says, "It cost me fifty bucks" or "The gun cost fifty bucks," he means the object of the commercial transaction, the gun mentioned in the previous sentence, FIREARM001, not just an arbitrary gun.

If Lefty says, "I've wanted one ever since I saw your new heater in the car," Knuckles is faced with several interpretations. Perhaps the gun is presently in the car, but the "seeing" took place somewhere else. Perhaps the "seeing" took place in the car. Knuckles' semantic analyzer will select an interpretation by using his knowledge of the times Lefty saw his various guns. This is necessary for Knuckles to identify the particular object and particular event that Lefty has mentioned.

By saying, "I've wanted one . . . ," Lefty may not be referring to FIREARM001 specifically but to weapons or pistols in general. Knuckles' semantics must decide which. Notice the difference between Lefty's saying "I've wanted one . . ." and "I've wanted it . . . ." In the latter case he is referring to FIREARM001 specifically.

In this chapter and the next, the various problems of semantic analysis will be discussed. A number of case studies will be used to describe examples of how semantic issues have been handled in natural language processors. This chapter has a different character than the chapter on syntax (Chap. 3). Chapter 3 is concerned primarily with mechanisms for applying rules of syntax (a grammar) to utterances; not much is said about what a grammar should include. In the present chapter, mechanisms are discussed in the case studies, but the overall organization is built around the problems of semantic analysis. Semantic-analyzer design has not matured to the point of syntactic-analyzer design, but then the semantic problem is much more complex.

## 4.1 Multiple Word Senses

Consider the following words: dog, cow, badger, squirrel, fly, horse, buffalo, chicken and snake. It may surprise you to know that this is a list of verbs. (I am indebted to Gene Lewis for this delightful list). Most words in English have more than one sense. Many of them have senses that are different parts of speech, like, "We had chicken for dinner" (noun), "He's turned chicken" (adjective), and "He chickened out when the fighting started" (verb).

In Chapter 3 we see that word senses, when they differ in their syntactic categories, can often be selected by syntactic analysis. A problem less well understood is that of selecting a word sense when its syntactic role is known. Table 4.1 shows the various senses of *fly* as a noun, and Table 4.2 shows it's senses as a verb.

### Table 4.1

#### Noun senses of *fly*

fly1:    a winged insect
fly2:    a fishhook dressed to resemble an insect
fly3:    the action of flying
fly4:    a garment closing, such as on trousers
fly5:    a baseball hit high into the air
fly6:    "on the fly"—in motion

### Table 4.2

#### Verb senses of *fly*

fly7:    to pass through the air with wings
fly8:    to flee, vanish
fly9:    to move quickly
fly10:   to hit a fly in baseball
fly11:   to operate an airplane
fly12:   to travel in an airplane
fly13:   "fly at"—assail suddenly
fly14:   "fly high"—to be elated
fly15:   "fly in the face of"—to act brazenly

**Table 4.3**

---

1. The gas killed all the flies but one (fly1)
2. Hand me that fly with the yellow feathers and spinner (fly2)
3. He hit an infield fly (fly5)
4. Let's go for a fly (fly3 if spoken by a pilot)
5. Let's go for a fly (fly1 if spoken by a tse-tse fly collector)
6. Knuckles was so busy he ate his lunch on the fly (fly6)
7. Knuckles was distracted and put his sandwich on the fly (fly1, fly2?)

---

These are the familiar senses of *fly*. There are a few more, but they are used less frequently than the ones shown here. One would expect nearly all fluent users of English to be able to use and understand every one of these senses of "fly."

The appropriate senses of words can usually be determined from the context. Table 4.3 has some examples of uses of various senses of *fly*. The peculiar thing about the·sentences is that the *context* differs radically from one sentence to the next. In sentence 1, we assume fly1 because that is the only one which can be killed; the context is specified by the verb. In sentence 2, the prepositional phrase, a modifier, eliminates all possible interpretations but fly2. Similarly, the modifier "infield" in sentence 3 eliminates all interpretations but fly5. Sentences 4 and 5 do not even use the text of the conversation but rather the identity of the speaker. The idiom "on the fly," fly6, is selected in sentence 6 not because of the verb "ate" or because of modifiers, but because of the similarity to the word "busy." In spite of the fact that "on the fly" is present in sentence 7, fly6 is not the selected interpretation. It is overridden by the special function "on" plays when used with the verb "put."

The complicating characteristic of context in semantic analysis is that any of the rules that prompted the selection of senses of fly in this example could be overridden by an appropriate context. None of the rules seem to be absolute, but are accepted unless some other interpretation which fits more of the facts is found. In appropriate contexts, one can imagine "killed" being used to suggest "rendered useless" when talking about fly2. "Infield flies" could be fly1s buzzing around the infield. A pilot could be a tse-tse fly collector on the side, or vise versa. Knuckles could be an imaginary character who rides a fly1 like a horse.

Many early natural language understanding programs did not deal with the problems of multiple word senses, in spite of the fact that most words have many senses. The natural language processors commonly circumvented multiple word senses by restricting the domain of discourse so severely that it was highly unlikely that a word would be used in more than one way. This was not a solution to the problem, but avoidance of it. Natural language processing technology has now reached a level of sophistication that no longer allows this pervasive problem of language to be avoided.

In the early 1960s a scheme was developed in linguistics for attaching some semantic rules to transformational grammar. The idea is to include "semantic markers" in the definitions of each sense of the words in the dictionary. The semantic markers attached to a word would be used to restrict the ways in which it could combine with other words. For example, three senses of "green" are having the color green, inexperienced, or unripe. The first sense of green must apply to physical objects. The second sense must apply to humans (as in "the green troops fresh from boot camp"). The third sense must apply to fruit. If the phrase "green x" were analyzed using semantic markers, the features of "x" would be checked to see which of the categories required by "green," PHYSICALOBJECT, HUMAN or FRUIT, the "x" best satisfies. This process selects one of the senses of "green." It could simultaneously select one of the senses of "x." If the "x" were "ball" with two senses—a spherical object and a large dancing party—the phrase "green ball" would select the interpretation of "a spherical object that has the color green."

Semantic markers have proved to be very useful in natural language processing. They have been widely applied and, in many cases, they select appropriate word senses successfully. There are problems with semantic markers, however. It may be the case that a noun, for instance, can fall within more than one category expected by an adjective. This was the case with "green" above, but we glossed over it. The senses of "green" are marked for PHYSICALOBJECT, HUMAN and FRUIT, respectively. The problem is that these categories are not mutually exclusive. Members of both the categories HUMAN and FRUIT must also fall into the category PHYSICAL-OBJECT. It was suggested above that the "best" match, meaning the most specific, be taken. It is entirely reasonable, however, for one to speak of a fruit or perhaps a person as having the color green. If this is so, how are the semantic markers to be handled?

One solution is to maintain a collection of all the interpretations which are not explicitly ruled out by local semantic marker checks. In addition to the local checks, a set of semantic markers describing the overall context could be maintained. These could be used to select among ambiguities that were not resolved at the local level. The difficulty with this solution is that sets of semantic markers describing the context can get unwieldy. It is also unclear as to when markers are added to or removed from the global lists (i.e., when does the context shift?), and how large a piece of discourse it should describe (a clause, a sentence, a paragraph?). Although semantic markers have been used for local word sense selection in many natural language programs, the author is not aware of any using semantic markers to describe larger contexts.

There are other word sense selection problems that semantic markers appear not to be very useful for. For example, the money sense of "bucks" is appropriate for the following:

He left twenty bucks in his other pants.

It seems that money is selected over deer because one cannot imagine getting twenty deer into one's pants. This sense selection is made on some sort of plausibility criterion. It does not seem amenable to treatment by semantic markers.


APPROACHES TO SELECTION


With a large vocabulary, the problem of making a word sense choice becomes very important. There are two general strategies to selecting from a set of choices: stop-on-success and try-all-possibilities. Computationally, they both have advantages.

*Stop-on-success*

The stop-on-success strategy requires that all the alternative interpretations of an input are ordered before the search begins. This ordering is critically important because the search stops as soon as a satisfactory interpretation is found. A heuristic grammar implemented in an ATN works this way. Many parses of a sentence may be possible, but the only one returned by a heuristic ATN grammar is the first one found. The "heuristics" in the grammar are embodied in the *order* that the grammar rules are applied. The same strategy can be applied to selecting word senses. For example, the global context of a word can be used to order the relevant senses. When a dictionary entry of a word is called for, the ordered list of its senses is scanned sequentially. The first sense that satisfies the local context constraints is selected as the appropriate sense.

The SAM program (which will be discussed more fully in chapter 6) orders word senses in this way. When the global context is recognized as patronizing a restaurant, two senses of "check" are given priority: the "bill indicating the amount due" and the "written order instructing a bank to pay as specified":

1) Knuckles asked the waitress for the check.
2) Lefty paid the bill with a check.

Local context selects one sense of "check" over another in sentences 1 and 2. Additional senses of "check" need never be considered unless the most strongly expected senses do not match. The other possible senses are given below:

CHECK1: exposure of a chess king to attack
CHECK2: a stoppage in the forward course of progress
CHECK3: a restraint
CHECK4: an inspection or investigation
CHECK5: a pattern in squares that resembles a checkerboard
CHECK6: a mark written beside an item to show it has been noted

CHECK7: a bill indicating an amount due
CHECK8: a written order instructing a bank to pay as
specified

When a context has been established that strongly favors some word senses over others, it intuitively seems that the other senses are not even considered except as a last resort. While playing chess, "check" (CHECK1) is strongly indicated and CHECK8 is not even consciously considered.

Another intuitive observation is that some word senses are never considered unless the listener has been specifically prepared by the context to expect them.

3) Lefty drank a check.

Sentence 3 is nonsensical, but the author found himself trying to force certain interpretations like some liquid form of CHECK7 or CHECK8. Looking back to the various senses, CHECK1, CHECK2 and CHECK3 were considered and rejected, but CHECK4, CHECK5 and CHECK6 never even occurred to the author (at least not consciously, which is certainly inconclusive). In the proper contexts, the author would have no trouble recognizing CHECK4, CHECK5 and CHECK6. It is interesting to note that if the sentence were changed to

4) Lefty drank his check.

an interpretation is made more readily, i.e., spending a paycheck on alcohol.

The unsettling feature of a stop-on-success strategy is that it is based on certainty. It implies the ability to decide "this is it, I need look no further." It does not directly support the possibility of selecting the best match among a number of imperfect alternatives. It is reasonable to suggest, however, that a best alternative selection can be used as a backup for stop-on-success. If decisions can be made with certainty most of the time, stop-on-success is still attractive. If stop--on-success is used, the critical problem becomes ordering the alternatives.

*Try-all-possibilities*

The try-all-possibilities strategy is attractive for two reasons. First, if one alternative out of the set of possibilities has an uncommon characteristic, that one characteristic may eliminate all the other possibilities immediately. If the number of possibilities is large, an uncommon characteristic can lead to a prompt selection. Suppose a speaker were to describe a person he saw in a crowd as being medium height, medium weight, dark hair, blue eyes, grey pants and a blue blazer. A listener may, with some difficulty, be able to select the person in question from among the possibilities. If, however, the person was described as having flowers tatooed on his cheek and a parrot on his shoulder, an immediate, "Oh, him" is likely. The identification could be made through set intersection. The person described is the one who (supposedly uniquely) has all the mentioned characteristics. If a very uncommon characteristic implies a set of one member, the other characteristics need not be considered. The catch with making use of uncommon characteristics is that the listener must order the characteristics. To do this effectively, the listener must know before the search is performed which characteristics are unusual among the possibilities.

The second reason that a try-all-possibilities strategy is attractive is that it can deal with imperfect matches. If the available data does not uniquely specify one alternative from the possibilities, it would at least indicate the prime candidates. Dealing with imperfect information has been a hallmark of natural language and AI in general, so this alternative is alluring. It is more reasonable, however, to concentrate on making more information available so a unique decision can be made. In many applications of intelligence, like detective work, making a list of candidates may be the best that can be done. Considering the candidates (bottom-up) can then direct the detective toward the kinds of information required for a unique selection, or at least to make a smaller list of candidates. When information gathering is troublesome, time consuming or otherwise expensive, an iterative try-all-possibilities strategy may be well advised.

The discussion above for both strategies assumed that there was one or more possibility to select and that the appropriate choice was among the possibilities (e.g., the word senses, the murder suspects) known to the decision maker. This is not always the case.

3) Lefty drank a check.

The sense of "check" used in sentence 3 (repeated here for convenience) is not one of the senses listed on page 00. If we were using a stop-on-success strategy, it would be necessary to note not only that this usage did not match any of the available alternatives because of an insufficient number of required feature matches, but there was also a required feature—namely, that this "check" must be a liquid—that was not matched. Likewise, the try-all-possibilities strategy would return no candidates rather than a best fit candidate.

## 4.2 Modifier Attachment

The following sentences are similar in that they all have the same sequence of phrases, namely, NP-V-NP-PP-PP-PP:

1. Knuckles rubbed out the man with the briefcase with Lefty's initials in gold letters.
2. Knuckles rubbed out the man in the picture on the motorcycle with the goggles.
3. Knuckles rubbed out the man with the briefcase at midnight behind the warehouse.
4. Knuckles rubbed out the man at midnight behind the warehouse with a stilleto.

Although these sentences all have the same sequence of phrase types, their structures are different. In the first sentence, "in gold letters" modifies "initials"; "with Lefty's initials" modifies "briefcase"; and "with the briefcase" modifies "man." In the second sentence, all the prepositional phrases modify "man." In the third sentence, "with the briefcase" modifies "man," but the other prepositional phrases modify "rubbed out." In the fourth sentence, all three prepositional phrases modify "rubbed out." It is clear that finding the proper place to attach a prepositional phrase to the word it modifies cannot be done by using syntax alone. It involves knowing the meaning of the phrases and the words they modify. In other words, it is a semantic problem.

Cases of ambiguity illustrate the problem further. In

Knuckles rubbed out the man in the picture in the hallway.

we know that the man is in the picture. But is the man in the hallway now or is the picture hanging in the hallway, or is the man pictured in a hallway, or was the rubbing out done in the hallway? The only way for a listener to answer these questions is to check what he knows about the situation. If the listener knew that a killing occurred in the hallway, either by being a witness or from the previous discourse, he or she could choose the appropriate interpretation. Natural language processors have been designed to deal with this problem in two ways. One, the approach taken for SHRDLU (see chapter 5) maintains a model of its world, and examines it to see which of the various interpretations make sense. The other approach is exemplified by LUNAR in which words are tabulated along with the modifiers that would make sense with them. The LUNAR (see chapter 5) approach cannot resolve alternative structures like that for the killing of the man in the picture in the hallway. The SHRDLU approach can handle this kind of attachment problem, but it requires searching the database repeatedly. Repeated searching of the database was acceptable for SHRDLU's small database, but it would be impractical with a large database like LUNAR's.

## 4.3 Noun-Noun Modification

One of the most difficult problems of semantic interpretation is when one noun is modified by another, as in the examples below:

    aircraft maintenance
    paper bag
    beer mug
    raspberry sherbet

Modification of a noun by another noun suggests that there is some relationship between the two nouns which is not stated explicitly.

The speaker assumes that the listener will infer the appropriate relationship. In the examples above, "aircraft maintenance" implies that maintenance *is performed on* aircraft; "paper bag" implies a bag *made of* paper; "beer mug" implies a mug *usually used for or designed for drinking* beer; and "raspberry sherbet" implies sherbet *that has the flavor of* raspberries. Notice that for each of these examples, the implied relationships are very different and also quite specific to the particular nouns.

The relationship between the nouns of a noun-noun modifier pair is often defined by context. An example that is particularly dependent on context is "Boston ships" (Thompson and Thompson 1975). "Boston ships" could imply ships sailing to Boston, ships sailing from Boston, ships built in Boston, or ships registered in Boston. A sufficiently detailed context could suggest an even more unusual implied relationship.

Nominalized verbs are often used in noun-noun pairs. When a nominalized verb is modified by another noun, the modifying noun is usually related to the nominalized verb as subject or object of the verb form. Examples are (from Finin 1979):

Subject:
    university purchases
    acid corrosion
    bird damage
Object:
    automobile purchases
    engine corrosion
    propeller damage

A third class of modifiers that have been grouped with noun-noun modification are called nonpredicating adjectives. These adjectives do not function as either nouns or adjectives. Common adjectives like "red" or "wet" can be used either as a prenominal modifier or as a subject complement.

the red ball    The ball is red.
the wet rag    The rag is wet.

Nonpredicating adjectives, however, cannot function as subject complements without changing their meaning. One can say, "electrical engineer" but not "the engineer is electrical" because "electrical" is a nonpredicating adjective. One can speak of a "criminal lawyer" and "a lawyer who is criminal," but the two forms mean different things showing that "criminal" is a nonpredicating adjective. Some adjectives function as common (predicating) adjectives when modifying some nouns, and nonpredicating adjectives when modifying others. A "nervous groom" is a "groom who is nervous," but a "nervous twitch" is not "a twitch that is nervous." Nonpredicating adjective modification, like noun-noun modification, requires inferring the appropriate relationship between the modifier and the noun it modifies.

Another complication with noun-noun modification is that a noun phrase may contain a string of several nouns. Consider the following examples:

    ice cream
    ice cream sandwich
    vanilla ice cream sandwich
    vanilla ice cream sandwich wrapper
    vanilla ice cream sandwich wrapper inspector

In addition to indentifying implied relationships between nouns, a language analyzer must identify which nouns modify which. These examples from Finin (1979) suggest the variety:

    water meter cover adjustment screw
        [[[water meter] cover] [adjustment screw]]
    ion thruster performance calibration
        [[ion thruster] [performance calibration]]
    boron epoxy rocket motor chambers
        [[boron epoxy] [rocket motor] chambers]]
    aluminum automobile water pumps
        [aluminum[automobile[water pumps]]]
    January automobile water pump cover shipments
        [January[[automobile[[water pump] cover]]shipments]

## 4.4 Pronouns

### THE UTILITY OF PRONOUNS

Both spoken and written language make frequent use of pronouns, and for good reason. Pronouns bind the sentences of a text or conversation together; they help to impose some coherence to the whole. Compare the following two sentences:

Knuckles was caught and Knuckles was fitted for a pair of concrete shoes.

Knuckles was caught and he was fitted for a pair of concrete shoes.

Besides seeming strange, the first sentence may leave some uncertainty in the listener's mind as to who the two "Knuckles" refer. They may both be the same person, Knuckles Smith, or perhaps Knuckles Smith got caught and Knuckles Wilson got the concrete shoes. In the second sentence, there can be no confusion. The use of the pronoun specifies that one individual was involved in two events, getting caught and getting fitted.

The other advantage of pronouns is that they provide an abbreviated reference. If a "monolithic CMOS technology universal counter circuit evaluation kit" has just been mentioned in a conversation, it is very handy to be able to refer to the object as "it"; this saves a lot of breath.

The problem with pronouns is, of course, that they impose a burden on the listener. Not much information is carried along with a pronoun: he, she, they, we, us, I, you, it. The listener learns from the pronoun that the item it refers to is either animate or inanimate, either male or female, either singular or plural. For all the things that pronouns could refer to, that is not much information! The burden is on the listener's semantic analyzer to learn more about the characteristics of the referent of the pronoun, then to identify the referent from candidates that were either mentioned in or implied by the preceding text.

## PRONOUNS AND REFERENCE

The use of a pronoun in most cases is an act of reference. This means that the pronoun is intended to stand for a particular concept that has come before in the conversation. (Actually, pronouns can also refer to concepts that follow the pronoun, as in "Lefty thought it was too heavy, but he bought a .45 anyway." This is much less common than referring to previously mentioned concepts.) Consider the following sentences:

Lefty bought a heater. The boys from Detroit were coming to town, so he decided he had better buy it. After all, they haven't been too friendly lately. Well, he got a great deal. It only cost $39.95 and it came with trading stamps.

The pronoun "he" is used repeatedly throughout this piece of text to refer to Lefty. "It" is used repeatedly to refer to the gun. Notice that the pronouns are not referring to the word "Lefty" or the word "heater." "Lefty" and all the instances of "he" refer to one concept—the particular person named Lefty; "a heater" and all the instances of "it" refer to another concept—a particular gun.

## REFERENCE TO IMPLIED SETS

Thinking of pronouns as references to concepts rather than to words or phrases has some implications for referring to concepts that have not been mentioned in the conversation.

Lefty bought a .45 and a .38. He took them wherever he went.

In this sentence, "them" refers to a set consisting of the .45 and the .38 mentioned in the previous sentence.

Lefty bought a .45 and a .38. They ought to be outlawed.

"They" does not refer to the same kind of set as in the last example. It refers here to the set of all .45's and all .38's or perhaps to the set of all pistols. Then again, it could refer to the set of all deadly weapons. One is not sure without more information.

> Lefty bought a .45 and an Almond Joy. They ought to be outlawed.

In this example, "they" almost certainly does not refer to the set consisting of the .45 and the Almond Joy. One would expect it to refer to something like the set of all .45's or all handguns, or all deadly weapons or some such set. It could possibly refer to something like the set of all candy bars.

The implication for the semantic processor for handling this kind of pronoun is quite serious. One possibility is that these various sets of which objects could belong must be generated as soon as the first references are made. The other possibility is that if semantic analysis cannot find a satisfactory referent for a pronoun among the concepts it has available, it could start generating new concepts that represent the various sets discussed above. Pronoun handling is a difficult problem in natural language processing even for the least exotic occurrences. Most of these more difficult cases are beyond the capabilities of current systems, but work is proceeding along these lines (Webber 1978b).

## REFERENCE LISTS

Pronouns are handled by many natural language processors in a similar fashion. As items are referenced in the text, the event of reference is recorded on a list along with a description of or pointer to the referenced concept. For example, if Lefty were talking to Knuckles, and Knuckles were recording the references, the list might look like the one below:

> I bought a heater. I got it for $39.95. It was too much.

> REFERENCE LIST (MOST RECENT FIRST): MONEY083, MONEY083, FIREARM047, PERSON993, FIREARM047, PERSON993.

When the semantic analyzer attempts to find the referent for a pronoun, it first gathers as much information as possible about the referent from the local context of the pronoun. Then the reference list is sequentially scanned from most recent to least recent until a referent is found that matches the description (stop-on-success strategy). The description of the referent of a pronoun is made from examining the role the pronoun is playing in the sentence. In the sentence "I got it for $39.95," the pronoun "I" refers to the buyer in a commercial transaction and "it" refers to an object that was bought. In scanning the reference list, FIREARM047 was originally referred to in the preceding sentence and is the object of a Commercial Transaction. FIREARM047 is therefore taken to be the referent of "it." Similarly, PERSON993 is the probable referent of "I." The new referents are added to the list for future pronoun references.

Simply adding references to a list as they occur in a left to right sweep does not always work. If there are several candidate concepts, all referred to in the same sentence, some candidates are more likely than others.

Lefty rubbed out Tiny. He was wearing a blue suit.

In this example, either Lefty or Tiny could have been wearing a blue suit. It is more likely that "Lefty" and "he" refer to the same person than "Tiny" and he." The reason is that a speaker tends to continue talking about the same subject. The subject of the first sentence is Lefty, so he will probably he the subject of the next sentence.

A purely syntactic method of pronoun resolution that used no semantic information other than number and gender was found successful about 85% of the time (Hobbs 1976). Although this is not very promising as the only pronoun resolution technique for a natural language processor, it is simpler than semantic methods that would perform as well. It searches parse trees of sentences in a breadth-first, left-to-right order for noun phrase nodes. It accepts the first one it finds that satisfies the number and gender constraints. It can be improved by adding more semantic constraints to the description of the referent.

Lefty rubbed out Tiny. He was being paid back for double-crossing the boys.

The "he" in this example refers to Tiny, in spite of the fact that Tiny is the object of the first sentence and "he" is the subject of the second sentence. The contents of the second sentence make it clear that "he" must refer to Tiny.

In mentioning the possible role of syntax in assisting with pronoun resolution, casual note was made of competing candidates of referents. Before that, however, the described technique for referent identification was to scan a list for a first fit, with no mention of competing candidates. If a semantic analyzer were to compare the appropriateness of several candidate referents, it would have to be able to establish a set of possible candidates. It is desirable, of course, to consider as small a candidate list as possible. One way to deal with this problem is to use the observation that nearly all pronouns refer to concepts that were referred to in either the current sentence or the immediately preceding sentence (true in 98% of the pronoun references found in text in one study [Hobbs 1976]). All others could be dropped from the reference list. Alternatively, the semantic system could highlight the most recently discussed regions of the memory structure. There is at least one natural language processor currently under development that has proposed to use this technique.

## REFERENCES TO EVENTS

All the pronouns discussed to this point refer to objects that were mentioned in the text or to sets of objects implied by the text. Pronouns can also refer to events that are described by clauses:

Lefty rubbed out Tiny. It started a bloody gang war that lasted for years.

In this example, "it" refers to the particular event of killing, KILLING-031, that was described by the previous sentence. Pronouns referring to events can have the same problems of extension to sets as were mentioned for object-referring pronouns.

Lefty rubbed out Tiny. They must be stopped.

"They" could refer to some group of miscreants to which Lefty belongs, or it could refer to a set of killings.

There are several cases in which pronouns are used to refer to elaborately described concepts:

> Knuckles suggested that they drive as far as the warehouse. They could then walk through the alley to State Street. Then they would take a bus to Cermak. The cops could never follow the trail. *It* was an appealing plan.

In this example, "it" refers to the entire scheme described in the four preceding sentences. The concept of the plan was not mentioned explicitly, but was implicit in the text.

## PRONOUNS WITHOUT SPECIFIC REFERENTS

In some cases pronouns seem not to have specific referents. The following examples:

1. You and one—any person: "you never know"

2. We—some vague group: "we don't do that here"

3. They—unspecified people: "they dug up the road today"

4. It—the weather: "It's raining in Florida"

5. It—the time: "It's time for another beer"

6. It—the general environment: "It was utter chaos at the PTA meeting"

### 4.5 Determiners and Noun Phrases

Determiners, e.g., an, the, some, every, reveal a great deal of information about the meaning of the noun phrases that they are in. In the past, many natural language processors simply ignored determiners.

As they have become more complete, however, the information implied by determiners has become very important.

## DEFINITE AND INDEFINITE NOUN PHRASES

The last section described the use of pronouns as references. Pronouns generally indicate a specific concept of which the listener is expected to be aware. Noun phrases that do not contain pronouns often work in a similar way.

1) Lefty bought a heater. *It* cost $39.95.
2) Lefty bought a heater. *The heater* cost $39.95.
3) Lefty bought a heater. *A good heater* can cost hundreds of dollars.

These three examples illustrate some of the ways that noun phrases can be used and how they relate to reference. Upon hearing the phrase "a heater" in the first sentence, the listener presumably creates a new concept in his or her mind, say, FIREARM048, to represent that particular gun. In example 1, the pronoun refers to FIREARM048, as was discussed in the last section. Notice the similar function that the phrase "the heater" has in example 2. Evidently, this noun phrase is used to refer to FIREARM048 just as the pronoun was. The referent of "the heater" may be a little easier to identify than the referent of a pronoun. "The heater" carries with it a partial description of the referent (the referent must be a heater, i.e., a firearm), and the wording of the noun phrase is similar to the wording of the last reference to the concept (a heater— the heater). Now contrast example 3 with example 2. Upon hearing "a good heater," the listener does not interpret this as a reference to FIREARM048. The distinction is in the determiner: the use of "the" versus "a." Noun phrases with definite determiners like "the" are generally used to refer to a concept that the listener knows. Noun phrases with indefinite determiners, like "a" or "an," generally introduce new concepts to the listener.

*References to Unmentioned Concepts*

It is worth noting that definite noun phrases, like pronouns, refer to concepts that the listener is aware of from a conversation. Say that Lefty and Knuckles were surveying the personal effects of one of their fallen comrades. If Lefty were to turn to Knuckles and say, "the watch cost $50," Knuckles would identify the referent of "the watch" was the one they were both looking at even though it had not been mentioned by either of them.

Now imagine Lefty in a pawn shop closely examining a pistol that he is thinking of buying. One would not be surprised if the broker said any of the following to him:

4) *The price* is $39.95.
5) *The safety* doesn't work.
6) *The firing pin* has been removed.

These noun phrases are references to specific concepts, as we can see from the definite determiner "the." However, they are somewhat different from the previously mentioned cases. In one case above the listener instantiates concept FIREARM048 when he or she hears "a heater." In the other case the listener instantiates a concept when he or she sees an object. The concepts are ready and waiting for the subsequent references. In examples 4, 5 and 6 the concepts corresponding to "the price," "the safety" and "the firing pin," respectively, may never have been referred to explicitly. It does seem reasonable, however, to suggest that Lefty knew, or at least assumed, that any gun he looked at would have a price, a safety and a firing pin. In order to resolve this kind of reference, the listener, or a natural language processing program, would have to hold more than the list of previously mentioned concepts as was described in the pronoun section. Concepts that have not been mentioned but are closely related to instantiated concepts must also be available for reference.

Examples 4-6 underscore one advantage that noun phrases with definite determiners have over pronouns for reference. Since a noun phrase can specify a more complete description of its referent, a wider range of concepts are made available for reference. Beyond the use of nouns and modifiers, a referent may be specified further by the

other definite determiners (this, these, that or those) and the posses-
sive determiners (my, your, our, his, her, their, its and one's).

## References to General Descriptions

In example 2 above, the noun phrase "the heater" both referred
to a previously mentioned concept and paralleled the phrasing of
"a heater," the original reference to the concept. This parallelism is
not always done:

7) Lefty bought a pearl handled heater. *The heater* cost $39.95.
8) Lefty bought a heater. *The gun* cost $39.95.
9) Lefty bought a heater. *The weapon* cost $39.95.
10) Lefty bought a heater. *The thing* cost $39.95.
11) Lefty bought a heater. *The piece of junk* cost $39.95.

Examples 7-11 illustrate references through definite noun phrases
that do not parallel the wording of the original reference. "The
heater" in example 7 is similar but not identical to the first reference,
"a pearl handled heater." "Gun" is a synonym of the first reference,
"heater." In example 9, "weapon" describes its referent in a more
general way than the first reference. "Weapon" denotes a general
class to which guns belong. "Thing" in example 10 is more general
still. We can design a natural language processor with a hierarchy of
concepts that shows that the set of all guns is a subset of the set
off all weapons. The set of all weapons is a subset of the set of all
things. In a comparison of a noun phrase description like "thing" to
the description of a referent like the one for "a heater," the two
would not immediately match. The supersets that the referent belongs
to could then be compared with the noun phrase description. If these
do not match, their supersets are compared with the description.
This would continue until a match is found or until the program
runs out of supersets.

The reference in example 11 probably should not be processed
this way. It is doubtful, however, that a language understander
maintains an explicit set of all pieces of junk. "The piece of junk"
in example 11 would instead invoke a description of a thing that

has undesirable properties. An examination of the possible candidate concepts for a referent shows that the concept FIREARM048 satisfies the part of the description that says it must be a thing. The undesirable characteristic part of the description is neither supported nor denied. If no better candidates are found, FIREARM048 is accepted as the referent, and the new information regarding the undesirable characteristic is attached to it. In this way, we see that a definite noun phrase can not only refer to previously known concepts, but can simultaneously add to the description of the referent.

### References to Events

All of the definite noun phrases discussed to this point have had concepts representing physical objects as their referents. Definite noun phrases are not limited to physical object referents any more than pronouns are. A noun phrase may refer to actions and events:

Fingers stole the racketeer's money.
12) *The theft* shocked the underworld.
13) *The event* shocked the underworld.
14) *The blunder* shocked the underworld.
15) *The fact that Fingers stole the racketeer's money* shocked the underworld.
16) *Fingers' stealing of the racketeer's money* shocked the underworld. (participle)
17) *For Fingers to steal the racketeer's money* shocked the underworld. (infinitive)

These sentences show ways in which a concept representing an event can be referenced. Examples 12 and 13 show the event being referred to with nouns that describe classes of events, "event" in 13 being a more general class than "theft" in 12. Example 14 shows the event being described as a "blunder" which identifies that the referent is an event with some unfavorable characteristics. In examples 15-17 the original sentence has been nominalized, transformed in some way so that the resulting structure behaves as a noun phrase. In example 15 the original sentence becomes a relative clause modifying "fact."

In example 16 the tense of the verb is changed, transforming the sentence into a participial phrase. In example 17, a rather awkward sentence, the tense of the verb is changed to the infinitive form. This similarity between the way events and objects can be referenced suggests that they should have similar representations. If there is a concept for each object, like FIREARM048, there should also be a concept to represent each event, like THEFT049. New questions are raised, however.

18) Fingers ripped open the empty satchel. *The fact that the satchel was empty* terrified Fingers.

Should a special concept describing the emptiness of the satchel in this example be ready and waiting for this reference? This example, as most of the examples in this section, represent phenomena that are just beginning to be studied for natural language processors.

A final caveat should be made before closing this section. Not all definite noun phrases imply a unique referent. We often say that we are going to "the grocery store," "the dentist," "the doctor" or "the bathroom," when in fact the speaker does not expect the listener to identify a particular referent. Apparently, noun phrases like these must be handled as special cases.

## QUANTIFICATION

The problem of quantification is one of selecting an appropriate interpretation for sentences like the following:

19) Every person in this room speaks a foreign language.
20) A foreign language is spoken by every person in this room.

Although the words used in these two sentences are nearly the same, they are often interpreted differently. Example 19 is usually interpreted as implying that every person knows some foreign language, but they may not all know the same one. Example 20 is usually interpreted as implying that the same language is known by every person. These interpretations are not always the selected ones, however.

An interesting study of quantification was done by Van Lehn (1978) in which he asked people for their interpretations of sentences with multiple quantifiers. One of the results was that the subjects could not immediately decide which interpretation was appropriate. In addition, the test subjects disagreed on what were the appropriate interpretations. These are very interesting results in that they imply that although people commonly deal with sentences with multiple quantifiers, they do not explicitly understand them.

Quantification is usually indicated by the determiners of noun phrases: a, an, each, every, all, etc. It is not limited to determiners, however. For example, "Give me the flight hours for all the planes that flew in February" leaves some doubt as to whether one total is required, or a figure for each plane. But the following resolves the ambiquity with the additional modifiers:

Give me the flight hours for all the planes that flew in February, listed separately.
Give me the flight hours for all the planes that flew in February, added together.

## 4.6 Ellipsis and Substitution

Ellipsis is the phenomenon of leaving some words of a sentence unsaid, to be "filled in" by the listener. Substitution is similar, but rather than just leaving the words unsaid, a dummy word is substituted for the omitted words.

1) Lefty bought three blackjacks. Knuckles bought *two*. (ellipsis)
2) Lefty drove a blue convertible. Knuckles drove *a yellow one*. (substitution)

In example 1 the word "blackjacks" has been omitted, ellipted, from the phrase "two blackjacks." In example 2, "one" has been substituted for the word "convertible."

Ellipsis and substitution are similar to pronoun reference and definite noun phrase reference in that they help to tie together the utterances of a discourse. They also allow the speaker to express himself or herself in fewer words by putting a heavier demand on the listener. The listener must first decide that an ellipsis or substitution has been made and then deduce what has been omitted.

Ellipsis and substitution (referred to here as *e* and *s*) are significantly different from the use of pronouns and definite noun phrases, however. *E* and *s* are not references to specific concepts, whether objects or events, that have been mentioned previously. Rather, they require the recall of the actual words and phrases of the preceding text. In fact, one of the primary uses of *e* and *s* is not to refer to exactly the same concept that was referred to previously, but to contrast the description of one thing with a previous description of another. In example 1, the ellipted noun phrase contrasts sets of blackjacks by the number of elements in the sets. In example 2, Lefty's and Knuckles' cars are shown to have the similar features of both being convertibles, but they are contrasted by their colors.

It is important to realize that in spite of the fact that *e* and *s* are not references in themselves, they could occur in a definite noun phrase that is a reference to a previously mentioned concept.

3) Lefty carried an argyle and a plain black sock filled with sand. Knuckles borrowed *the argyle one*.

In the analysis of the first sentence of example 3, among the concepts that are instantiated in the listener's model of the situation are, say, SOCK002, which is an argyle sock filled with sand, and SOCK003, a plain black sock filled with sand. When the listener analyzes "the argyle one" in the second sentence, he or she first must resolve the substitution. The listener discovers that "the argyle one" should be interpreted as "the argyle sock filled with sand." This is the extent of the substitution analysis. The listener then realizes that the completed noun phrase is definite, a reference to a previously mentioned concept, namely, his or her concept SOCK002. *E* and *s* are not in themselves references to concepts, but neither do they preclude the possibility of an ellipted noun phrase simultaneously being a reference.

### STRUCTURAL ELLIPSIS

The kind of *e* and *s* described to this point is commonly found in written or formal text as well as spoken conversations. It is characterized by a syntactic unit such as a noun phrase or verb phrase that has had some or all of its constituents omitted, and other constituents may have been replaced to affect a contrast. There are two other types of ellipsis that have been dealt with by some natural language processing programs. To keep them straight, the type of ellipsis described above will be referred to as *substructure ellipsis*. It is typified by occurring in a nearly completely specified sentence but for the omission of some substructure.

The second form of ellipsis will be called *superstructure ellipsis*. In superstructure ellipsis, nearly the entire sentence is omitted, with only a substructure remaining:

4a) How much cash did you get from the First National Bank?
   20 grand
4b) Downtown Savings and Loan?
   10 grand

Example 4b shows a superstructure ellipsis. Notice that all that has remained after the ellipting is part of the noun phrase (the determiner "the" has been deleted) of the object of a prepositional phrase that modifies the verb. The sentence superstructure that that noun phrase fragment would ordinarily hang from has all been omitted. Superstructure ellipsis is very common in conversations, and some natural language interfaces to databases have attempted to deal with it.

What makes the problem even more interesting is that substructure ellipsis and superstructure ellipsis can occur in the same utterance:

5a) What is the price per item if I buy 5 blackjacks?
   $10.
5b) 50?
   $8.50

The phrase "50" in example 5b implies both a substructure and superstructure ellipsis. The result of resolving the superstructure ellipsis is the sentence, "what is the price per item if I buy 50?" This question contains the substructure ellipsis "50," which is intended to mean "50 blackjacks."

## PRAGMATIC ELLIPSIS

Another phenomenon which has been called ellipsis in the natural language literature is quite unlike structural ellipsis. The author calls this type *pragmatic ellipsis*, because the listener only realizes that something has been omitted from his or her knowledge of the world (pragmatic knowledge). Once again, dealing with this type of ellipsis has been important in natural language interfaces to databases.

6a) How many maintenance actions were performed on plane 6 in 1971?

6b) How many maintenance actions were performed on plane 7?

Example 6 is typical of the kind of questions that are asked of an aircraft maintenance database. Notice that question 6b is syntactically complete, which is to say that there are no structural components missing. However, the question does not mention explicitly a time period of interest. A natural language processor would typically translate the question into a formal database query. The formal query would specify that only records for maintenance actions need be considered, and only the records for plane 7 need be considered. If such a query were executed on a very large database, and there were records on plane 7 for the last twenty years, the search could take hours and possibly require mounting scores of magnetic tapes. If this is what the user intended, so be it. More likely, the user intended to know about plane 7's maintenance history for 1971. The time period restriction was expected to be carried over from the context established in the previous sentence. The time period phrase is structurally optional, but it is nearly always either stated explicitly or implied.

There are several ways to look at the problem of recognizing the occurrence of a pragmatic ellipsis. PLANES (Waltz and Goodman 1977) stored templates of the components of expected queries. The templates had uses other than for pragmatic ellipsis, but for that problem the semantic constituents found in the user's sentence were compared to the templates for the best match. If the best match were a complete match—every constituent in the template matching a constituent in the sentence—the sentence was considered to be free of pragmatic ellipsis. If the best match did have some omissions in the sentence, PLANES would attempt to fill in the ellipted phrase with the most recently used phrase of the same type. If there were no predecessors, it would ask the user for clarification.

Woods (1978) discussed the approach of using "smart quantifiers." After a formal query has been constructed, the smart quantifiers use information on the size of the database to estimate the size of the database search. If the search is unusually large, corrective action is taken.

A third approach is based on the assumption that in the course of a conversation, one question will tend to be pretty much like the last one. Instead of building a new conceptual structure for each input sentence, the structure for the preceding sentence is assumed. The only components of the old conceptual structure that are changed in the analysis of the new sentence are those components that have been denied explicitly. In example 6, for instance, the resulting structure for the second question is the same as the one for the first sentence except that "plane 6" has been denied by "plane 7." Nothing in the second question has denied the date component, "in 1971," so it persists. It is consequently used in the construction of the query for the second question.

Pragmatic ellipsis must be resolved at the level of the meaning of user inputs, the same level at which references are resolved. Substructure and superstructure ellipsis, on the other hand, require that at least some remnants of the syntactic structure of the previous discourse be preserved. This adds a new facet to what we must consider as the context.

## SUBSTITUTES FOR VERB PHRASES

7) Lefty beats his wife. Knuckles does too.

In example 7, the verb "do" is acting as a substructure substitute for the verb phrase "beats his wife." But whose wife does Knuckles beat? His own wife or Lefty's wife? We realize that it is more probable that Knuckles beats his own wife rather than his colleague's wife. This is further evidence that the whole verb phrase "beats his wife" is carried over without the prior resolution of the pronoun reference.

8) Lefty beats his wife, Trixie. Knuckles does too.

Example 8 illustrates that the complete syntactic structure of an ellipted constituent is not necessarily carried over intact for the ellipsis. If we know that Knuckle's wife's name is Bubbles, then the implied verb phrase is "beats his wife," not "beats his wife, Trixie." In fact, even if we do not know anything about Knuckles' wife, we can assume that her name is not Trixie. The point is that in spite of the fact that recognition of the constituent that has been ellipted or substituted for relies heavily on syntactic structure, it also requires a significant amount of semantic and pragmatic checking.

## 4.7 Case Frames

Most events share a common structure. They typically have an agent and recipient, and they occur at a particular time. They may involve an instrument and may involve a movement from one point to another along a path. These various elements that "flesh out" the event depicted by a verb are usually found in the subject, object or direct object slots or in prepositional phrases. If a preposition introduces a particular kind of phrase, like a time phrase, the preposition can be one of a small set (in, on, before, after and between are possible for time phrases; without, against, upon and under would not be used). Some of the "fleshing out" details are required in a sentence, others are optional. The verb "slice" must have an agent and an object; the time, instrument and other details are optional. Furthermore, as with the time phrase, particular kinds of details are required in particular places in the sentence.

The individual types of details are called cases. A verb can be described with sets of the kinds of cases that may be associated with it (agent, instrument, recipient, etc.), which of these are optional or required, and the characteristics that the case role fillers are expected to have (e.g., the agent must be animate, etc.). The collection of optional and required cases for a verb is called a case frame. They are identified in the sentence by case markers, which are clues as to whether a particular case is likely to turn up as a subject, an object or following one of a set of prepositions. Such descriptions have been used to describe verbs in several natural language systems.

Some linguists theorize that there is a small number of cases that can be associated with verbs. They further theorize that the set of types is universal to all languages. Finally, one sentence can have no more than one filler for each case role (conjoined noun phrases are treated as one—in "John and Bill sliced the hams," the agent role is filled by "John and Bill").

A sentence may include many details that need not be included in the case frame for a verb. A survey article on case systems (Bruce 1975) suggests that several alternative criteria have been used to determine which details can appropriately be called cases of the verb. They are:

1. A case is necessary to distinguish different senses of a verb. The verb "run" may have two case frames, one for the "locomotion" meaning of run with no object case marker, and a different case frame for the "operate" meaning that would have an object case marker.

2. A case provides information necessary to identify an event uniquely.

3. A case must be known, whether it is mentioned explicitly or inferred.

4. A case is a property whose value is usually specified for a particular event.

5. A case is a detail relevant to the domain of discourse.

Linguists have tried to develop classifications of permissible meanings of cases that would have wide applicability to verbs. There is much disagreement on what classifications are best, but most case systems designate somewhere on the order of ten or twenty cases. A typical case system is that of Fillmore (1968). A sentence (S) is composed of a modality (M) and a proposition (P):

$S \to M + P$

The modality of the sentence indicates tense, mood, aspect and negation of the proposition. The proposition consists of the root form of the verb (V) and its cases (Ci):

$P \to V + C1 + C2 + C3 + \ldots + Cn$

Each case has a noun phrase (NP) and an identifying case marker (K) which can be considered as some sort of function on the words of the sentence:

$Ci \to K + NP$

The case markers may be as simple as a set of legal prepositions or it may be more involved. There are also restrictions on the meaning of cases. This is the debated classification referred to above.

| | |
|---|---|
| Agent | —instigator of the event |
| Counter-agent | —force of resistance |
| Object | —entity that moves or changes |
| Result | —entity that comes into existence through the action |
| Instrument | —stimulus or cause of an event |
| Source | —place from which a thing moves |
| Goal | —place to which a thing moves |
| Experience | —thing which receives or experiences the effect of the action |

In Fillmore's Case System above, meaning restrictions are not sufficient to describe all cases of all verbs, but they do have wide applicability both in English and other languages. These meaning restrictions, which are semantic restrictions, illustrate the close interconnections between syntax and semantics.

The cases that attach to verbs can be found in a variety of places in the sentence. Case frames make no reference as to where in the sentence a case will be found. They just describe what the case markers will be and the semantics of the cases. The following illustrates a variety of ways to combine the cases of a verb.

(a) Genghis Khan drove his army from the steppes of Mongolia to the forests of Europe in the thirteenth century against primarily unmounted resistance with the adept horsemen of the Golden Horde.

(b) In the thirteenth century, Genghis Khan drove his army to the forests of Europe from the steppes of Mongolia with the adept horsemen of the Golden Horde against primarily unmounted resistance.

(c) Genghis Khan, in the thirteenth century, drove his army against primarily unmounted resistance from the steppes of Mongolia to the forests of Europe with the adept horsemen of the Golden Horde.

Although the position of the cases vary between sentences, the cases and case markers are the same. They are listed below:

| Noun Phrase | Case Marker | Case |
|---|---|---|
| Genghis Khan | subject | agent |
| his army | object | object |
| the steppes of Mongolia | "from" | source |
| the forests of Europe | "to" | goal |
| primarily unmounted resistance | "against" | counter-agent |
| the adept horsemen of the Golden Horde | "with" | instrument |

The limitations of this case system are revealed when one attempts to specify more details about the event. Some fit the case system, but others do not have a case provided for them. If, for example, the path the army took was specified ("through the desert and over the mountains"), perhaps it should have case status, but it cannot in this system.

## 4.8 Concept Decomposition

When we use language to communicate ideas, each word is capable of communicating a great deal of information. The verb *buy*, for instance, invokes a detailed concept of trading money for goods. It usually, though not necessarily, implies a number of other ideas such as the buyer, the seller and the location and time of the transaction. In addition to the various people involved and things used (like money), there is a particular set of actions involved. The buyer turns ownership of some money over to the seller, who gives the buyer ownership of goods.

The same event can be described in various ways, but if one is to recognize that several different descriptions all mean the same thing, they should all invoke the same internal representation.

1) Lefty bought a blackjack from Knuckles for ten dollars.
2) Knuckles sold Lefty a blackjack for ten dollars.
3) Lefty paid ten dollars to Knuckles for a blackjack.
4) Knuckles charged Lefty ten dollars for a blackjack.

If these sentences are all to produce essentially the same internal representation, the verbs "bought," "sold," "paid" and "charged" must all map into the same structure. One suggestion for accomplishing this is to have a small set of primitive actions used to describe the events depicted by verbs in the language. Once any of the above sentences have been said and analyzed into its structure of primitive actions, it no longer matters in which form the concept was communicated. The structure is the same for all of them. Incidentally, people apparently do something like this, evidenced by the fact that it is much easier to remember concepts than it is to remember exact wordings.

The two leading proponents in natural language processing of decomposing words into structures of primitives and building larger conceptual structures from these are Schank (1972) and Wilks (1975). Both were working on translation. Translating text from one language to another cannot be accomplished on a word-by-word basis. If there is a word that describes a particular concept in one language, there very well may not be a corresponding word for the concept in another language. After the text in the source language decomposed into a structure of primitives, translation to the target language is done from the structure. Consequently, the source text is used to build a conceptual structure and the target text is composed from the conceptual structure.

Schank proposed that the number of primitives necessary for building conceptual structures to describe verbs is small. He proposed the set shown in Table 4.4, maintaining that, although these may not be exactly the right primitives, the order of magnitude of the number of primitives is right.

**Table 4.4**
**Schank's 11 Primitive Acts**

| | Schank's 11 Primitive Acts |
|---|---|
| ATRANS: | transfer of an abstract relationship such as ownership or control |
| PTRANS: | physical transfer of an object |
| PROPEL: | application of a physical force to an object |
| MOVE: | movement of a body part of an animal by the animal |
| GRASP: | grasping of an object by an actor |
| INGEST: | taking an object inside an animal by the animal |
| EXPEL: | expulsion of an object from inside an animal by the animal |
| MTRANS: | transfer of information between animals or within an animal (for example, remembering) |
| MBUILD: | construction of new information from old information by an animal |
| SPEAK: | production of sounds |
| ATTEND: | focusing a sense organ toward a stimulus |

**References and Further Reading**

Bruce, B. "Case Systems for Natural Language." *Artificial Intelligence* 6 (1975):327-60.

Bullwinkle, C. "Levels of Complexity in Discourse for Anaphora Disambiguation and Speech Act Interpretation." In *Proceedings of the International Joint Conference on Artificial Intelligence*. Cambridge, Mass.: MIT, 1977.

Charniak, E. "A Framed PAINTING: The Representation of a Common Sense Knowledge Fragment." *Cognitive Science* 1 (Oct. 1977a):355–94.

_____. "Inference and Knowledge in Language Comprehension." In *Machine Intelligence* 8, edited by E.W. Elcock and D. Michie. New York: Holsted Press, 1977b.

_____. "On the Use of Framed Knowledge in Language Comprehension." *Artificial Intelligence* 11 (1978):225-65.

Fillmore, C. "The Case for Case." In *Universals in Linguistic Theory*, edited by E. Boch and R. Harms. New York: Holt, Reinhart and Winston, 1968.

Finin, T.W. "The Semantic Interpretation of Noun-Noun Modification by Computer." Ph.D. thesis proposal, University of Illinois, May 1979.

Grosz, B.J. "The Representation of Use of Focus in a System for Understanding Dialogs." In *Proceedings of the International Joint Conference on Artificial Intelligence*. Cambridge, Mass.: MIT, 1977.

Halliday, M.A. and Hasan, R. *Cohesion in English*. London: Longman, 1976.

Harris, L.R. "User Oriented Data Base Query with the Robot Natural Language Query System." *International Journal of Man-Machine Studies* 9 (1977): 697-713.

Hayes, P. "Semantic Markers and Selectional Restrictions." In *Computational Semantics*, edited by E. Charniak and Y. Wilks. New York: North Holland Publishing Co., 1978.

Hobbs, J. "Pronoun Resolution." Research Report 76-1. New York: City College, 1976.

_____. "38 Examples of Elusive Antecedents from Published Texts." Research Report 77-2. New York: City College, 1977.

Moore, J. and Newell, A. "How Can Merlin Understand?" In *Knowledge and Cognition*, edited by L.W. Gregg. Potomac, Md.: Lawrence Erlbaum Associates, 1974.

Nash-Webber, B. and Reiter, R. "Anaphora and Logical Form: On Formal Meaning Representation for Natural Language." In *Proceedings of the International Joint Conference on Artificial Intelligence*. Cambridge, Mass.: MIT, 1977.

Samlowski, W. "Case Grammar." In *Computational Semantics*, edited by E. Charniak and Y. Wilks. New York: North Holland Publishing Company, 1978.

Schank, R.C. *Conceptual Information Processing*. New York: American Elsevier, 1975.

Sheridan, P.B. "On Dealing with Quantification in Natural Language Utterances." *International Journal of Man-Machine Studies* 10 (1978):367-94.

Sidner, C. "A Progress Report on the Discourse and Reference Component of the PAL." Cambridge, Mass.: MIT Artificial Intelligence Laboratory, 1978.

Thompson, F.B. and Thompson, B.H. "Practical Natural Language Processing: The REL System as Prototype." In *Advances in Computers*, vol. 13. New York: Academic Press, 1975, edited by M. Yovits and M. Rubinoff.

VanLehn, K.A. "Determining the Scope of English Quantifiers." AI-tr-483. Cambridge, Mass.: MIT Artificial Intelligence Laboratory, 1978.

Waltz, D. and Goodman B. "Writing A Natural Language Data Base System." *Proceedings of The International Joint Conference on Artificial Intelligence*. Cambridge, Mass.: MIT, 1977.

Webber, B.L. "Description Formation and Discourse Model Synthesis." In *Proceedings of Theoretical Issues in Natural Language Processing—2*. Urbana, Ill.: University of Illinois, 1978a.

Webber, B.L. "Discourse Model Synthesis Preliminaries to Reference." Cambridge Mass: Bolt Beranek and Newman Inc., 1978b.

_____. "A Formal Approach to Discourse Anaphora." Report 3761. Cambridge, Mass.: Bolt Beranek and Newman Inc., 1978c.

Wilks, Y. "An Intelligent Analyzer and Understander of English." *Communications of the ACM* 18 (May 1975):264-74.

Woods, A.W. "What's in a Link: Foundations for Semantic Networks." In *Representation and Understanding*, edited by D.G. Bobrow and A. Collins. New York: Academic Press, 1975.

# 5. Implemented Semantic Analyzers

## 5.1 Case Study: SHRDLU

Winograd's SHRDLU (1972) is certainly one of the most widely
known natural language processors. It addressed a broad range of
problems of language understanding. Its domain of discourse was the
now famous blocks world. The blocks world consisted of a table with
a number of blocks of various sizes, shapes and colors. The user
could direct the program, which knew itself as SHRDLU, to pick up
blocks and move them around on the table.

The semantic analysis of SHRDLU translated syntactic tree fragments into statements in MICROPLANNER, a language for use with
databases that store knowledge in the form of assertions and theorems.
These database manipulations had the effect of returning values for
use with other statements or for answering questions. The database
could also be altered to reflect the execution of a user command to
move the blocks.

### MINGLING SYNTACTIC AND SEMANTIC ANALYSIS

SHRDLU begins the analysis of a user's sentence with a syntactic
parse. The entire sentence is not parsed in one process, however. The
syntactic parse continues until a meaningful unit has been parsed;

then semantic routines are called to analyze that unit. If there are no objections to the unit on semantic grounds, the syntactic parse will continue; otherwise, the semantic routine informs the syntactic parser that there is a problem and a different parse should be tried.

The semantic procedures that are called are specific to the type of phrase that has just been parsed. For example, two semantic procedures are called during the parsing of a noun phrase. The first is called just after the parser has identified the head noun. This procedure builds a MICROPLANNER description of the noun phrase fragment from the dictionary definitions of the noun and its modifiers.

The definitions of words in the dictionary are in the form of procedures. When the parsed-head-noun semantic procedure is called, it in turn calls the definition procedures of the words of the noun phrase in right to left order. For the phrase "a red cube," the definition procedures of the words of the noun phrase are called in right to left order. The procedure for "cube" is called first; it sets a semantic marker register to BLOCK and sets a MICROPLANNER description register to the MICROPLANNER statements that specify a cube. Next, the definition procedure for "red" is called. This procedure checks the semantic marker list to verify that the object described so far is the kind of object that "red" can modify. If there is a semantic marker discrepancy, the noun phrase is rejected. If there is no problem, as in the case of "red cube," the MICROPLANNER statements for "red" are added to the description register. The definition procedure for "a" sets the noun phrase DETERMINER register to INDEFINITE, SINGULAR.

SHRDLU then returns to syntactic parsing, looking for post-nominal modifiers such as prepositional phrases and relative clauses. After each one is found, the post-nominal-modifier semantic procedure is called. It checks for semantic marker compatibility and adds the MICROPLANNER representation of the modifier to that of the rest of the noun phrase.

When all of the post-nominal modifiers have been semantically analyzed, the database is queried for an object or objects matching the MICROPLANNER description implied by the noun phrase. An interesting case arises for definite singular noun phrases, like "the blue block." The database is queried, and if only one object is returned, all is well. If more than one object is returned, however, there is a problem. The phrase indicates a unique object. SHRDLU then looks back at the objects mentioned in previous discourse for a reference matching the description. This would be the proper interpretation for a series of commands like, "Pick up a blue block. Put *the blue block* in the box."

The definition programs for pronouns do the same thing. They search the preceding dialog for their own antecedents. The noun substitute "one," as in "the blue one," does the same.

Semantic interpretation routines are called after the identification of several structures, among them, main verb, clause, clause modifier, prepositional phrase and comparative phrase.

Encoding word definitions and interpretation rules as procedures has brought much criticism to Winograd's work. Winograd cited the advantage of procedurally encoded knowledge as providing a high degree of flexibility. The flexibility, though, can cause problems in that the procedures are difficult to keep consistent and are hard to alter.

Once the user's question or command was understood, SHRDLU had to respond. A command like "Put the red block on the blue block" might be a simple movement, or it could be more complex. If the red block and the blue block both had other blocks on top of them, they would have to be cleared before the command could be carried out.

The impact of SHRDLU is largely due to the fact that it was one of the first systems to deal with many sophisticated issues of language analysis simultaneously: parsing, semantics, references to the previous discourse, knowledge representation and problem solving. It has been criticized, however, on the grounds that its solutions to these problems are highly dependent on the very restricted domain of the blocks world.

## EXAMPLE OF DIALOG*

*The text and figures in this section are reprinted by permission of Academic Press, Inc., from Terry Winograd, *Understanding Natural Languages*, 1972, pp. 8-15.

SAMPLE DIALOG

This section contains a sample of a dialog with the language understanding system. It carries out actions and answers questions about a simple scene containing a table, hand, and box, and several blocks and pyramids. The lines in lower case were typed in by a person, and the lines in upper case are the computer's response. Indented lines are comments describing some of the features being exhibited.

The dialog was carried out in real time with the response of the "robot" displayed on a CRT screen. Figures are included to show the state of the scene at various points.

1. pick up a big red block.
OK.

> The system answers "OK" when it carries out a command. In order to pick up the red block, it had to clear it off by finding a space for the green one and moving the green one away. Figure 5.1 shows the scene when the command was given, Figure 5.2 shows the green block being put out of the way, and Figure 5.3 shows the end result.

2. grasp the pyramid.
I DON'T UNDERSTAND WHICH PYRAMID YOU MEAN.

> There are three pyramids in the scene, so the program does nothing.

3. find a block which is taller than the one you are holding and put it into the box.

> The system has to figure out what is meant by "one" and "it," as well as using deduction to decide which block it is holding.

BY "IT," I ASSUME YOU MEAN THE BLOCK WHICH IS TALLER THAN THE ONE I AM HOLDING.

> Printed out to keep us informed.

OK.

> The hand has to set down the red block to pick up the taller blue one. Figure 5.4 shows the result.

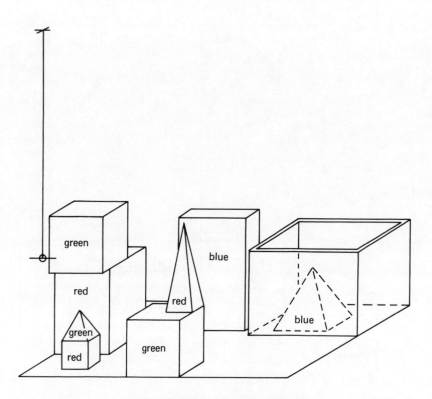

**Figure 5.1 "Pick up a big red block"**

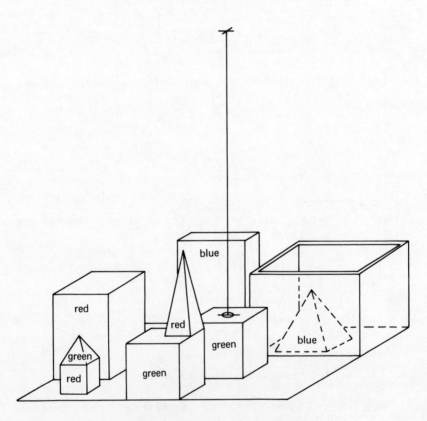

**Figure 5.2 "Pick up a big red block"**

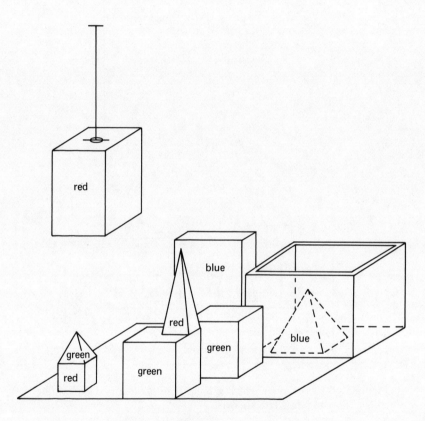

**Figure 5.3** "Pick up a big red block.
OK."

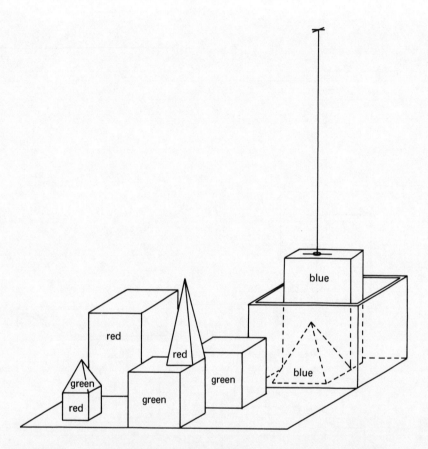

**Figure 5.4** "Find a block which is taller than the one you are holding and put it into the box.

By 'it,' I assume you mean the block which is taller than the one I am holding.

OK."

4. what does the box contain?
THE BLUE PYRAMID AND THE BLUE BLOCK.

5. what is the pyramid supported by?

> Earlier the system responded to "the pyramid" by saying "I don't understand which pyramid you mean." Now it knows that we must mean the one which was just mentioned.

THE BOX.

6. how many blocks are not in the box?

> Negatives such as "not" and "no" are handled whether they appear in clauses or noun groups (such as "no boxes").

FOUR OF THEM.

7. is at least one of them narrower than the one which i told you to pick up?

> The phrase "at least one of them" must be analyzed to refer to the previous question, and "the one which . . . " must also refer to blocks. Noun groups can have complicated numbers, such as "at least one," "more than three," "exactly seven," etc. The memory of past events is used to deduce which block is "the one which I told you to pick up." Notice the complicated grammatical structure in which "the one" is actually the object of a clause embedded two levels deeper.

YES, THE RED CUBE.

8. is it supported?

> Passives can be used without a "by . . . " phrase.

YES, BY THE TABLE.

9. can the table pick up blocks?
NO.

> The semantic rules make this a nonsensical question which therefore must be false.

10. can a pyramid be supported by a block?
YES.

> The deductive system finds an actual example, so it knows this is possible.

11. can a pyramid support a pyramid?
I DON'T KNOW.

> The question makes sense, but there is no example in the scene, so there is no easy way to tell without being able to examine the robot's programs.

12. stack up two pyramids.
I CAN'T.

> The robot tries and fails.

13. the blue pyramid is nice.
I UNDERSTAND.

> This data is added to the data base.

14. i like blocks which are not red, but i don't like anything which supports a pyramid.
I UNDERSTAND.

> Two new theorems are created for proving things about "liking."

15. do i like the box?
NO.

> The box supports whatever it contains, including a pyramid.

16. do i like anything in the box?
YES, TWO THINGS: THE BLUE BLOCK AND THE BLUE PYRAMID.

> Presumably, we like anything which is nice, and the blue block is certainly not red.

17. will you please stack up both of the red blocks and either a green cube or a pyramid?
OK.

> Logical connectives such as "and," "or," "either," etc., are handled in both the grammar and semantics.

A command is executed even if it looks like a question. The robot carries out the command by the series of steps shown in figures 5.5 through 5.8. It puts a green cube on the large red block (note that it chooses the green cube with nothing on it), then removes the small pyramid from the little red cube, so that it can use that cube to complete the stack as specified.

18. which cube is sitting on the table?
THE LARGE GREEN ONE WHICH SUPPORTS THE RED PYRA-MID.

Ordinarily, the system would be satisfied with calling this "a big green cube," but since we asked "which cube" it has to be more specific in naming it. The use of substitute nouns (such as "one") and pronouns in answers makes the discourse more natural.

19. is there a large block behind a pyramid?
YES, THREE OF THEM: A LARGE RED ONE, A LARGE GREEN CUBE AND THE BLUE ONE.

20. put a small one onto the green cube which supports a pyramid.
"A small one" must contrast with the earlier phrase "a large block," so this means "a small block."
OK.

21. put the littlest pyramid on top of it.
Words like "littlest" are not in the dictionary but are interpreted from the root forms like "little." The scene now looks like Figure 5.9.
OK.

22. does the shortest thing the tallest pyramid's support supports support anything green?
The grammar can handle words like "support" which are both verbs and nouns without getting confused, and can understand possessives. To compute the answer, see Figure 5.10 for the scene.
YES, THE GREEN PYRAMID.

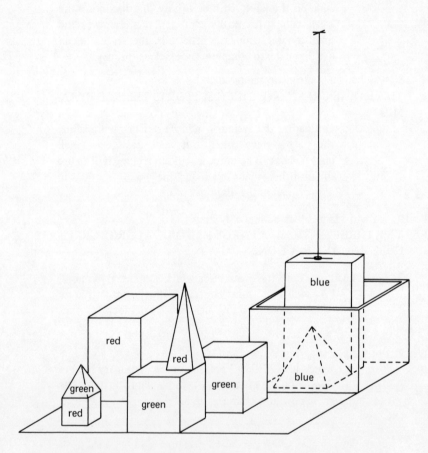

**Figure 5.5** "Will you please stack up both of the red blocks and either a green cube or a pyramid."

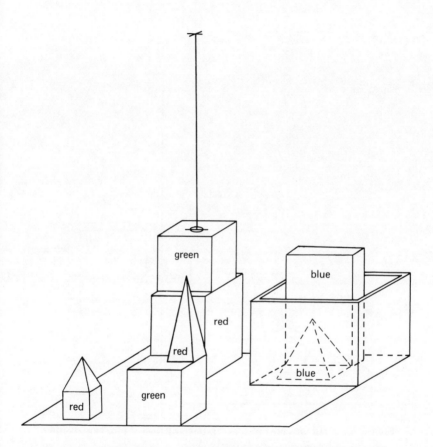

Figure 5.6 "Will you please stack up both of the red blocks and either
a green cube or a pyramid."

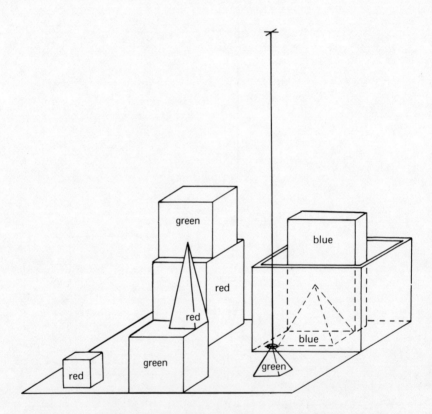

**Figure 5.7** "**Will you please stack up both of the red blocks and either a green cube or a pyramid.**"

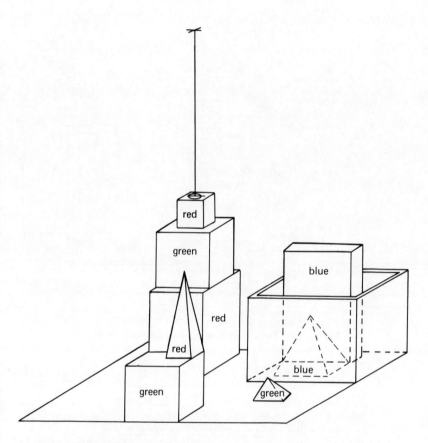

Figure 5.8 "Will you please stack up both of the red blocks and either
a green cube or a pyramid.

OK."

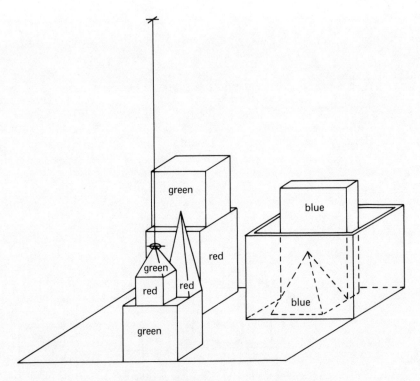

**Figure 5.9 "Put the littlest pyramid on top of it.**
**OK."**

23. what color is it?
BY "IT," I ASSUME YOU MEAN THE SHORTEST THING THE
TALLEST PYRAMID'S SUPPORT SUPPORTS.

> If we had asked "what size is it?" the system would
> have assumed that "it" meant the green pyramid, but
> nobody would ask the color of something which was
> just called "the green pyramid," so it had to look
> farther for the reference of "it."

RED.

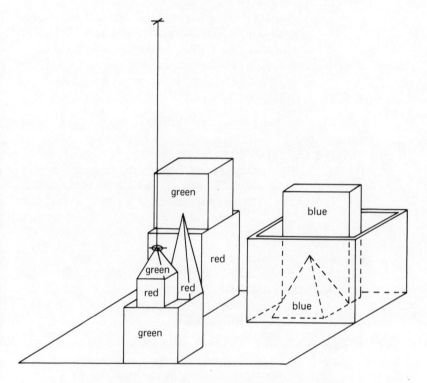

**Figure 5.10** "Does the shortest thing the tallest pyramid's support supports support anything green?"

24. how many things are on top of green cubes?
I'M NOT SURE WHAT YOU MEAN BY "ON TOP OF" IN THE PHRASE "ON TOP OF GREEN CUBES."
DO YOU MEAN:
1 - DIRECTLY ON THE SURFACE
2 - ANYWHERE ON TOP OF?

> When there are several interpretations and none is clearly better, the system has to ask the user for more information. The paraphrases were included with the

dictionary definition of "on," and the request for more information occurs automatically when the heuristics for resolving ambiguities aren't sufficient. A request like this can also occur when the meaning of a pronoun such as "it" or "they" is unclear.

THREE OF THEM.

25. had you touched any pyramid before you put the green one on the little cube?

YES, THE GREEN ONE.

The system deduces from its memory what event is being referred to, and can relate other events to it in time. The analysis includes complex tenses of verb groups, and there are special facilities for keeping track of the various forms of irregular verbs like "have."

26. when did you pick it up?

WHILE I WAS STACKING UP THE RED CUBE, A LARGE RED BLOCK AND A LARGE GREEN CUBE.

A time is described by naming the main goal which was being worked on.

27. why?

The system remembers immediately previous sentences to understand questions like this and the following ones.

TO GET RID OF IT.

By keeping track of selected parts of the original subgoal tree, the system has some understanding of its own motives.

28. why did you do that?

TO CLEAN OFF THE RED CUBE.

"That" refers to the action mentioned in the answer.

29. why did you clear off that cube?

Here, "that" means the one just referred to.

TO PUT IT ON A LARGE GREEN CUBE.

30. why did you do that?

TO STACK UP THE RED CUBE, A LARGE RED BLOCK AND A LARGE GREEN CUBE.

31. why did you do that?
BECAUSE YOU ASKED ME TO.
> It remembers what it did, not how the request was worded.

32. how did you do it?
> "It" refers to the action mentioned in the last question, rather than the answer.

BY PUTTING A LARGE RED BLOCK ON THE TABLE; THEN LETTING GO OF IT; THEN PUTTING A LARGE GREEN CUBE ON IT; THEN LETTING GO OF THAT CUBE; THEN PUTTING THE RED CUBE ON THAT CUBE; THEN LETTING GO OF THAT CUBE.
> This is a description of the top-level subgoals used to achieve the goal.

33. how many objects did you touch while you were doing it?
> Time references can refer to a time span, using words like "while."

FOUR OF THEM.

34. what did the red cube support before you started to clean it off?
THE GREEN PYRAMID.
> By remembering what has been moved, it is possible to deduce things about earlier states of the scene. We can use complex nestings of clauses like "before you started to clean it off."

35. there were five blocks to the left of the box then.
> "Then" must refer to the time mentioned in the last sentence.

NO, ONLY FOUR OF THEM: THE RED CUBE, TWO LARGE GREEN CUBES AND A LARGE RED BLOCK.
> Earlier in the dialog, information about "liking" was accepted at face value. But the system knows that it has complete information about the basic properties of objects, including location. It checks any statements about location or other such properties to see whether it agrees or disagrees.

36. put the blue pyramid on the block in the box.
> This is syntactically ambiguous, but is understood without ambiguity since the parsing corresponding

to "put the blue pyramid which is on the block in the box" does not make sense in the current scene, while "put the blue pyramid on the block which is in the box" does. We can see the situation in Figure 5.11 and the result in Figure 5.12.

OK.

37. is there anything which is bigger than every pyramid but is not as wide as the thing that supports it?

The system understands quantifiers such as "every," "any," "some," etc., and structures such as "bigger

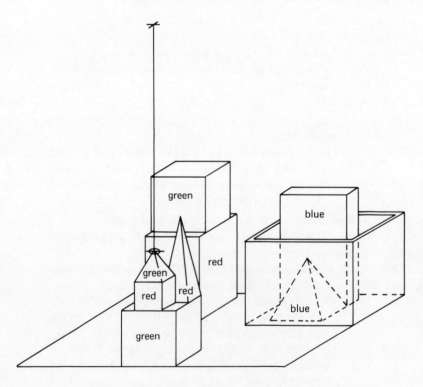

**Figure 5.11 "Put the blue pyramid on the block in the box."**

than," "as wide as," etc. Here "it" refers to a noun
group within the same sentence but two levels up in
the parsing tree.

YES, THE BLUE BLOCK.

39. does a steeple
SORRY, I DON'T KNOW THE WORD "STEEPLE." PLEASE TYPE
TWO SPACES.

> The system interrupts immediately when it sees a
> word it can't figure out. The two spaces are to clear
> the input buffer of anything typed after the message
> was sent but before the typist saw it.

40. a "steeple" is a stack which contains two green cubes and a
pyramid.

> The quotation marks indicate that we are defining a
> new word.

I UNDERSTAND.

41. are there any steeples now?
NO.

> The new definition is used as a description to recognize
> steeples.

42. build one.
OK.

> The description given in the definition is enough to
> deduce a plan for building new objects as well as
> recognizing them. The word "one" means "a steeple,"
> and the plan is carried out. First, one of the large green
> cubes is cleared off by removing the red cube and two
> pyramids. Then the two green cubes and the tall red
> pyramid are stacked up to fit the description. Figures
> 5.13 through 5.16 show the initial state, some interme-
> diate steps, and the result.

43. call the biggest block "superblock."
OK.

> We can also give objects names.

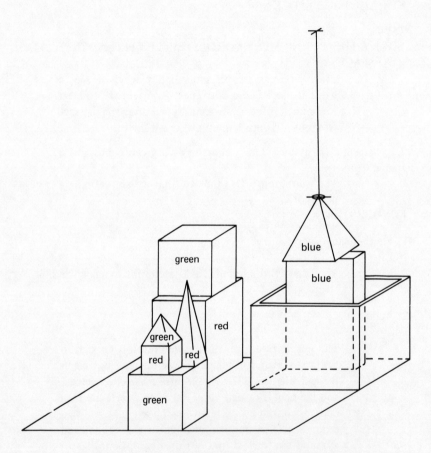

**Figure 5.12** "Put the blue pyramid on the block in the box.
OK."

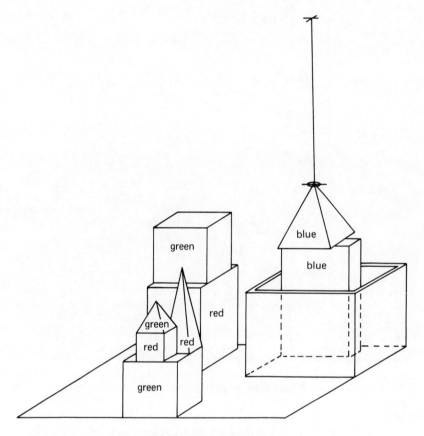

**Figure 5.13 "Build one."**

44. have you picked up superblock since we began?
   YES.

45. why did you drop it?
   BY "IT," I ASSUME YOU MEAN THE SUPERBLOCK.
   I CAN'T EXPLAIN A NON-EXISTENT EVENT.
   There is no record in memory of any block being
   dropped.

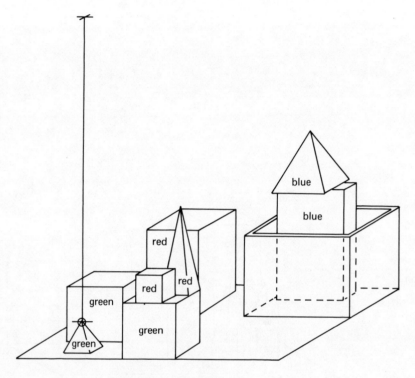

**Figure 5.14 "Build one."**

46. is there anything to the right of the red pyramid?
YES, FOUR THINGS: THE BOX, THE RED CUBE, THE BLUE
PYRAMID AND THE BLOCK NAMED SUPERBLOCK.

> Once an object has a name, the name is used to help
> identify it in responses.

47. thank you.
YOU'RE WELCOME!

> The special idiom-defining capabilities allow us to in-
> clude such pleasantries without modifying the gram-
> mar.

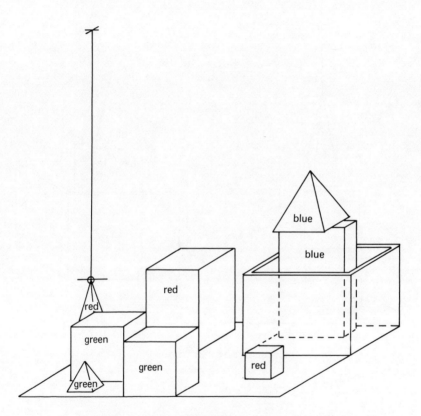

**Figure 5.15 "Build one."**

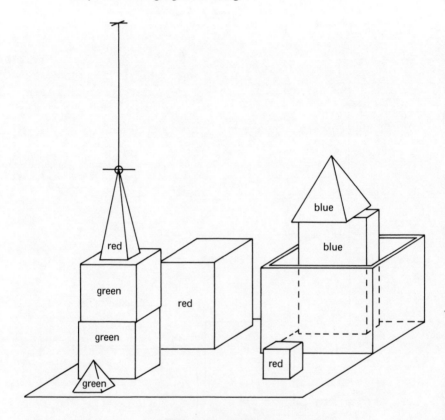

**Figure 5.16 "Build one.**
**OK."**

## THE DIALOG IN PERSPECTIVE

The dialog with SHRDLU is certainly impressive. It demonstrates
SHRDLU's ability to handle a broad range of concepts and sentence
constructions. There is no doubt that SHRDLU represented a significant advance in natural language processing technology.

When reading a dialog like the one above, there is a tendency for
the reader to overgeneralize, to consider programs to be more capable

than perhaps they are. This is easy to do, in part because there are no examples given of where the program fails to understand the user.

The dialog with SHRDLU is "typical" of the dialogs that it is capable of conducting. However, the user must be quite familiar with the capabilities of Winograd's program to carry on a smoothly flowing dialog like this one. The linguistic coverage was not such that a user could have used it successfully without being quite familiar with the forms and vocabulary that it would accept. Similarly, its conceptual coverage did not extend beyond what was indicated in the dialog.

In addition to the contributions that Winograd's program represented (which were significant), it also represents a missed opportunity. This program would have been ideal for user testing. SHRDLU could have been given an initial configuration of blocks on the table, and users could have been given drawings of desired final configurations. The users would then attempt to talk SHRDLU through rearranging the blocks. The dialogs from these tests would have provided an excellent demonstration of the capabilities and limitations of the program. Also, the transcripts of the user tests would have provided a detailed profile against which other natural language processors could have been compared. As it is, the capabilities and limitations can only be inferred from a few properly handled examples. Inferring performance on this basis is notoriously uncertain. Unfortunately, the program is no longer operational, so its performance will probably never be known.

## 5.2 Airline Guide

In the late 1960s Woods (1967, 1968) described a new approach to the semantics of question answering that was more powerful and complete than any that had come before. It was the semantic approach that would later be used in the LUNAR program that has been widely acclaimed and frequently referenced in the natural language processing literature.

Woods' semantic technique was described in terms of building a natural language interface to a machine-readable version of the

*Official Airline Guide.* The *Airline Guide* can be thought of as a fixed format database with each entry specifying a flight. Information about each flight included the origin, destination, flight number, arrival and departure times, the day of the week, whether meals are served, the operating airline, the service classes, whether the flight is nonstop and more. The work focused on semantics. A syntactic component was assumed that provided the semantic component with parsed sentences. A primitive parser was built but much of the semantics work was done from handmade syntactic parses.

## TRANSFERABLE SEMANTIC ANALYSIS

The output of the semantic analysis was a formal query that could then be passed on to a retrieval component. The advantage of separating semantic analysis from the database was that the same semantic techniques would be transferable to databases that had different structures and contents. This work was an advance in the effort to deal with natural language interfaces to databases as they actually exist, as opposed to specially constructing a database for a natural language system (as its predecessor natural language systems had done). It was also one of the first to deal with the problems of quantification, which were treated more completely in this program than in many programs that followed. Woods' semantic techniques also supported a new view of semantics.

The study of semantics in the early 1960s focused largely on the role of semantics in disambiguating syntactic analysis, that is, selecting one syntactic structure (the one that makes sense semantically) from a number of possible syntactic structures. It was viewed in the abstract, largely separate from the specific domain of discourse. A later view of semantics that has gained acceptance among those interested in natural language processing is that semantics must be more specific, concepts must be related to some representation of reality. For a natural language interface to a database, reality was assumed by Woods to be the information represented in the database. The purpose of his semantic techniques was to relate words and the syntactic structures in which they appear to the concepts and relationships that they reference in the database.

The semantic programs worked on a syntactic tree representation of an input sentence. A query was build in terms of procedures that represent the conceptual primitives of the database (these are not to be confused with the primitive acts mentioned in the last chapter). The primitives are the predicates, commands and functions that can be included meaningfully in the database query. An example of a primitive predicate is as follows:

CONNECT (FLIGHTNUMBER, CITY1, CITY2).

If flight FLIGHTNUMBER flies from CITY1 to CITY2, then CON-NECT returns true; otherwise it is false. CONNECT is a procedure that would scan the database, or a fragment of it to determine if such a flight is in the database. An advantage of representing primitives as procedures is that they can perform arbitrarily complex computa-tions, allowing the system designer to include deductive routines as primitives.

Only two primitive commands were built into the program, LIST and TEST. LIST prints the names of the objects, and test prints a response to the user based on whether a proposition was true or false. Primitive functions return actual database values such as the arrival time of a given flight at a given airport.

## SYNTHESIZED DATABASE QUERIES

The semantic procedures that Woods devised gather information from four sources from which to build queries: verbs and their cases, nouns, noun modifiers and determiners. The verb of a sentence and its cases usually designate propositions:

1) Does AA-57 fly from Boston to Chicago?

The verb "fly" indicates the semantic primitive CONNECT, and the predicate (CONNECT AA-57 BOSTON CHICAGO). Since the sentence is a true-false question, the proposition specified by the verb is to be tested in the database:

(TEST (CONNECT AA-57 BOSTON CHICAGO)).

In question 1 each of the noun phrases, AA-57, BOSTON and CHICAGO, name explicit data elements. However, when a common noun (e.g., "flights," "city," "airline") is used to refer to a class of data elements, it is necessary to determine (1) what class is indicated by the noun, (2) whether there are restrictions on the class, as specified by modifiers of the noun, and (3) which or how many members of the class are expected to satisfy the proposition of the main verb of the sentence. The determiner and quantifier of a noun phrase, such as "the," "a," "every," "at least four," specifies which or how many members should satisfy the proposition. This information is called the quantification.

In the question

2) Is AA-57 an American Airlines flight?

the proposition is that flight AA-57 is the same as or an element of a set of something designated by the noun phrase "an American Airlines flight." The head noun of the phrase is "flight," so we know that the phrase refers to the database domain FLIGHT. The modifying compound noun "American Airlines" restricts the class of data elements under consideration from all FLIGHTS to only those that have an owner relation to the data element AMERICAN. (The owner relation is assumed, since that is the only way an element of the AIRLINE domain can be related to the elements of the FLIGHT domain in this database. For a more complex database, finding the implied relationship between data elements is not so straightforward.)

Let the variable X represent a member of the class of flights. X is a flight owned by American. In Woods' notation this is represented as

X/FLIGHT: EQUAL (OWNER(X), AMERICAN).

The determiner of the variable for the noun phrase indicates what quantification was intended. The determiner for the noun phrase is "an." This corresponds to the quantifier SOME, meaning that for at least one of the members of the class of flights that American Airlines owns, the  proposition of the verb holds. By considering noun phrases with different determiners, we can see how the intended quantifications vary:

| Phrase | Quant. | Verbal Description |
|---|---|---|
| AN AMERICAN AIRLINES FLIGHT | SOME | PROPOSITION HOLDS FOR AT LEAST ONE MEMBER OF THE CLASS |
| EVERY AMERICAN AIRLINES FLIGHT | EVERY | PROPOSITION HOLDS FOR EACH MEMBER OF THE CLASS |
| THE AMERICAN AIRLINES FLIGHT | THE | THE CLASS IS ASSUMED TO HAVE ONLY ONE MEMBER AND THE PROPOSITION HOLDS FOR THAT |
| HOW MANY AMERICAN AIRLINES FLIGHTS | COUNT | COUNTS THE NUMBER OF MEMBERS OF THE CLASS THAT SATISFY THE PROPOSITION |
| MORE THAN 4 AMERICAN AIRLINES FLIGHTS | GREATER (N, 4) MANY | PROPOSITION HOLDS FOR MORE THAN 4 MEMBERS OF THE CLASS |

The final query generated for the question is

```
(TEST ((FOR SOME X/
    FLIGHT: EQUAL (OWNER (X), AMERICAN);
    EQUAL (AA-57, X))))
```

## SEMANTIC INTERPRETATION FROM SYNTACTIC TEMPLATES

The semantic procedures work by having four sets of rules, one for each kind of information taken from the sentence. The rules consist of two parts, a syntactic template part and a semantic interpretation part. The syntactic template part is compared to the syntactic structure of the question. If they match, the semantic interpretation part of the rule is added to the developing query. After all rules whose templates match the sentence have been applied, the query is complete. The following example will illustrate how this works:

3) Does American have a flight which goes from Boston to Chicago?

See Figure 5.17. The query building begins by locating determined noun phrases. In this question there is only one, "a flight which goes from Boston to Chicago." If there were more than one in a sentence, the program would start with the most deeply embedded. In Figure 5.18 the determiner rule matches the determiner in the noun phrase.

Next the template parts of head noun rules are matched against the structure of the noun phrase. One rule is found to match; see Figure 5.19.

The interpretation part is substituted for ⟨CLASS⟩ in the query fragment. This gives

(FOR SOME X1/FLIGHT:⟨CLASS⟩;⟨PROPOSITION⟩)

The ⟨CLASS⟩ that X1 can range over has been further restricted by the relative clause "which goes from Boston to Chicago." There are no determined noun phrases in the clause except for the relative pronoun, and relative pronouns do not affect quantification. Consequently, no determiner rules, head noun rules or noun modifier rules are examined. However, two matches are found in the verb rules; see Figure 5.20. The terminals ⟨FLIGHT⟩ and ⟨PLACE⟩ indicate classes to which the head noun of a noun phrase must belong in order for the template to match. Since the templates of two rules match the noun phrase, their semantic interpretation parts are

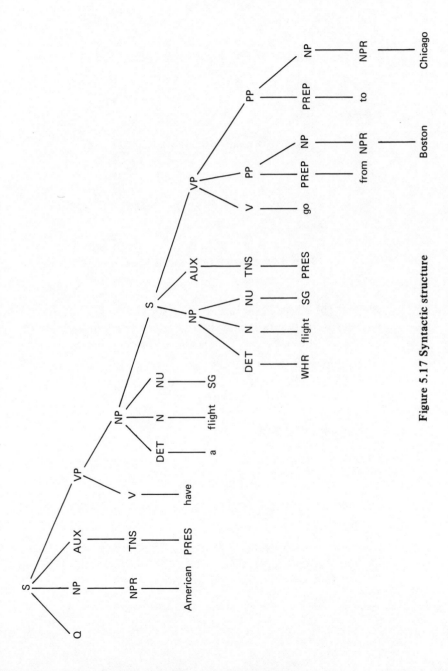

**Figure 5.17 Syntactic structure**

**Figure 5.18 A match from the determiner rules**

**Figure 5.19 A match from the head noun rules**

ANDed. The data element names are substituted for the appropriate variables in the semantic interpretations, and these are inserted as class restrictions on the noun in the developing query, giving:

```
(FOR SOME X1/
   FLIGHT:CONNECT (X1, BOSTON CHICAGO)
      AND ARRIVE (X1, CHICAGO)
   ⟨CLASS⟩;
   ⟨PROPOSITION⟩)
```

There are no further restrictions on the noun phrase so ⟨CLASS⟩ is eliminated. The verb rules are now compared against the main clause, and one is found to match; see Figure 5.21. The interpretation is substituted for the ⟨PROPOSITION⟩ in the developing query, giving:

```
(FOR SOME X1/
   FLIGHT: CONNECT (X1, BOSTON, CHICAGO)
   AND ARRIVE (X1, CHICAGO);
   EQUAL (OWNER(X1), AMERICAN))
```

Finally, since the question is a true-false one, the function TEST is wrapped around the query. TEST returns a yes or no answer depending on the outcome of the query. The final query is:

```
TEST ((FOR SOME X1/
    FLIGHT: CONNECT (X1, BOSTON, CHICAGO)
            AND ARRIVE (X1, CHICAGO);
    EQUAL (OWNER (X1), AMERICAN)))
```

As a second example, consider the following question:

4) Which flight from Boston to Chicago leaves Boston at 8:00?

See Figure 5.22.
    Final query:

```
(FOR THE X1/
    FLIGHT: CONNECT (X1, BOSTON, CHICAGO)
    AND DEPART (X1, BOSTON)
    AND EQUAL (DTIME (X1, BOSTON, 8:00));
    LIST (X1))
```

This query means that there is assumed to be one flight in the database from Boston to Chicago that leaves (DTIME) at 8:00. It is to be found and printed.


## 5.3 LUNAR


LUNAR (Woods 1973; Woods, Kaplan and Nash-Webber 1972) was a natural language program designed as an interface to a database that described the moon rock samples brought back by the Apollo astronauts. It was originally called LSNLIS (Lunar Sciences Natural Language Information System), but the more pronounceable LUNAR has been adopted. It was designed as an aid to lunar geologists and has received wide acclaim for its capabilities. LUNAR is one of the most frequently cited works on natural language processing.

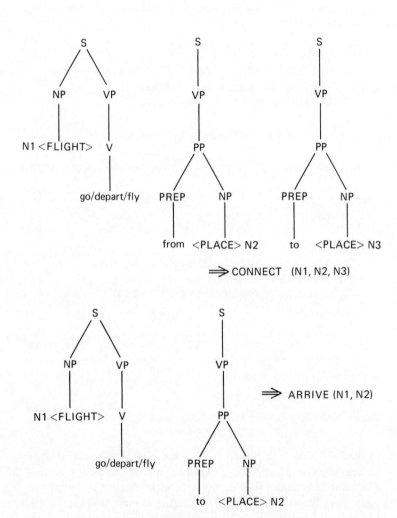

**Figure 5.20 Two matches from the verb rules**

from Noun Modifier Rules

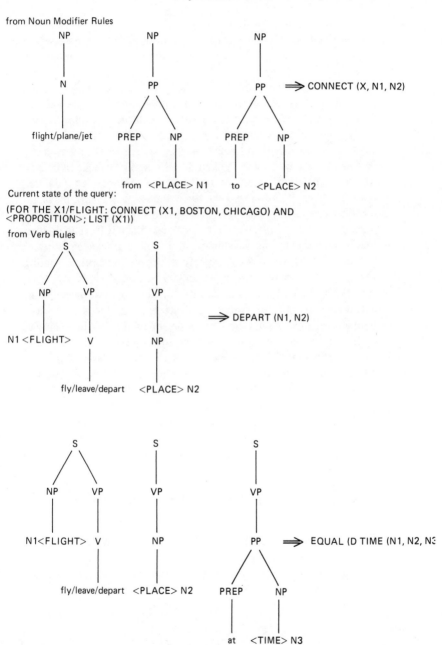

Current state of the query:

(FOR THE X1/FLIGHT: CONNECT (X1, BOSTON, CHICAGO) AND
<PROPOSITION>; LIST (X1))

from Verb Rules

**Figure 5.22 (continued)**

The second simplification that the LUNAR database allowed was in the database query language. A more complex database would require much more sophisticated algorithms for more complicated searches.

The last simplification was that a large vocabulary was not required to identify the data elements. The data elements of the sample identifier and source identifier domains could be recognized generically. Sample identifiers are composed of an "S" followed by five digits (e.g., S10002), and source identifiers are a "D" followed by two digits followed by a hyphen and three digits (e.g., D70-237). The concentration domain consists of real numbers and the tag domain has small integers. Of the three remaining domains, the phase has only five distinct elements, and the units of measure domain has a small number of elements (certainly less than 100). The domain that would add to the vocabulary of the natural language system, and hence to its size, is the chemical constituent domain. Considering that the entire system had a vocabulary of 3,500 words, including synonyms, the chemical constituents domain must not have had an extravagant number of unique data elements. If this is contrasted with a database of equivalent size for personnel records, for example, each entry would have a unique name (or at least few duplications) so a 13,000-entry database would need a vocabulary of at least 13,000 words. Other fields, like street names in addresses and the names of cities of birth, would also increase the vocabulary significantly. This certainly complicates the analysis programs.

These remarks on the simplifying aspects of the database of LUNAR are meant to put the achievements of the designers into perspective, certainly not to detract from them.

## STAGES OF ANALYSIS IN LUNAR

The natural language analysis for LUNAR was done in three independent procedures. The first was a powerful ATN syntactic parser. The syntactic parser, then, worked quite effectively at mapping many surface forms into the same parsed form. This gave the semantic program a fairly uniform structure to operate on.

A sentence, as parsed by the parser, was sent on to the semantic program for translation into a query. Since the parser included no semantic knowledge, there would inevitably be some errors in the parse. One common error was the attachment of prepositional phrases. If a head noun were followed by two prepositional phrases, the first phrase may modify the head noun or the object of the first prepositional phrase. An example of each is below:

"the car by the house with a flat tire"
"the car by the house with a chimney"

A third possibility is that the prepositional phrases do not modify the noun at all, but a verb elsewhere in the sentence as in:

"I drove the car at top speed for an hour."

The only way to attach prepositional phrases properly to the words they modify is to include some information as to the meaning of the phrases when parsing. As mentioned, LUNAR does not do this so the semantic program must grope through the parse when trying to couple words with their modifiers.

The third stage of analysis in LUNAR was the execution of the query produced by the semantic analyzer. This stage will not be discussed further here.


## SEMANTICS IN LUNAR AND THE AIRLINE GUIDE

Except for the minor difference of working with parses that may not be correct, the semantic program for LUNAR is an enlargement of the semantics developed for the Airline Guide prototype. The operation of LUNAR's semantic component will not be described again because it is so similar to the Airline Guide. Some of the differences are worth pointing out, however. The two semantic programs are designed for different domains—moon rocks and commercial airline flights. All the rules for verbs, nouns and noun modifiers must be different in the different domains of discourse.

The airline domain allowed a relatively rich collection of verbs: planes fly, arrive and depart, meals are served and so on. Moon rocks do not do much, so the only verbs in the system refer to commands to the system, like give and list.

The noun rules and noun modifier rules were different in content between the two systems. Proper nouns (meaning here words that designate specific data elements) were used less frequently in LUNAR than in the airline program, because concepts could not be named readily (or the names were not remembered readily). More often, they were described. One did not find the users referring to S10023 and D70-244 in LUNAR as fluently as one would expect them to refer to Boston, 8:00 p.m. and American Airlines in the airline program. As a result, the capability to handle noun modifiers, including relative clauses, was very important in LUNAR. References to samples were frequently in the form, "What is the average concentration of Rb in the samples *that contain phosphorus*?"

The determiner rules were extended significantly in LUNAR over those in the airline program. The determiner rules for the airline program allowed the specification of the quantifiers SOME, EVERY, THE, COUNT and the specification of quotas. LUNAR included these quantifiers and also handled the quantification of mass nouns (nouns that designate noncountable objects like water and aluminum), numerical functions on the data elements such as average, maximum and minimum, numerical elements such as average, maximum, minimum and age (which computes the age of a sample from the concentration of certain isotopes). The determiner rules are also responsible for identifying the existence of anaphoric references and calling functions to resolve them.


ANAPHORA

LUNAR differentiates between two kinds of anaphoric reference (references to previously mentioned concepts). The first kind, semi-anaphor, is a reference by a noun phrase to part of a preceding noun phrase:

"Give me all analyses of sample 10046 for hydrogen"
"Give me them for oxygen"

The second command contains a semi-anaphoric reference to the noun phrase "all analyses of sample 10046 for hydrogen," but "for oxygen" is intended to be used in place of "for hydrogen."

Semi-anaphoric references are recognized by the occurrence of a noun substitute modified by a prepositional phrase or relative clause. A reference list is kept of all noun phrases. The method of resolving a semi-anaphor is to compare the noun phrase containing the noun substitute to the previous noun phrases. If the semantic and syntactic structures match a saved noun phrase, the saved noun phrase is taken as the antecedent.

A complete anaphor is one which has no modifiers on the noun substitute. If the noun phrase has a noun as in "those samples," matching with antecedents is done on the basis of the noun. If no noun is present in a noun phrase, the semantic interpretation of the rest of the sentence is examined for possible semantic types that might apply to the pronoun. If one is found, an antecedent is searched for on the basis of the semantic type.

## EVALUATION

LUNAR was one of the few systems that was ever evaluated in any way. The evaluation was very informal and uncontrolled, but when a number of geologists asked questions of it, LUNAR was able to answer about 80% of them. After minor corrections were made to the program, this was improved to 90%. The questions were limited to those that were relevant to the database, but there were no other restrictions on the inputs. The success rate for nongeologists was lower because they tended to let their questions drift out of the range of the database. The utterances were further limited to strict database queries. None of the other kinds of utterances expected in a dialog were allowed (see chapter 7 on discourse).

### 5.4 Case Study: ROBOT

ROBOT (Harris 1977) (later called INTELLECT) is one of the first database question-answering systems to be available commercially. It consists of an ATN-based syntactic parser followed by semantic analysis that results in a formal query language representation of the sentence. It has two unique features. The first is a means for dealing with the large vocabularies necessary with most question-answering domains while at the same time keeping the natural language processor portable. The second is a means of selecting intended word sense for ambiguous words.

INTELLECT handles the large vocabulary problem by building an inverted file of data element names. Each entry in the file indicates the data domains in which the name occurs. INTELLECT's dictionary consists primarily of common English words. The domain-specific vocabulary is, for the most part, found in the inverted file. Since an inverted file can be made automatically, the task of adapting ROBOT to a new database, i.e., its portability, is greatly facilitated. This is also an aid for keeping the natural language component current as the database is updated.

In addition to the data names that actually occur in the database, the inverted file can contain other words or phrases that are interpreted as data element names. For example, the data element in the database representing *Ford* may be *FD*. One would want to include *Ford* as a synonym for *FD*. Also, the term *New England* may be interpreted as the list of states, New Hampshire, Vermont, Maine, Massachusetts, and Connecticut. The language processor can then answer questions about "New England workers," even though the locations of the workers are stored by specific states. It reportedly takes approximately one week to adapt INTELLECT to a new database.

Some data element names may appear in more than one data domain. For example, "New York" could appear in both a city domain and a state domain:

1) Who lives in New York?
2) Which of the New York people live in Buffalo?

The intended meaning of "New York" in sentence 1 is ambiguous when it is taken out of context. The intended meaning may be clear from context, but ROBOT cannot determine that. However, in sentence 2, "New York" must refer to the state domain. ROBOT disambiguates the term by building two queries, one with each interpretation for the ambiguous term. If one query returns no hits and the other returns some hits, the successful query is taken as the appropriate interpretation. This scheme is practical in the limited domains to which ROBOT has been applied.

## 5.5 Case Study: Preference Semantics

Wilks (1973, 1975) designed and built a program for translating English paragraphs to French. The primary goals of the program are to (1) select the appropriate senses of the words, (2) select the appropriate case marker function of prepositions and (3) select the appropriate referents for pronouns. In the domain of translation to French, if these goals are not met, the errors are usually reflected in improper translations.

The most significant characteristics of Preference Semantics is that it explicitly considers alternative interpretations of text fragments. It measures the "semantic density," which is the degree to which one element of text satisfies the preferences of its neighbors. It then selects one interpretation over others based on semantic density (i.e., the "preferred" interpretation).

The preferences work by storing a lot of knowledge in the system about words and their preferred functions and expected case relationships between verbs and classes of noun phrases. Wilks calls the structures that represent word definitions formulas.

There is a different formula for each sense of each word. Formulas for nouns depicting objects would typically describe the physical characteristics of the object and the typical actions in which it would play a part. Formulas for verbs specify the general class of the action, the preferred types of case fillers for the action, and a representation of the action itself. Between the definitions of nouns and verbs, it is clear that there is a lot of redundancy. For example, the instrument case for the verb "sew" would describe a needle and the formula for "needle" would indicate that it is usually used for sewing. If "needle" were to be considered as a candidate instrument for the verb "sew," the formulas would match very well. In Wilks' words, the semantic density would be high. If some other object having physical characteristics similar to a needle were considered, say a fish bone with a hole in it, there would be some matching, but the semantic density would not be as high as with a needle. The idea of preference semantics is that even though "sew" prefers the instrument "needle," it could accept the fish bone if that were the best alternative.

On the other hand, coupling "sew" with the verb sense of "needle" —to incite to action by repeated gibes—would have a very low semantic density. In this way, the elaborate word sense definitions and high redundancy in the sentence both permits flexible inter- pretations and eliminates ambiguities. Pronoun referent identification is also facilitated. There is a large amount of information about the referent available from the context of the pronoun.

## 5.6 Case Study: SOPHIE

SOPHIE, SOPHisticated Instructional Environment (Brown, Burton and Bell 1974; Brown and Burton 1975; Burton 1976; Brown and Burton 1978), was a study of the application of natural language and inference techniques to computer-aided instruction. It was im- plemented to provide students with an electronics troubleshooting environment and help them to develop their troubleshooting tech- niques. SOPHIE had a simulation of a power supply circuit. It would generate a malfunction for the supply, then determine the consequences of the malfunction. For instance, if a capacitor was proposed to be shorted, the circuit simulation would be run and the effect on other components would be measured. If a resistor, for instance, was now found to be dissipating more power than it was rated for, SOPHIE would "blow" the resistor and rerun the simula- tion. Eventually, the simulation would stabilize. The student would then troubleshoot it.

Troubleshooting consisted of the student suggesting that measure- ments be taken, or components be removed or replaced. Whenever the circuit was altered, the simulation was repeated to reveal the consequences of the change. After component changes, the parameters of the circuit were examined for the propagation of failures. The results were reported back to the student.

SOPHIE also had the ability to recognize inappropriate changes to the circuit and run hypothetical changes. If the student suggested that a component be replaced, SOPHIE would ask specific questions about the nature of the malfunction. If the student was not at least partially correct, the part would not be replaced. Hypothetical situations suggested by the student were simulated, but the simulation was not rerun to propagate faults. The student could also ask for the specifications of parts, control settings or ask for help.

SOPHIE had several impressive characteristics. It could run simulations, abstract them and be able to use the results. It could develop hypotheses and it could make suggestions based on what the user had discovered. These capabilities are interesting to study in themselves, but our main interest is SOPHIE's language analysis. The range of SOPHIE's capabilities shows that a powerful language analyzer was required. In order to be useful for CAI, it also had to be fast—a response had to be made within a few seconds.

Syntactic analysis was considered to be an unaffordable luxury for SOPHIE. The syntactic parse would take time and not yield much information about the meaning of the sentence. A grammar was designed that would not search for syntactic constituents like noun phrase, verb phrase and preposition, but would instead search for semantic constituents or pieces of meaning. SOPHIE's grammar searched for constituents like REQUEST, FAULT, INSTRUMENT, JUNCTION/TYPE, or NODE/NAME. The mechanism, called a semantic grammar, worked just like a syntactic parser. It could build a parse tree just like a syntactic grammar, but the nodes were labeled differently. This approach gave direct access to the semantics of the sentence. It was also very fast; parse times were typically 100ms to 1 sec. Each grammar rule was coded as a LISP procedure. The grammar operated top-down in a recursive descent fashion. Each grammar rule procedure, equivalent to a nonterminal in the grammar, could generate the semantic representation of the subtrees that its nonterminal dominated. Figure 5.23 shows the parse of the following sentence:

What is the voltage of the collector of Q5?

Procedures representing fragments of the semantic interpretation of the sentence are shown next to the nonterminals where they are

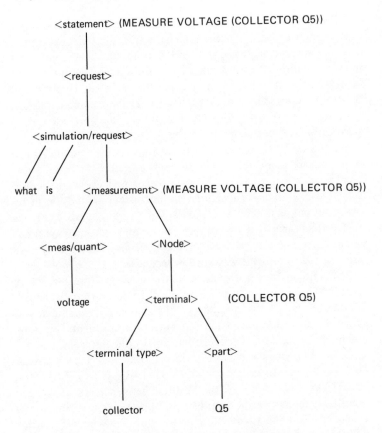

**Figure 5.23 Semantic parse tree for "What is the voltage of collector Q5?"**

produced. The final semantic interpretation procedure is shown next to the root, ⟨statement⟩.

SOPHIE also had the ability to skip words if they did not match the grammar rules (in the example, "the" and "of" were skipped). This made it possible to do at least a partial analysis of sentences that exceeded the range of the grammar, thus making SOPHIE appear more robust. There was, of course, the danger of skipping words that would change the meaning of the sentence significantly.

## 5.7 Case Study: LIFER

The LIFER, Language Interface Facility with Ellipsis and Recursion (Hendrix 1977), parser was designed to enable the construction of natural language interfaces to databases. It is based on the idea that when conversation is limited strictly to questions about a small domain, one can identify the meanings of the questions fairly accurately. The parser works quite well when it operates on a grammar designed by people who are well informed about linguistics and the vocabulary and structure of the domain of discourse. Problems are likely to arise, however, if the LIFER parser is applied to a domain by an inexperienced user. One of the applications of LIFER is the LADDER–Language Access to Distributed Data with Error Recovery–(Hendrix, Sacerdoti, Sagalowicz and Slocum 1978; Sacerdoti 1977) system which is designed to answer questions regarding a naval command and control database. Another application is to a database describing an academic department in a university.

### LIFER's SEMANTIC GRAMMAR

LIFER is a semantic grammar-based parser that attempts to match a question from the user to sentence templates. An example of a template from LADDER is below:

WHAT IS THE ⟨ATTRIB⟩ OF THE ⟨SHIP⟩?

In order for the user's question to match this template, the question must begin with "what is the." ⟨ATTRIB⟩ and ⟨SHIP⟩ are nonterminals. (Hendrix calls them "metasymbols.") The nonterminal ⟨SHIP⟩ will match any phrase that is marked as belonging to the class of ships. For example, the submarine *Nautilus* and aircraft carriers *John F. Kennedy* and *Constellation* are marked as ships. ⟨ATTRIB⟩ matches phrases that are marked as descriptors, such as length, displacement, or class. The template matches sentences such as the following:

What is the length of the Constellation?
What is the displacement of the Nautilus?
What is the class of the John F. Kennedy?

Whenever this template matches the user's question, the following query is generated:

((NAM EQ ⟨SHIP⟩) (? ⟨ATTRIB⟩))

The query is a command to the database component to find the value of the ⟨ATTRIBUTE⟩ for the ship whose name (NAM) is equal (EQ) to the name terminal under ⟨SHIP⟩. For the question

What is the length of the Constellation?

the query is

((NAM EQ CONSTELLATION) (? LENGTH))

A different dictionary is built for each application domain of the LIFER parser. The dictionary holds a list of all the words that can correspond to attributes in the domain of discourse. Many attributes, such as length, displacement and class, are single words that correspond directly to attributes. Some attributes may be described by more than one word, such as home port, power type and hull number. Further, an attribute may be specified by synonyms. For example, location and position both describe the location of a ship.

Now, say a user wanted to know the length, home port and hull number of the *Constellation*. He or she could ask

What is the length of the Constellation?
What is the home port of the Constellation?
What is the hull number of the Constellation?

but would rather ask

What is the length, home port and hull number of the Constellation?

The list of attributes, "length, home port and hull number," could be allowed by adding a new nonterminal and two new parsing rules. The nonterminal ⟨ATTRIBUTE⟩ is added to correspond to a set of

⟨ATTRIB⟩'s. It may be a set of only one ⟨ATTRIB⟩, or more than one. The rules and templates are:

1. ⟨ATTRIBUTE. → ⟨ATTRIB⟩ ⟨ATTRIBUTE⟩
   ⇒ add(? ⟨ATTRIB⟩) to set
   for a list of ⟨ATTRIB⟩'s

2. ⟨ATTRIBUTE⟩ → ⟨ATTRIB⟩ AND ⟨ATTRIBUTE⟩
   ⇒ add(? ⟨ATTRIB⟩) to the
   set of questions formed
   from ⟨ATTRIBUTE⟩

3. ⟨ATTRIBUTE⟩ → ⟨ATTRIB⟩
   ⇒ ((? ⟨ATTRIB⟩))
   an ⟨ATTRIB⟩ found by
   itself is a set of one member

The sentence template is changed to:

TEMPLATE 1: WHAT IS THE ⟨ATTRIBUTE⟩ OF THE ⟨SHIP⟩

For the sentence,

What is the length, home port and hull number of the Constitution?

the final parse tree is the one shown in Figure 5.24.

## SEMANTIC GRAMMARS AND SYNTACTIC REGULARITIES

The purpose of these three expansion rules for ⟨ATTRIBUTE⟩ is, of course, to allow the user to join a list of attributes together in the question. This allows the user to ask one compound question instead of three simple ones. One deficiency of this kind of parsing scheme is that it does not state a general rule about joining elements. It is specific to ⟨ATTRIBUTE⟩. If the user is to be allowed to join ⟨SHIP⟩'s

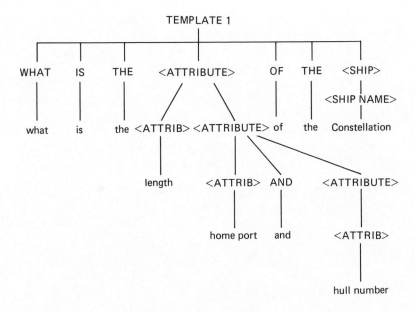

**Figure 5.24 Semantic parse tree**

in the same way, a new set of three rules must be written specific to ⟨SHIP⟩. And this is true for each nonterminal that one would want to join. It is much more appealing to give the system a general capability for joining elements. However, if the system designers remember to write the joining rules for all the appropriate nonterminals, the appearance to the user would be the same as if a general procedure for joining elements did exist in the system.

This raises another point—that of the expertise required of designers of a natural language processing system. One of the important design features of a natural language processing system is how difficult it would be to adapt to different applications areas. For example, consider the problems of adapting a system built to answer questions on a naval command and control database to a database on the business records of a corporation. The domain is totally different, so the vocabulary and the concepts would be totally different. But, the language would have very much the same structure in both applications. A description of the structure of language is not carried from application to application by LIFER. It must be redescribed in each application by the application developer. The developer's level of expertise must be high in both understanding the content of the application and the structure of English.

The syntax of English is not embedded in LIFER, but that is not due to oversight. The difficult problem of analyzing an English utterance is in semantics: relating words to their meanings. Two sentences with the same words could be structured differently, giving different meanings. The general meaning of sentences fitting the template

THE (ATTRIBUTE) OF THE (SHIP)

can be determined by the system. By dealing with structural variations after identifying semantic components, the system makes the relationship to meaning easier to establish. The resulting system is syntactically weak, but semantically adequate. It has been argued that for interfaces to databases, the user's questions will also be syntactically limited, so in actual operation, the weakness in syntax would not be noticed by users. The advantage of this approach is that it permits the rapid implementation of a natural language processor. A skilled application designer can have a LIFER-based system on a new database application within a few weeks.

## PRONOUNS AND ELLIPSES

LIFER also has the ability to deal with some forms of pronominal and elliptical references. The techniques for the two phenomena are complementary.

1) What is the length and hull number of the Constellation?
2) The home port?

The second user utterance above is a superstructure ellipsis, presumably a shortened form of "what is the home port of the Constellation?"

LIFER can analyze this ellipsis correctly. It first tries its top-level sentence templates. "The home port" would fail to match any of them. It then examines the parse tree of the previous sentence. If the ellipsis can be made to match the fragment of the parse tree, the ellipsis is inserted into the tree and a new query is formed and executed; see Figure 5.25.

Similarly, if the user entered the elliptical phrase "of the Nautilus" this would be substituted for the OF THE ⟨SHIP⟩ tree fragment in the previous question. Note, however, the "for the Nautilus" would not be parsed because of the seemingly insignificant discrepancy of substituting "for" for "of." The grammar could be redesigned to accommodate this anomaly. Here, again, the operation of LIFER depends largely on the skill and foresight of the application designer, rather than including this common substitution in LIFER itself.

### 5.8 Case Study: The Linguistic String Project

The Linguistic String Project, LSP (Sager 1967, 1972, 1973), has developed a parser that is based on the linguistic string theory of English grammar. We shall not discuss the details of linguistic string grammar, but rather its implementation by LSP. The implemented grammar consists of three components: a dictionary, a set of context-free productions and a set of restriction rules. The restriction rules represent the grammar information that cannot be captured efficiently in the context-free rules. There are rules for such restrictions as subject-verb number agreement and semantic marker agreement between a verb and its object (e.g., in "John eats each day," "each day" is rejected as the object of "eats" because it is not edible).

The LSP-implemented grammar is probably the most complete grammar of English implemented to date. Its vocabulary of 8,000-9,000 words is also much larger than most implementations. The parser applies the rules of the context-free grammar component in a conventional top-down fashion. Nondeterminism and multiple parses are handled by backup. The parser can save well-formed substrings, thus alleviating the problem of parsing a substring repeatedly and each time resulting in the same parse. Each restriction rule is associated with one or more of the context-free productions.

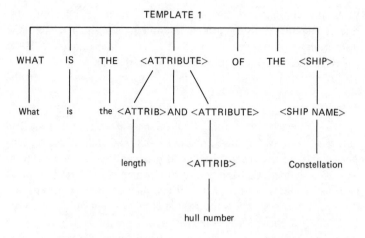

Semantic parse structure of sentence 1

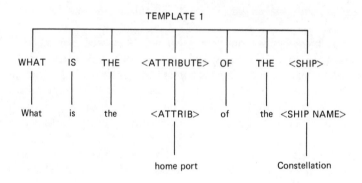

Semantic parse structure assumed for sentence 2

**Figure 5.25**

When the context-free component concludes the application of a rule corresponding to the production of a node in the parse tree, the restriction rules attached to the context-free rule are executed. If the newly parsed constituent satisfies all the restrictions, the parse continues. If a restriction is violated, the constituent is rejected, and the context free component backs up.

The LSP grammar has been applied to the problem of analyzing text and constructing a formatted database from its contents. The text was from two sources, pharmacology and radiologist reports. The benefit of a program that could produce such a database from text is, of course, that the conceptual content of the text becomes more available to users. Alternatives include free text retrieval, document retrieval, and retrieval based on concept clustering. Free text retrieval suffers from the effects of syntactic variability in the statement of concepts. Document retrieval forces the user to search sets of retrieved documents when only one particular fact in a document is of interest. Concept clustering, if done statistically, is prone to errors based on word choice. If it is done manually, it requires a great deal of effort by workers who are sufficiently familiar with the technical field to be able to identify references to concepts.

For these applications, the general implemented grammar was augmented to reflect the specific rules of the sublanguage of the specific domains. The general grammar of English has word categories such as noun, verb and preposition as the lowest level nonterminals in the grammar. However, not all possible sentences that are well formed in the general grammar are well formed in the sublanguage. For instance, in the pharmacology sublanguage, the verb "transport" can accept an object from the noun subclass of ions (e.g., "ion," "K+") but not from the noun subclass of pharmacological agents (e.g., "drug," "digitalis," or "gyncosides").

To reflect these semantic constraints, new lowest level nonterminals are added to the grammar. These new nonterminals group the traditional word categories into semantic classes. It was also observed that some word class ambiguities that were present in the general grammar did not warrant attention in the sublanguage.

In addition to changes at the lowest level of the grammar, sublanguage-specific changes were made at the highest level, the sentence level of the grammar. Sentences were classified according to their subject-verb-object types.


## SEMANTIC GRAMMAR WITH SYNTACTIC REGULARITIES

The effect of these sublanguage-specific alterations was the conversion of a syntactic grammar into a semantic grammar. The resulting semantic grammar has a fundamental advantage over the other semantic grammars implemented. It retains most of the productions of a general syntactic grammar. This means that the regularities of syntactic analysis were, for the most part, preserved and applied to the new semantic grammar. This contrasts with most other semantic grammars where, as we have seen in other case studies, regularities like determiners on noun phrases and "anded" constructions conjoining two structures are lost in the semantic grammar. The advantages of a semantic grammar are still achieved.


### 5.9 Case Study: PLANES

PLANES, Programmed LANguage-based Enquiry System (Waltz 1975; Waltz and Goodman 1977), is a natural language interface to a large database. The database is the Navy's 3-M database which holds the maintenance and flight records for all naval aircraft. It is on the order of a trillion bits, and grows by the equivalent of 100 magnetic tapes of data annually. The purpose of the PLANES project has been to explore the possibilities of building a natural language interface to the database.

The normal operation of PLANES entails three steps. First, the user's question is typed in and it is analyzed for its semantic content. Next, a formal query is constructed. The formal query is used to generate a paraphrase of the user's question as PLANES has understood it. Last, if the user accepts the paraphrase, the query is performed on the database and the results are presented to the user.

SEMANTIC CONSTITUENT SCAN

PLANES makes little explicit use of syntactic information. Its analysis of a user's sentence is a left to right scan for "semantic constituents." A semantic constituent is a phrase that can (usually) be mapped directly into some part of the formal query, such as a predicate or return field. The semantic constituents include such items as PLANETYPE, TIMEPERIOD, MALFUNCTIONCODE and so on. The analysis is implemented with an ATN. The top level, shown in Figure 5.26 is a one-state network which calls various subnets to analyze the input for semantic constituents (this view, though somewhat simplified, is essentially correct).

1) How many A7's flew three or more catapult flights in May 1971?

In the analysis of example 1, the first semantic constituent found is the question word "how many," found by the subnet QWORD. Next, "A7's" is identified as a class of attack aircraft by the PLANETYPE subnet. ACTION recognizes "flew." A subnet for FLIGHTS identifies "three or more catapult flights," and TIMEPERIOD picks up "in May 1971." These constituents are now held in registers. The only structural information that is retained is the order in which the constituents were found in the sentence. Since there is a PLANETYPE between the question word and verb, PLANES will return the aircraft serial number field. However, because this is a "how many" question, PLANES will count the number of elements in the return field and display the count to the user.

The one-state ATN at the top level calls each subnet repeatedly during the analysis of the sentence. This is done without regard to whether the constituent that the subnet parses has been identified elsewhere in the sentence. What this is, then, is a top-down analysis technique that does not make use of expectations at the top level!

This seemingly unusual approach to analysis does have some justification. One of the goals of PLANES was to be very tolerant of user inputs not necessarily stated in standard English. The idea was that the sentence-level structure (syntax) of inputs would tend not to be well formed, while the semantic-constituent level would be

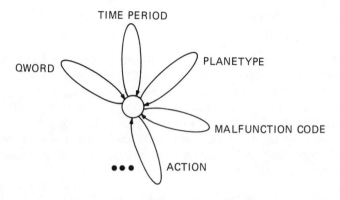

**Figure 5.26**

fairly grammatical. PLANES expected to see rampant pragmatic ellipsis and deletion of verbs, case markers and determiners. It was designed to be sufficiently robust to identify semantic constituents and build queries in spite of such adversity. It was presumed that the difficulty of designing a detailed grammar for English that would condone such a cavalier attitude toward standard syntax would not warrant the advantages. Instead, it was decided to ignore most of the constraints of English syntax.

The inefficiency of pushing to many subnets that do not eventually accept a phrase of the input sentence can also be improved. A predicate could be attached to each push arc to test the next word of the input string. If there is a string that could be parsed by the subnet that starts with the next word, the push would be executed. If the subnet under consideration could not parse a string starting with the next word, the push would not be made. A manual count of arc transitions indicated that this one-word lookahead would reduce the total number of arcs tested in the parse of a sentence by a factor of ten. A lookahead to the next content word, overlooking prepositions and determiners, would result in a reduction of arcs tested by a factor of 100. This would resemble a bottom-up analysis strategy at the sentence level, but a top-down strategy when parsing semantic constituents in the subnets.

CONCEPT CASE FRAMES

After the semantic constituents of the user's sentence had been collected, the collection was examined from the point of view of whether it constituted a complete query as it stood. If so, it was passed on to the query-generation routines. If not, the missing constituents were filled in from the context. The context in this case was the set of semantic constituents used in the previous query with each constituent labeled by semantic type. If a TIMEPERIOD was missing, as in,

2) How many A7's had unscheduled maintenance?

the TIMEPERIOD constituent from the previous query would be used again.

The decision as to whether a user's question actually specified a complete query without borrowing constituents from the context was made on the basis of "concept case frames." Concept case frames were strings of constituents of reasonable queries. Example 1 is repeated below with its constituents labeled:

| How many | A7's | flew | three or more catapult flights |
|----------|------|------|-------------------------------|
| QWORD | PLANETYPE | FLY | FLIGHTS |

in May 1971
TIMEPERIOD

For this query to be judged complete, a set matching "QWORD PLANETYPE FLY FLIGHTS TIMEPERIOD" had to be found among the concept case frames.

*Substructure Ellipsis and Pronouns*

There were several ways in which a mismatch could have occurred. First, the constituent between the QWORD and verb might be missing;

this is labeled an ellipsis and the constituent filling that function in the preceding sentence is used. Second, one of the constituents could be missing, having been replaced by a pronoun. In this case, the concept case frame that most closely matches the pattern of constituents for the current sentence is used. If there is a one-constituent difference between the current sentence and a concept case frame, that constituent is taken as the referent of the pronoun.

3) What maintenances were performed on plane 3 in May 1971?
   [QWORD MAINTTYPE MAINTACTION PLANETYPE TIME-PERIOD]

4) What maintenances were performed on it in August 1973?
   [QWORD MAINTTYPE MAINTACTION PRONOUN TIME-PERIOD]

Question 3 specifies a complete query without recourse to context. A concept case frame would match its string of semantic constituent types. The string of constituents for example 4 would nearly match the same concept case frame. The previous PLANETYPE, PLANE 3, would be substituted for the PRONOUN constituent.

*Pragmatic Ellipsis*

Another kind of incomplete match to concept case frames was with the occurrence of a pragmatic ellipsis:

5) What maintenances were performed on plane 48?
   [QWORD MAINTTYPE MAINTACTION PLANETYPE]

The TIMEPERIOD constituent has been ellipted from this example. The constituent string would nearly match the concept case frame that matched example 3, the TIMEPERIOD being the only discrepancy. This could be filled in from context (i.e., the TIMEPERIOD constituent of the previous query).

*Superstructure Ellipsis*

The last case of an incomplete match to concept case frames was in the event of a superstructure ellipsis. A superstructure ellipsis like the one below would be recognized by the absence of a verb:

6) Plane 50?
   PLANETYPE

Instances of superstructure ellipsis were handled by using the entire constituent string of the previous sentence (after it had undergone pronoun and ellipsis resolution) and replacing the constituents mentioned in the current sentence.

If for some reason the pronoun and ellipsis routines were not successful, a clarification dialog would be initiated with the user to remedy the problem.

## THE QUERY GENERATOR

After application of the concept case frames, the semantic constituents were passed to the query generator. The query generator produced query predicates from the semantic constituents, each constituent being interpreted independently of the others. The fields to be returned from the query, as mentioned above, were taken from the noun phrases that fell (or had been ellipted) between the question word and verb. PLANES maintained a list of the files in which each data field occurred. The file lists of the fields mentioned in the predicates and return fields were intersected to determine which files needed to be searched. This process also identified more involved queries, like those involving joins.

After the query had been built by the query generator, it was given to the paraphraser. The paraphraser generated an English paraphrase for the user's approval. Upon approval, the query was executed and the results were returned to the user.

## PROBLEMS FROM IGNORING SYNTAX

PLANES was fairly proficient at resolving ellipsis and pronoun reference. Its main deficiencies lay in word sense selection and modifier attachment. PLANES relied heavily (too heavily) on its world of discourse to eliminate problems of word sense selection.

7) How many flights did plane 3 make in June?
8) How many maintenances were performed in June?

In PLANES, "make" is always interpreted as "fly," and "perform" is interpreted as indicating "maintenance action." This causes no problems in examples 7 and 8, but examples 9 and 10 below could not be handled. Due to the fact that semantic constituents were parsed independently, there was no mechanism available for the appropriate sense of the verb to be selected based on the other constituents in the sentence.

9) How many flights did plane 3 perform in June?
10) How many maintenance actions did work center 3 make in August?

PLANES did not have an organized approach toward attaching prepositional phrases to nouns that they modify. The semantic constituent subnets would, for example, interpret "hours" as flight hours, and "NOR hours" or "NOR" as not-operationally-ready hours. The phrase "hours of NOR" was interpreted as a flight hours constituent and a not-operationally-ready hours constituent. A slight change to the subnets could have corrected this. The phrase "hours for plane 3 of NOR" would have required massive changes. The point is that the policy of allowing head nouns and modifying prepositional phrases to be broken apart and analyzed independently ignored an important generalization of language: modifiers help to describe some particular thing, and they must be attached properly.

## 5.10 Case Study: RENDEZVOUS

RENDEZVOUS (Codd 1974, 1978) is a natural language interface to a relational database. Its most distinguishing characteristic is that it assumes that the queries specified by users may be incomplete, improperly understood or based on false assumptions. To remedy these problems, RENDEZVOUS can, when the need arises, retreat from full natural language communication to a more restricted form of communication. The dialog capabilities of RENDEZVOUS will be discussed later, but first its semantic capabilities will be described.

RENDEZVOUS is unusual among its contemporaries in that it is a semantic grammar, but is not top-down. The other semantic grammars discussed in this chapter are primarily top-down, many having been implemented with ATNs. RENDEZVOUS's grammar is implemented with a production system-like mechanism. It consists of rewrite rules which, through repeated application, transform the user's questions into formal database queries.

One of the goals of RENDEZVOUS's language analysis program is to be able to accept questions whether they are stated in standard English or not. It can accept sentence fragments and phrases with such words as determiners omitted. The overall scheme for achieving this flexibility is to analyze phrases in user inputs with only minimal regard to the syntactic or semantic context. Thus, a phrase is analyzed in the same way whether it occurs in a complete sentence or in a sentence fragment. In this respect RENDEZVOUS is similar to PLANES.

### PROBLEM OF LARGE VOCABULARY

Another interesting aspect of the RENDEZVOUS semantics is that it recognized that the vocabulary necessary for a large database may be only partially understood by the interface. This contrasts with most natural language processors in which every word that is acceptable in a user's question must be in the system dictionary.

Word recognition in natural language processors is commonly done in one of two ways. The first is that all acceptable words are entered in a dictionary, usually accompanied by the syntactic or semantic characteristics of the word. If one of the words in the user's sentence is not in the dictionary, it must be deleted, replaced by a synonym or defined before the sentence can be analyzed. The dictionary approach seems reasonable because it is similar to the large recognition vocabularies that humans seem to have. It is unattractive from an implementational point of view. One database, although a restricted domain, may have an enormous number of words used as data elements. For this kind of database, it is unfeasible for every word to be entered in a dictionary. Keeping the dictionary consistent with the database contents can also be a problem.

The second approach to the vocabulary problem is to use the database itself as a dictionary. The nonnumeric data fields could be inverted, providing an index of all the words used in the database and the fields in which they occur. A natural language program could maintain a dictionary of frequently used words. If a word cannot be found in the dictionary, the data element names are checked. The syntactic and semantic routines may also make use of which fields the words occur in. ROBOT (Harris 1977) and CO-OP (Kaplan 1977) use this approach.

The database-as-dictionary approach has deficiencies as well. The most striking is that an inverted index must be maintained. This could be very expensive in terms of storage space, often doubling the required storage. This makes the inversion technique unattractive.

RENDEZVOUS does not use either technique, but assumes that users may give data element names that it will not recognize. The data type of an unknown word may be inferred from the context, or the user may be asked to identify its data type.

## BOTTOM-UP SEMANTIC GRAMMAR

The analysis of user inputs by rewrite rules is done deterministically: there is no provision for backup in case of analysis errors. Cases of ambiguity are resolved through interaction with the user as soon as they are detected.

1) How many Whitney shipments have a ship date 6/10/75?

The date in example 1 can be interpreted as either June 10 or October 6. Also, RENDEZVOUS can interpret the question in two ways (assuming 6/10/75 means June 10, 1975):

2) Count the number of suppliers named Whitney who, on June 10, 1975, sent a shipment.

3) Count the number of shipments sent on June 10, 1975 by a supplier named Whitney.

They are then presented to the user who selects the intended interpretation.

The chapter on syntax pointed out that a bottom-up parse would likely result in building a large number of temporary structures for parses of phrases that would not contribute to the overall parse of the sentence. The production system-like mechanism of RENDEZVOUS's grammar is a semantic grammar. More specific information is required to trigger a semantic rule than a syntactic rule. As a result, few semantic rules get triggered that should not be.

The rewrite rules consist of two parts: a left-hand side (LHS) and a right-hand side (RHS). The LHS contains a pattern that is matched against the source string; the LHS may also contain some Boolean functions. The RHS usually contains one, but possibly more than one, replacement string. If the LHS pattern matches and the Boolean functions are true, the string that matches is replaced by the RHS replacement.

The RHS may contain alternatively the name of a function to be executed. The value returned by the function is used in the rewrite string. This provides greater flexibility than simple declarative rules. The RHS may also include a control code which specifies where in the string the next matching operation should begin. If no control code is given, the next match begins at the first word following the newly installed replacement string.

4) HOW MANY → C

Example 4 shows a very simple replacement rule. If the string matches the LHS, "HOW MANY," those two words are replaced by "C," meaning count. The next match would be attempted starting with the word in the string immediately to the right of "HOW MANY." Example 5 shows snapshots of an input string before and after the application of this rule; the arrow indicates where the next matching rule should begin:

5) How many Whitney shipments have a ship date after or during 6/10/1979?

C Whitney shipments have a ship date after
↑
or during 6/10/1975?

The time phrase in example 5 would match the rule given below:

6) AFTER OR (IN, ON, DURING) (⟨NUMVALUE⟩, ⟨YEAR⟩, ⟨DATE⟩) →⟩ DATE⟩ = D400

The LHS of this rule (the part of the rule to the left of the arrow) contains alternative elements written in parentheses. The first alternative specifies that one of the words "in," "on" or "during" must occur. The second alternative in the pattern specifies that there must be a word belonging to one of the word classes NUMVALUE, YEAR or DATE. This pattern matches the phrase "after or during 6/10/1975" with "6/10/1975" being in the class DATE. The matched string is replaced by the RHS. The RHS consists of two literal strings, "DATE" and "⟩=," and a function, D. The function can take up to three arguments, but in this case only one argument will be supplied. The 4 designates that the word matching the fourth pattern constituent will be passed to D as its first argument. The 0's indicate null values for the second and third arguments. The fourth constituent of the LHS is the word matching (⟨NUMVALUE⟩, ⟨YEAR⟩, ⟨DATE⟩), namely, "6/10/1975." D analyzes this date and returns the date expressed in a RENDEZVOUS standard format.

The rewrite rules are grouped into eight classes. The rule classes are applied to the user's input one at a time, making eight passes over it. They are shown below:

| Class | Purpose |
|---|---|
| 1 | query type |
| 2 | dates |
| 3 | general idioms |
| 4 | domain-specific phrases |
| 5 | negation and comparators |
| 6 | relation names, attributes, values, parentheses |
| 7 | introduce join terms |
| 8 | remaining attributes and values |

## CLASSES OF DIALOG

If RENDEZVOUS had any doubts about its analysis of the user's question, it initiated a dialog to clarify them. Six classes of dialog are supported. The first class is *clarification dialog*. Clarification dialog can be initiated for many reasons, for instance, spelling errors, ambiguities such as those illustrated above, fuzzy values and semantic overshoot. A fuzzy value is a word like "recently" which would initiate a dialog to determine its exact interpretation. Semantic overshoot are references to concepts that are outside the range of the database:

7) Who are the managers of the Monterey projects?

Here the word *managers* indicates that the user is attempting to reference a concept that is not included within the range of the database.

The second class of dialog is menu-driven dialog. When the language analysis is complete, it passes its formal query representation of the user's question to the menu driver. The menu driver scans the formal query for omissions. If any are found, menus specific to the kind of missing information are presented to the user. Dialog through specific menus is designed to repair any omissions quickly. The use of menus restricts the user's inputs so that new ambiguities or misinterpretations are not introduced at this stage.

The third dialog class is verification. An unambiguous English paraphrase is generated from the formal query, and then the user is asked to verify the accuracy of RENDEZVOUS's interpretation. In order to change the paraphrase, the user entered the fourth dialog class.

The fourth class is the query editor. The editor is menu driven and allows the user to change his or her original question, change the system's paraphrase or throw them both out and start over.

The fifth class is the presentation of the query output to the user. The most interesting case here is when the query returns an empty relation. In that case RENDEZVOUS will attempt to provide an explanation. If any predicates were never satisfied, that fact is relayed to the user. An example from Codd (1978) is given below:

8) Q: Is there any supplier named Jones and rated excellent who, during March 1976, sent a shipment of a part named cam to a project named Mojave located in Monterey?

A: There is no supplier in the database satisfying your query. Note that in the database there is
(1) no part named cam,
(2) no project named Mojave located in Monterey, and
(3) no supplier named Jones rated excellent.

The last class of dialog is *continuation dialog*. In this class, the user is asked the following:

In regard to your present query, what additional information would you like to have? If none, just hit the "send" key.

This strategy neatly sidesteps most of the problems of references and ellipses. Whatever is mentioned by the user in the continuation dialog is either added to the current query or it replaces terms in the current query.

## 5.11 Case Study: ELI

Two versions of ELI (Riesbeck 1975; Riesbeck and Schank 1976; Gershman 1977) have been implemented. The description given here includes some characteristics of both programs.

### MOTIVATION BEHIND ELI'S ARCHITECTURE

A large part of the literature about ELI is devoted to the motivation for its design. The premise behind ELI is that it should reflect, wherever possible, the kind of processing that humans apparently do. Since little is known about how humans process language, the architecture of ELI relies heavily on introspection. Specifically, the ELI model of language processing opposes the assumption (made by many linguists) that a separate syntactic parse is done. ELI is designed under the premise that semantics drives the understanding process and syntax is of secondary importance. ELI does syntactic processing only when the semantic routines require it.

Some of the assumptions on which ELI is based are quite persuasive. Syntactic analysis usually produces many possible structures for a sentence. These are based on such problems as modifier attachment and word sense selection. People do not appear to select from several alternative interpretations of a sentence, but are constrained by the context so that they rarely notice the possibility of ambiguity. The context usually specifies uniquely which sense is intended by a word. The dialog and the listener's model of the world usually specify where modifiers should be attached as soon as they are heard. In order for context to determine the speaker's intentions as soon as the words are heard, ELI is run by expectations. ELI uses what has been parsed so far to describe what is expected to be found next. Language analysis is driven by the fulfillment of expectations.

### EXPECTATION-BASED PARSING

The parsing technique used in ELI does not fall neatly into any of the classes mentioned above, but it does have some characteristics in common with each of them. First, the importance of expectations implies top-down analysis. A top-down parser uses what it has already parsed to govern the tests it will apply to the next input word or phrase. ELI does this, too, but the expectations in ELI simply may not apply to the next word, but to some constituent farther down the sentence. Another difference is that top-down mechanisms, typified by ATNs, are usually used to capture regularities in the language. The structure of a noun phrase, regardless of its meaning, is a regularity captured by a syntax parsing ATN when the structure of all noun phrases is described in one ATN subnet. The structure of a reference to a concept, say, a time period, is captured in a subnet of a semantic grammar ATN. These recognizable regularities expressed in ATNs give them the advantage of "perspicuity," clarity and ease of understanding. ELI attaches all of its expectations to word senses. Regularities are not factored out. As a result, the grammar is difficult to understand. This can result in a grammar that is difficult to develop and maintain, since the expectations of one word may interact with those of other words.

Second, ELI has some characteristics in common with production systems. The definition of a sense of a word consists of an expectation part and an action part. These resemble the pattern and action parts of a production system. While processing a sentence, new expectations are placed on an expectation list. As each new word is considered, the expectations are tested to see if they have been satisfied. If one has, its action part is executed and the expectation is removed from the expectation list. The action parts are primarily responsible for building complete or partial structures that represent what has been understood. ELI differs from the production system-like rules of RENDEZVOUS in that ELI scans the sentence left to right, making as many decisions as it can as early in the parse as possible. RENDEZVOUS does not always scan left to right.

Third, the use of a production system-like mechanism generally denotes an essentially bottom-up parse. This is not true with ELI because the production rules (the expectations) are dynamic. The set of rules that may apply at some point in the processing is highly dependent on the context that has been established.

As an example, consider the verb "leave." The rules for processing "leave" include provisions for the following senses:

1) John left the restaurant.
2) John left the waitress a tip.
3) John left quickly.
4) John left the waitress.
5) John left a dollar.

When "leave" is encountered, a structure is built to represent a physical movement, as in the senses in examples 1 and 3. Rules are activated that indicate that if the subject of the sentence is a human, it should be taken as the agent of the leaving event. Also, the point of departure for leaving is indicated as a location-type noun phrase. A third rule is activated that specifies that if the sentence has an object, a special procedure is to be called. This procedure is responsible for selecting the appropriate sense of "leave." If the category of the first noun phrase following the verb is LOCATION, the sense implied by example 1 is assumed. The LOCATION is built into the representation. If the semantic category is MONEY, as in example 5, the physical movement structure that was built earlier is discarded and a new structure is built. The new structure represents a transfer of ownership, in this case of money.

If the semantic category of the object noun phrase is HUMAN, as in examples 2 and 4, two interpretations are possible. Example 2 denotes a transfer of ownership, and 4 denotes a physical movement. ELI temporarily retains the existing physical movement representation, but activates a new rule. This rule states that if another noun phrase is found following the object, a transfer of ownership representation should replace the physical movement structure.

## EXPANDING ELI's LINGUISTIC COVERAGE

ELI-2 expanded on the ELI processing model through better treatment of noun phrases and treatment of certain "surprise" constructions such as appositives and certain types of prepositional phrases.

The normal word processing strategy of ELI is changed in ELI-2 for parsing noun phrases. Ordinarily, all the test parts of the active rules are collected in one large pool of rules. When a new word is read, all the tests in the pool are checked. The ones that are satisfied are executed. Noun phrase analysis in ELI-2 is different in that not all expectations are available simultaneously.

6) large Chinese restaurant

The analysis of this noun phrase begins with "large." Rules associated with "large" expect to modify a physical object. An expectation rule to this effect is activated. This expectation is pushed on a modifier stack. "Chinese" sets up two expectations. If it modifies a physical object, it is interpreted as made in China. If it modifies a person, it is interpreted as being a Chinese citizen. The two "Chinese" expectations are pushed on the modifier stack. Putting them on the stack leaves them accessible, but makes the "large" expectation inaccessible. "Restaurant" has an expectation that looks to the left, called a backward expectation. If the word to the left of "restaurant" can be interpreted as a restaurant type, it is interpreted that way. Backward expectations are generally more specific than forward expectations so the backward ones are checked before the forward ones. "Chinese" can specify a type of restaurant, so it and its expectations are popped off the modifier stack. A structure is built representing a Chinese restaurant.

The expectation for "large" is now at the top of the stack. The Chinese restaurant concept satisfies the physical object test. A representation for a "large Chinese restaurant" is then built and the analysis is complete.

The expectation rules are actually organized in a slightly more complex fashion than just explained. The expectations are separated into six levels:

1. Words
2. Active
3. Optional
4. Expert
5. End of Phrase
6. Trap

Word expectations test for specific words such as particles; for example, if "pick" has been seen, a word expectation for "up" would be set. Active expectations are those that should be satisfied later in the text. Optional expectations may not be satisfied. Expert expectations are generated by the control program rather than specific words; they are designed to deal with surprise phrases as in examples 7 and 8:

7) Lefty, *the president of the Optimists Club*, left town today. (appositive)
8) Knuckles *of the Chicago gang* went into hiding. (prepositional phrase)

End of Phrase expectations are designed to recognize situations that indicate that the current phrase has been fully parsed.

Trap expectations are essentially for error recovery. If the input is not handled by one of the other types of expectations, a trap is activated.

### References and Further Reading

Brown, J.S. and Burton, R.R. "Multiple Representations of Knowledge for Tutorial Reasoning." In *Representation of Understanding*, edited by D.G. Bobrow and A. Collins. New York: Academic Press, 1975.

_____. "A Paradigmatic Example of an Artificially Intelligent Instructional System." *International Joint Man-Machine Studies* 10 (1978):323-339.

Brown, J.S.; Burton, R.R.; and Bell, A.G. "SOPHIE/A Sophisticated Instructional Environment for Teaching Electronic Troubleshooting." Report .2790, A1 Report 12. Cambridge, Mass.: Bolt, Beranek and Newman, 1974.

Burton, R.R. "Semantic Grammar: An Engineering Technique for Constructing Natural Language Understanding Systems." Report 3453, ICAI Report 3. Cambridge, Mass.: Bolt, Beranek and Newman, 1976.

Codd, E.F. "Seven Steps to Rendezvous with the Casual User." In *Data base Management*, edited by J.W. Klimbie and K.L. Koffema. New York: North Holland Publishing Company, 1974.

Codd, E.F.; Arnold, R.S.; Cadiou, J.M.; Chang, C.L.; and Roussopoulos, N. "Rendezvous Version 1: An Experimental English-Language Query Formulation

System for Casual Users." Report RJ2144(29407). San Jose, Calif.: IBM Research Laboratory, 1978.

Gershman, A.V. "Conceptual Analysis of Noun Groups in English." In *Proceedings of the International Joint Conference on Artificial Intelligence*. Cambridge, Mass.: MIT, 1977.

Goldman, N. "Conceptual Generation." In *Conceptual Information Processing*, edited by Schank. New York: American Elsevier, 1975.

Grishman, R. "The Implementation of the String Parser of English." In *Natural Language Processing*, edited by R. Rustin. New York: Algorithmics Press, 1973.

Grishman, R.; Sager, N.; Raze, C.; and Bookchin, B. "The Linguistic String Parser." In *Proceedings of NCC*. Montvale, N.J.: AFIPS Press, 1973.

Harris, L.R. "User Oriented Data Base Query with the ROBOT Natural Language Query System." *International Journal of Man-Machine Studies* 9 (1977): 697-713.

Hendrix, G.G. "Human Engineering for Applied Natural Language Processing." In *Proceedings of the International Joint Conference on Artificial Intelligence*. Cambridge, Mass.: MIT, 1977.

Hendrix, G.G.; Sacerdoti, E.D.; Sagalowicz, D.; and Slocum, J. "Developing a Natural Language Interface to Complex Data." In *ACM Transactions on Database Systems*, 1978.

Hirschman, L.; Grishman, R.; and Sager, N. "From Text to Structured Information—Automatic Processing of Medical Reports." In *Proceedings of NCC*. Montvale, N.J.: AFIPS Press, 1976.

Kaplan, S.J. "On the Difference Between Natural Languages and High Level Query Languages." *Proceedings of the ACM 78*. Washington, D.C. AMC 1978.

Miller, H.G.; Hershman, R.L.; and Kelly, R.T. "Performance of a Natural Language Query System in a Simulated Command Control Environment." *Advanced Command and Control Architectural Testbed, Code 832*. San Diego, Calif.: Naval Ocean Systems Center, 1978.

Rieger, C.J. "Conceptual Memory and Inference." In *Conceptual Information Processing*, edited by R.C. Schank. New York: American Elsevier, 1975.

Riesbeck, C.K. "Conceptual Analysis." In *Conceptual Information Processing*, edited by R.C. Schank. New York: American Elsevier, 1975.

Riesbeck, C. and Schank, R.C. "Comprehension by Computer: Expectation-Based Analysis of Sentences in Context." Research Report 78. Yale University, 1976.

Rubin, A. "Grammar for the People: Flowcharts of SHRDLU's Grammar." Memo 282, 1973. Cambridge, Mass.: MIT Department of Artificial Intelligence, 1973.

Sacerdoti, E.D. "Language Access to Distributed Data with Error Recovery." In *Proceedings of the International Joint Conference on Artificial Intelligence*. Cambridge, Mass.: MIT, 1977.

Sager, N. "Syntactic Analysis of Natural Language." In *Advances in Computers* vol. 8, edited by F.L. Aot and M. Rubinoff. New York: Academic Press, 1967.

_____. "Syntactic Formatting of Science Information." In *Proceedings of the Fall Joint Computer Conference*. Montvale, N.J.: AFIPS Press, 1972.

_____. "The String Parser for Scientific Literature." In *Natural Language Processing*, edited by R. Rustin. New York: Algorithmics Press, 1973.

Sager, N. and Grishman, R. "The Restriction Language for Computer Grammars of Natural Language." *CACM* 18 (July 1975):390-400.

Schank, R.C. *Conceptual Information Processing*. New York: American Elsevier, 1975.

_____. "Identification of Conceptualizations Underlying Natural Language." In *Computer Models of Thought and Language*. R.C. Schank and K.M. Colby. San Francisco: W.H. Freeman, 1973.

_____. "Representation and Understanding of Text." In *Machine Intelligence* 8, edited by E.W. Elcocks and D. Michie. New York: Holsted Press, 1977.

Waltz, D.L. "Natural Language Access to a Large Data Base." In *Advance Papers of the Fourth International Joint Conference on Artificial Intelligence*. Cambridge, Mass.: MIT, 1975.

Waltz, D.L. and Goodman, B.A. "Writing a Natural Language Data Base System." In *Proceedings of the International Joint Conference on Artificial Intelligence*. Cambridge, Mass.: MIT, 1977.

Wilks, Y. "An Artificial Intelligence Approach to Machine Translation." In *Computer Models of Thought and Language*, edited by R.C. Schank and K.M. Colby. San Francisco: W.H. Freeman, 1973.

_____. "An Intelligent Analyzer and Understander of English." *Communications of the ACM* 18 (May 1975):264-274.

_____. "Making Preferences More Active." *Artificial Intelligence* 11 (1978): 197-223.

_____. "Parsing English II." In *Computational Semantics*, edited by E. Charniak and Y. Wilks. New York: North Holland Publishing Co., 1976.

_____. "A Preferential, Pattern-Seeking, Semantics for Natural Language Inference." *Artificial Intelligence* 6 (1975):53-74.

Winograd, T. "A Procedural Model of Language Understanding." In *Computer Models of Thought and Language*, edited by R. Schank and K. Colby. San Francisco: W.H. Freeman, 1973.

_____. "Procedures as a Representation for Data in a Computer Program for Understanding Natural Language." MAC TR-84. Ph.D. thesis, MIT, 1971.

_____. *Understanding Natural Language*. New York: Academic Press, 1972.

Woods, W.A. "Procedural Semantics for Question-Answering Machine." In *Proceedings of the Fall Joint Computer Conference*. Montvale, N.J.: AFIPS Press, 1968.

_____. "Progress in Natural Language Understanding–An Application to Lunar Geology." In *Proceedings of the National Computer Conference*. Montvale, N.J.: AFIPS Press, 1973.

_____. "Semantics and Quantification in Natural Language Question Answering." Report 3687. Cambridge, Mass: Bolt, Berenak and Newman, 1977.

_____. "Semantics for a Question Answering System." Ph.D. thesis, Division of Engineering and Applied Physics, Harvard University, 1967. (also Report NSF-19 Harvard Computation Laboratory)

Woods, W.A.; Kaplan, R.M.; and Nash-Webber, B. *The Lunar Sciences Natural Language Information System: Final Report*. Report 2378. Cambridge Mass.: Bolt, Beranek and Newman, 1972.

# 6. Representing Knowledge about Objects and Events

One of the broadly accepted themes in current natural language work is that language understanding is largely a memory-based process. Syntactic analysis, for example, is the recognition of allowable structure in an utterance. Semantic analysis is partly the recognition of references to particular objects of events and partly the synthesis of unusual concepts from familiar ones.

When language understanding goes beyond the boundaries of single sentences, different structures are recognized. According to current theories, if a familiar event is being described, such as going to a restaurant, understanding the description involves recognizing the similarities and differences between the current description and a description of a stereotype of a trip to a restaurant. If a new car is being described, the description is understood in terms of recognizing the similarities and differences between this particular car and a stereotypical car.

Along another dimension, language understanding is embedded in a form of discourse. The form of discourse may be, for example, a conversation, a story or and essay. Specific rules govern the proper use of these forms. Understanding language involves interpreting the language in terms of the discourse in which it is embedded. Here again, understanding is facilitated by the recognition of the way in which the form is being used, its similarity to and differences from a stereotypical use of the form.

Syntax and semantics were discussed in previous chapters. The organization and use of knowledge for understanding situations, objects and events are discussed in this chapter. The organization and use of knowledge about the conventions of the form of discourse will be discussed in the next chapter.

If understanding is largely a recognition process, then one of the primary problems of understanding is the organization of a large memory. A frequently used technique for memory organization is to store differences between descriptions of related concepts rather than complete descriptions of each concept. The description of cars in general is a stereotype of a car, also called a conceptual prototype. A description of a particular car, like Lefty's car, would be compared to the prototype. Once Lefty's car has been mentioned, current theories suggest that the listener forms a mental image of it. It is a pretty vague image, but the listener assumes it has four wheels, is perhaps a sedan, and is perhaps a certain color. It is probably a fairly sound machine, not brand new, but not a clunker either. These are the default values of the listener's concept of a prototype car.

Without information to the contrary, the listener assumed a description of Lefty's car as being like his or her prototypical car. But the listener hears that it is a '68 Buick, and the concept of Lefty's car diverges from the prototype. Perhaps the listener imagines a car somewhat less sound than the prototype, rusting around the wheel wells and along the rocker panels. The finish now appears weather beaten, and the dimensions have grown from the prototype size to the extravagant size of higher priced cars in the days of cheap gas. To make these changes, the information for doing so was stored somewhere in the listener's mind. Perhaps there is a separate prototype for old cars. Perhaps there are transformations attached to his or her car concept. One transformation is used to add the rust and fade the finish (the old-car transformation). Another transformation to increase the dimensions and perhaps add some chrome, power windows and air conditioning (the large-car transformations invoked on learning it is a Buick). It may be that the listener pictures two alternative cars, one a clunker and another a beautifully preserved automobile with a high gloss finish and a smoothly running engine. Some deviations from the defaults in the prototype are accepted as being quite unsurprising. If the listener hears that Lefty's car is green, he or she simply notes the information. Other deviations require a more involved explanation. If the listener hears that a door is dented, there may be an explanation at hand: an accident. A very unusual deviation would also require an explanation, but there may not be one ready. If the listener hears that the car is equipped with an ejection seat, or it is 27 feet long, he or she may pause, unable to locate a reasonable explanation and may ask for one.

We seem to store and handle a great deal of information when understanding language. We seem to have default descriptions of objects, and ways of changing those descriptions as more information becomes available. Some information does not fit in easily with the defaults, so probable scenarios, ready and waiting, may be used to explain discrepencies. Furthermore, when a divergence from the prototype is unexpected and cannot be explained away, it causes attention to be focused on that detail.

The memory organization described above has been used in a number of natural language programs (as well as in other fields of artificial intelligence). The knowledge structures come by several names: frames, scripts, schema, and methods. These structures were first described in an artificial intelligence context by Minsky (1975), who called them frames. He discussed frames in general terms, primarily in the context of using frames for vision. A number of groups who were trying to bring more knowledge into the process of language understanding quickly adopted the concept of frames. Frames could organize the knowledge into convenient clusters of information. But many new problems are generated by the use of frames.

## 6.1 The Structure of Frames

There is no universally accepted format for frames, but some general remarks can be made. Generally, a frame is composed of a group of slots, each slot bearing one aspect of the description of the concept that the frame represents. For example, in a frame representing the concept CAR, one would expect slots for the manufacturer, the model, the color, the engine size, the date of manufacture and the owner. Certainly, many other slots could be imagined. Each of these slots could be given a value for a particular car: the manufacturer is GM, the model is Buick Le Sabre and so on. So far, this frame looks like a data type in a formatted database.

The slots in a frame are not limited to taking values. As an alternative, slots can carry default values. As mentioned above, the default values are assumed unless the program has been presented with evidence to the contrary. But even among default values, there may be some distinctions worth noting. For example, the default for the engine size may be an average engine size, say, 285 cubic inches. It may be that no car is made with a 285 cubic-inch engine. It may still be a reasonable default because it is "typical" in some sense. The color, on the other hand, would most likely be an arbitrary color. It might be the most common color, or it might just be one of the possible colors. One would not expect the default color to be some sort of "average" color, similar to an average engine size. These kinds of slot default values could have appropriate comments appended to them, identifying which kind they are. One might like to note, for example, that there really is no such thing as a 285 engine. Similarly, values instantiated for a particular car, like its being green, might have attached comments. A getaway car driven from a bank robbery may be described as, "I think it was green." One would want to attach a comment indicating that instantiated value with a moderate confidence level, or perhaps add a comment noting the source or sources of the information.

Another feature of slots in frames is that they may have procedures attached for various reasons. The procedures may be classified into two groups, those executed automatically and those executed only on demand. An example of an automatic procedure (commonly called a demon) is one that is executed whenever a slot is being instantiated with a value. If a value is being added to the manufacturer slot, a demon could be waiting to verify that the value is one of the known manufacturers. If not, corrective action may be taken by attaching a comment to the value or possibly interacting with the user to see if the manufacturer's name is an appropriate interpretation. Frame system management programs typically have provisions for attaching demons to be executed when values are added to a slot, when values are deleted and when values are read.

In one system, KRL (see below), procedures that are attached to slots that can be executed on demand are called servants. Servants are only executed if they are explicitly invoked by some other procedure. For example, there could be several servants attached to the same slot, all having the same result of instantiating the slot with a value. The servants could each go about the task in a different manner. One might ask the user for a value, another might deduce their value from other information, and so on. The procedures are written as servants so that the appropriate servant can be chosen for the given circumstances. The ability to have servants in addition to demons allows the frame system designer to determine whether procedures will be executed under the control of the frame (demons) or under the control of procedures external to the frame (servants).

In order for a collection of frames to work effectively, they must be related to one another. In the discussion above, the reader might get the impression that the values of slots are simple words. Slot values are more commonly pointers to other frames representing other concepts. The value of the manufacturer slot, instead of being a value like "GM," could be a pointer to a frame that represents the General Motors Corporation.

Another kind of relationship between frames is the subset/superset or generality/specificity links. The frame for CAR would have a superset slot with a pointer value that points to the frame VEHICLE. The link indicates that a car is a type of vehicle. Similarly, a specific car, CAR003, the car that was seen driving away from the bank robbery last week, has a superset pointer to CAR. CAR003 is a specific instance (one particular car) of the general class of objects described in the CAR frame. The car frame describes a general class of objects that is a subset of another general class of objects, VEHICLE.

Providing frames with links to more general and more specific frames permits some economy in representation and interpretation rules. CAR003 is a more specific description of a CAR, so every slot in CAR also applies ot CAR003 unless there is information in the CAR003 frame to the contrary. If all we know about the CAR003 frame is that it is green, we need not copy all the other slot values from CAR into CAR003. If the engine size of CAR003 is requested, the link to CAR is followed and the default is returned (of course, the default value is accompanied by a comment that it is a default and so it is just a reasonable value, not an actual value).

The same object represents different things from different points of view. One could view a car as a mode of transportation, a product of sophisticated technology, a status symbol or a relic from a bygone era. One could think of the car as a specialized concept under each of these general concepts, inheriting different kinds of information from each.

In addition to sharing information between frames, the generality/specificity links can be used to make semantic interpretation rules as general as possible. Assume that a rule could be written to interpret the phrase "gas powered car" as a CAR frame with a fuel slot instantiated with the concept GASOLINE:

1)   <FUEL> "powered" "car"
    -->      BUILD CAR frame
             SET FUEL slot to <FUEL>

If this strategy is followed, another similar rule would be required for interpreting "gas powered plane," "gas powered bus," "diesel powered truck" and "kerosene powered jet." There is an obvious regularity among these phrases that can be better captured by the following rule:

2) <FUEL> "powered" <VEHICLE>
    -->      BUILD <VEHICLE> frame
             SET FUEL slot to <FUEL>

If the vehicle is actually a car, its generality links are followed in search of whether VEHICLE is a more general concept. Since it is, CAR is used for <VEHICLE>, the rule pattern matches, so the action part is executed.

## 6.2 Matching

Knowledge representations are made more complex to either facilitate their use or allow some capabilities that were not possible with simpler representations. For example, representing complex descriptions of individuals in terms of comparisons with prototypes increases storage efficiency by factoring out common knowledge. It also allows interpretation rules to apply to the prototype and all the individuals that are instances of it, rather than requiring a separate rule for each individual. As another example, multiple descriptions of the same concept made from different points of view allow descriptions to be tailored to their uses.

Along with greater flexibility and expressiveness, complex representations require complex handling. In particular, the problem of concept comparison becomes quite involved. A concept comparison program generally operates on two concepts—a pattern and a candidate. The goal of the concept comparison may vary with the application, but one of several questions may be answered:

Does the candidate match the pattern exactly?

Is the candidate equivalent to the pattern?

What subconcepts would have to match in order for the candidate to be equivalent to the pattern?

If a match must be made, how would the constituents of the candidate map into the constituents of the pattern?

The most straightforward comparison is one which asks if the candidate is the same thing as the pattern. If the pattern is a green Buick and the candidate is a green Buick, they match. If the candidate is a green Buick with a dented door, a body flaking with rust and an engine that knocks, it will still match the pattern. As long as all of the features of the pattern are accounted for, the pattern and candidate are said to match.

If the concept comparison program were given a pattern for a green car, and a candidate is described as a green Buick, the candidate would not match the pattern identically. However, if a Buick is known to be a kind of car, then a green Buick is an equivalent concept to a green car. New complexity is added to the comparison process to allow this deduction. If the pattern were a green vehicle, more deduction would be required. A Buick is a car, and a car is a vehicle. Allowing this sort of deduction without any bounds permits the possibility of combinatorially explosive searches. It is clear to humans that a Buick is a vehicle, but a program may have to do a lot of searching to establish the fact.

The kind of deduction just described is the simplest that one can imagine. It involves just checking a feature of a prototype against a feature of a concept's prototype, or the prototype's prototype, on up the inheritance hierarchy.

Deduction could be used for a more indirect line of reasoning. Say the concept comparison program had a pattern "owns a car," and the candidate was a frame for a person. If the frame listed the person as owning a car, or owning a Buick, it can be handled by the methods described above. But instead, if the frame has "owns an automoblile class vehicle registration," a different kind of deduction is called for. The system must find a rule or chain of rules leading to the fact that someone's owning a vehicle registration means that the person owns a vehicle.

The problem with deduction is that it is not certain what should be investigated, and when the investigation should be continued or abandoned. Deduction is often combinatorially explosive, and so it may not be practical in all situations.

## 6.3 Frame Activation

The use of frames involves three problems. The first is deciding when a particular frame is relevant to the conversation and so should be activated. The second, the converse of the first, is deciding when an active frame is no longer relevant to the conversation. This problem can be particularly difficult to deal with in situations where many frames may be active simultaneously; for example, a conversation could begin on one subject, take a short digression on another subject, then return to the first subject. The third problem is dealing with situations for which no explicit frames exist. The rules normally embodied in the frames, for recognition, context switching and so forth, must somehow be inferred. The inference could be based on more general frames. This approach assumes that some frame will always be relevant, but, depending on the novelty of the situation, the active frame may not be very explicit or detailed. Another possibility is that new frames could be synthesized when needed through analogy to more familiar situations. Relatively little work has been done on frame synthesis.


## 6.4 Viewpoints

A viewpoint is a set of features about a concept that are clustered around a common theme. A car might be viewed as a gleaming, chrome-bedecked status symbol, or as a mode of transportation. The set of features relevant to one viewpoint can be distinct from the features of another. The features relevant to a car from a status symbol viewpoint include its cost, physical appearance, how clean it is and how fast it can go. The features relevant to a car viewed as a mode of transportation include its typical operating speed and operating cost, maneuverability and safety. Each viewpoint has attributes that may not be particularly relevant for the other.

Viewpoints are mappings, or rules of correspondence, from the information about one concept to the information about another concept. In the example of the car, selected features of the car are mapped onto the generic description of the concept of a mode of transportation. The mapping for this kind of viewpoint is one of specialization. All the aspects of the mode of transportation concepts are relevant to the car seen as a mode of transportation. Each particular instance of a mode of transportation—a car, a train, a plane— will add some aspects to the description that are particular to that instance.

Another kind of mapping between concepts is one in which only some of the information transfers from concept to concept. For example, one kind of commercial event involves two individuals, a transfer of money and a transfer of goods. The concepts of buying and selling are certainly related to commercial events; however, they are not more specialized descriptions of it. There is a mapping from buy to commercial event (and the other way), but it is not simple inheritance. "Buy" represents a mapping from the information about the commercial event through the perspective of the participant who gives up the money and gains the goods. "Sell" is through the perspective of the other participant. Notice how these mappings differ from a specialization, such as that of a commercial event where the item involved is a car. For this event, bargaining over price and options is added to the general information about commercial events.

A third kind of mapping is a forced perspective. Some examples are seeing a shoe as a hammer, a coffee cup as a pencil holder or a magnetic tape as a paperweight. This kind of mapping occurs frequently in human problem solving. It is certainly distinct from the other two kinds of mapping mentioned above. One way to implement a forced perspective is to attach a mapping function to the desired object. A mapping function could be attached to the concept of hammer, for instance. If a hammer is needed, but none is available, the mapping function could be applied to other candidate objects that are available, say, a piece of paper, an egg and a shoe. The one which readily accepts the mapping would be taken as the hammer substitute. It is also reasonable to assume that the mapping function affects perception. The features of a shoe that can be mapped to the desired features for a hammer substitute may never be noticed until a hammer substitute is needed, and the shoe is considered as a candidate.

## 6.5 Case Study: FRL

FRL, Frame Representation Language (Roberts and Goldstein 1977a), is a system that facilitates building and using frames. The information represented in an FRL frame is divided into slots that can contain any number of *facets*. Typical facets of a slot are the value, default value, if-added, if-removed and if-needed demons and a demon that checks the value facet against a set of requirements. These demons are part of the control structure of FRL. At the discretion of the designer, servant procedures can also be added as facets of slots. The data associated with facets can be commented as mentioned above.

| Frame | Slot | Facet | Data | Comment |
|-------|------|-------|------|---------|
| CAR | | | | |
| | MANUFACTURER | | | |
| | | $VALUE | | |
| | | $DEFAULT | GM | (TYPE: typical) |
| | | $REQUIRED | [MEMBER: VALUE GM CHRYSLER FORD AM TOYOTA | |
| | ENGINE | | | |
| | | $VALUE | DATSUN...)] | |
| | | $DEFAULT | 285 ci | (TYPE: average) |
| | COLOR | | | |
| | | $VALUE | | |
| | | $DEFAULT | WHITE | (TYPE: typical) |
| | INSTANCE | | | |
| | | $VALUE | (CAR001 CAR002 | |
| | A-KIND-OF | | CAR003...) | |
| | | $VALUE | VEHICLE | |
| CAR003 | | | | |
| | MANUFACTURER | | | |
| | | $VALUE | DATSUN | (CONFIDENCE: low) |
| | COLOR | | | |
| | | $VALUE | GREEN | (CONFIDENCE: moderate) |
| | A-KIND-OF | | | |
| | | $VALUE | CAR | |

**Figure 6.1 Two Small Frames**

The frames in FRL are organized into one large tree, based on generality (A-KIND-OF) and specificity (INSTANCE) links. The most general concept in FRL is THING; all the frames in the system are instances of THING. All inheritance between frames is done through this tree. One feature of the FRL frame tree should be noted. We often think of a tree like the one in Figure 6.2, where each node in the tree has one and only one ancestor, except the root which has none. Node D and node E each have one ancestor, C, which in turn has one ancestor, B. A is the ancestor of B, and since A is the root, it has no ancestors. This follow from the definition of a tree with *undirected* arcs.

The tree in Figure 6.3 has *directed* arcs, similar to the directed A-KIND-OF links in FRL frames. Notice that one node can have more than one ancestor. Node D has two immediate ancestors, B and C. In FRL, a frame with multiple ancestors, like node D, would inherit slots from both ancestors. Likewise, nodes F and G would inherit slots from B and C through D. This capability allows a certain degree of viewpoint orientation. In other words, if one wants to view a D (a car) as a B (vehicle), slots are inherited only through B. If a D (car) is to be viewed as a C (status symbol), slots are inherited only through C.

## 6.6 Case Study: KLONE

KLONE, Knowledge Language ONE (Brachman 1977, 1978) is a discipline for knowledge representation that formalizes some of

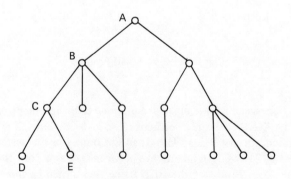

**Figure 6.2 A tree with undirected arcs**

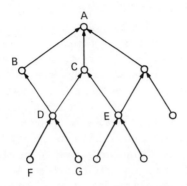

**Figure 6.3 A tree with directed arcs**

the uses of semantic nets. Before describing the refinements of KLONE, we need a brief description of semantic nets.

Semantic nets is a knowledge representation technique that was the workhorse of knowledge representation through the 1970s. Semantic nets are structures built of nodes and directed links. The nodes represent concepts, and the links represent relationships between concepts. Along with the nodes and links must be procedures for interpreting the nets. In spite of the enthusiastic acceptance of semantic nets, there has been no uniformity in the way they are used. No conventions have been widely accepted for assigning concepts and relationships to nodes and links (although many conventions have been proposed).

KLONE, as a discipline for the use of semantic nets, specifies restrictions on the kind of relationships links can represent. There are corresponding repercussions in the procedures that interpret the nets. One of the most significant contributions of KLONE is the differentiation it makes between (1) which concepts are members of a certain class and (2) what it means to be a member of that class. These two descriptions are called the *extension* of a class and the *intension* of a class, respectively.

Intension and extension deserve some attention before explaining how KLONE deals with them. The intensional description of a class describes the attributes a thing must have in order to qualify as a member of the class. The class of automobiles, for example, may include in its intensional description a number of wheels (usually 4, conceivably 3), a power plant (usually an internal combustion engine), a steering mechanism (usually deflecting the front wheels, rarely deflecting the rear wheels) and a braking mechanism. A lot more information could certainly be attached to the concept of an automobile, especially about its default description.

The intensional description then goes beyond this collection of attributes to describe structure. The structure specifies how the various attributes of the class are interrelated. A car has wheels, an engine, a steering mechanism and a braking mechanism, but unless they are structured properly, the collection is not a car. The power plant must cause the wheels to turn. The wheels are in contact with a surface, causing the car to move. The steering mechanism deflects the wheels, causing a change in the direction of motion of the car. The brakes slow the rotation of the wheels. This augmentation is needed to differentiate a car from a heap of disconnected parts. This is also the most difficult part of the intensional description, not yet fully solved by KLONE.

The extension of a class is the set of individuals or subclasses that are members of the class. One of KLONE's major contributions is the way it makes a clear distinction between the description of the attributes of a class and the description of the attributes of an individual member of a class. Consider the description of the power plant of cars in general, and the engine of Lefty's car in particular (for simplicity, let's assume that all cars have internal combustion engines—part of the intensional description of the class of cars). Lefty's car's engine is 350 cubic inches, the actual value of the piston displacement of that particular engine. In general, car engines vary from about 70 to about 400 cubic inches. This restriction on the range of values for engine displacement is part of the intensional description of the class of cars. It is a different kind of knowledge from the actual value of the displacement of the engine in Lefty's car. Therefore, one difference between classes and individuals is that while classes usually describe the possible values of an attribute, individuals usually give the particular value of an attribute.

Another distinction is in what is called in KLONE the modality of an attribute. Take headlights on cars. They are usually present, but a functioning member of the class of cars could be devoid of headlights. Since most cars have them, the attribute HEADLIGHTS may be specified in the intensional description of the class of cars, but with a comment that this attribute is optional when determining class membership. The optional/required distinction is the modality of the attribute with respect to the class. With a particular car, on the other hand, it makes no sense to speak of optional headlights. Either the car has them or it does not.

Another distinction is in default values for attributes. Classes have default values, individuals do not.

The important point here is that a distinction must be made for defining classes versus defining individuals. The interpretation procedure must be able to determine if a range of permissible values is being described (as with a class) and when a particular value is being given (as with an individual).

KLONE represents knowledge in a way that is very much like FRL. In fact, it would be straightforward to implement KLONE in FRL. The distinction between KLONE and FRL, however, is that KLONE is a *discipline* on the kind of facets that a slot can and should have. With FRL, the user is free to confuse the difference between, say, restricting the possible values in a class and expressing a particular value in an individual. When subscribing to the discipline of KLONE, such an error would not be made.

### 6.7 Case Study: KRL

KRL, Knowledge Representation Language (Bobrow and Winograd 1977), like FRL, is a language embedded in LISP that facilitates building frame-oriented systems (they are actually called units in KRL, but, to be consistent with the terminology of other systems, we shall refer to them as frames). The philosophy behind KRL is somewhat different from that behind FRL. KRL is built around certain commitments about what a knowledge base should look like based on psychological descriptions of human memory. Like FRL, KRL allows one frame to inherit information from another, more general frame. Generic frames that describe classes of concepts, like CAR, are called prototypes. Instance names describing particular objects, like CAR003, are described through a comparison to a prototype. In other words, the instantiated information in an instance frame shows the points of variance between the instance and its prototype.

One important point of divergence between FRL and KRL is how the frames are interrelated. Whereas FRL organizes all frames into one large generality/specificity hierarchy, KRL has no such single organizing structure. This is because the psychological evidence on memory structure does not support such a monolithic structure. KRL has several types of frames, among them basic, abstract, specialization, individual, and manifestation frames.

Basic frames are descriptions of mutually exclusive sets of things. Nothing can be an instance of more than one basic frame; dog and bacteria could be two basic frames. An abstract frame describes a set of concepts that are not physical¹ objects; a travel event or a family could be considered abstract. A specialization frame refines a description of a class; it can refine either a basic frame or an abstract one. A specialization of the basic frame, DOG, could be Dalmation or Collie; a traveler is a specialization of the basic frame PERSON; a flying-event is a specialization of the abstract travel event.

KRL makes no commitment and gives no guidance as to what concepts should be abstract, basic or specialization. Notice that if dog and bacteria were both basic (suggested as examples in Bobrow and Winograd 1977), animal could not be basic. Animal, dog and bacteria are not mutually exclusive sets, and all basic frames must describe mutually exclusive sets. Animal, then, must be abstract.

One of the advantages of basic frames is that they can limit searching. Say we were trying to establish that Lefty's car was a kind of VEHICLE, and VEHICLE is a basic frame. The A-KIND-OF links are followed from the frame for Lefty's car (CAR003), through its ancestors, and finally reach the VEHICLE frame. Now assume that we wish to establish whether the dog that woke up Lefty this morning (DOG014) is a VEHICLE (odd as this may sound, this kind of checking is done frequently during semantic analysis —consequently, it should be efficient). The A-KIND-OF links can be followed from DOG014 through its ancestor frames in search of the VEHICLE frame. Since DOG014 is not a specialization of the concept VEHICLE, the A-KIND-OF links must be followed all the way up to the root of the frame tree to show that DOG014 is not a VEHICLE. But with DOG and VEHICLE both being basic frames, much less searching is required. The A-KIND-OF link is followed from DOG014 to DOG. Since DOG and VEHICLE are basic frames, their extensions are mutually exclusive sets, so DOG014 is shown to not be a VEHICLE after a shorter search.

If one were attempting to decide whether DOG014 was a CAR, which is not a basic frame, the A-KIND-OF links would first be followed from CAR to its basic ancestor, VEHICLE. Then the A-KIND-OF links would be followed from DOG014 until either the CAR frame was found or a different basic frame was found.

The basic, abstract and specialization frames are generic descriptions. They describe collections of things and are the prototypes mentioned above. Individual frames, in contrast, describe particular individuals like the *Queen Mary*, the chewing gum stuck on Lefty's shoe, the millionth Ford Mustang or Genghis Khan. Individual frames are described in terms of prototype frames and inherit properties from prototype frames.

Manifestation frames are partial descriptions of individuals. For example, a manifestation frame could describe an individual from a particular point of view (e.g., how Knuckles is viewed as a traveler by the airlines). Another manifestation frame would describe what is known to be an individual but whose identity is not known. The person singing bawdy songs out on the street at 2 a.m. last night is a manifestation of someone, but one does not know who.

Some interesting steps have been taken toward the matching problem in KRL. First, the concept comparison program can specify limits on search time and depth. If the comparison program has reached its allowable limits, no further search is permitted. Second, it can return an admission of ignorance or a statement that the allocated resources were exhausted. Third, KRL, as well as some other representation languages, has the provision for attaching procedures to frames especially for expediting the matching and deduction process. One mentioned in the description of KRL is a special procedure for establishing ownership, which could be used in problems like the vehicle registration mentioned above.

## 6.8 Case Study: GUS

GUS, Genial Understander System (Bobrow, et al. 1977), is a natural language program written to study the use of frames in natural language processing. GUS's most distinguishing characteristic is that its dialog with the user can be fairly loosely structured.

GUS's domain of discourse is that of an airline reservation agent. A user comes to GUS with a trip in mind, and GUS helps select appropriate flights for the trip. The domain of discourse is very narrow, and the range of language covered appears very narrow. However, these were not the goals behind GUS. What GUS does seem to be able to do is engage in a fairly loosely constrained dialog (the structure of the dialog is loosely constrained, but the language itself is tightly constrained). This capability is based on an understanding of what the dialog will be about. Its knowledge is organized into KRL frames.

GUS's frames embody expectations of what the dialog will be about. At the top level, GUS will find out the name of the user, the current date and a description of the trip. The trip consists of a home port, a foreign port, a flight from the home port to the foreign port, a flight back and a stay at the foreign port. The two flights are specified by a starting place, a destination, an arrival time, a departure time and a travel date, the actual flights that have been proposed by GUS and the one accepted by the user. GUS goes through its expectations, asking the user for each piece of information, one after the other. For example, the foreign port is the same as the destination of the outbound flight, the starting point of the return flight, and it is the place at which the traveler will temporarily stay between flights. As soon as the foreign port is identified by the user, a demon attached to foreign port executes and fills in the other slots.

GUS is usually in control of the dialog because it asks the user questions and the user answers them. The user may give more information than asked for, however:

1) GUS: Where do you want to go?
   USER: I want to go to San Diego on May 28.

The user's answer here gives the date of the flight as well as the destination. GUS uses the expectations in the frames to decide what to do with the "May 28." The user may also take complete control of the dialog by asking a question instead of answering one.

The knowledge structure based on the program's frames and augmented by the user's description of the flights desired constitutes a model of the trip that the user wants to take. The semantic programs in GUS can use this model to identify the things, places and events that the user refers to and to interpret the intent of elliptical utterances.

### 6.9 Case Study: SAM and PAM

#### SAM

SAM, Script Applier Mechanism (Schank and Abelson 1977), is a program designed to demonstrate the utility of encoding specific knowledge about familiar events. The knowledge is encoded in frames called scripts. Scripts are used in understanding events by providing prototype descriptions of them. If a narrative about a familiar event leaves out some information, assuming it to be inferable by the listener, the inference is made based on the contents of a script.That is what SAM does, and Schank and his group, further suggest that people do the same.

A trip to a restaurant is such a familiar event that, according to the theory, it warrants a detailed script. When one goes to a coffee shop, he or she enters, decides where to sit and sits down. The waitress then brings a menu, or perhaps one is on the table. The patron reads it, decides what he or she wants and orders it. The patron waits while the food is prepared. When it is served, the patron eats it. The he or she gets up, leaves a tip, pays for the food and leaves the coffee shop. There are several roles played in the script, those of patron, waitress, cashier and cook. Several props are expected as well—tables and chairs, menus, food, dishes, glasses and silverware.

The more familiar an event is, the more detailed and specific the script will be. It could have alternative tracks for different kinds of restaurants and contingency plans for problem situations like the restaurant being out of the desired dish or how to respond when food is served that has been prepared unsatisfactorily.

One of the advantages of a script in language analysis, as mentioned above, is that it provides a means for inferring omitted steps of a sequence of events:

1) Lefty went to DeLux Lunch and ordered a fish sandwich. It cost two dollars. He left at 12:45.

A restaurant script could fill in several details about story 1. It is not stated, but Lefty probably consulted a menu before ordering, probably had to wait as it was prepared, probably ate it, probably left a tip, and probably paid for the meal before he left. After hearing this story, the question "Has Lefty had lunch?" can be answered. Notice that the answer does not lie in the text of the story, but in the text of the script that the story invokes.

2) Knuckles sauntered into DeLux Lunch. He told the waitress that he wanted a chili-dog with lots of onions.

Scripts can be used to understand the reference "the waitress" above. Ordinarily, definite noun phrases like this one are used to refer to a concept that has already been introduced. There was no previous mention of a waitress in the story, but "the waitress" is understandable. When a script is invoked, the roles and props described in it are as available for reference as if they had been mentioned in the text.

Another advantage of scripts is that they present a packetized means for interpreting words with multiple senses. Reference to a check in a restaurant most probably means either the bill sense or money order sense.

As with other frames, there must be a means of activating and deactivating scripts. Evidence favoring activating a script could include descriptions of meeting preconditions (e.g., hunger for a restaurant script), instrumental references (e.g., taking a subway to a restaurant), being physically located in a script-specific location (e.g., being in a restaurant) or references to components of the script (e.g., roles or events mentioned in the script). SAM looks for more than one reference to a script before activating it. This way, fleeting references, like "Knuckles stopped off at DeLux Lunch before going to the game," do not invoke an entire restaurant script.

Deactivating a script is simplified by the fact that scripts have standard exit points. One normally exits the restaurant script by leaving a restaurant.

SAM uses a few scripts to understand some simple stories. The methodology for which SAM was written is to write a program to show that there are stories in which scripts could be used. Stories and the necessary scripts are written simultaneously. SAM can generate extensive paraphrases of the stories (inserting the events that were omitted from the narrative) or shorter summaries. To demonstrate that the paraphrases are based on an understanding of the narrative, they can also be generated in several different languages.

There has been no attempt in SAM to demonstrate any degree of completeness in understanding stories about events. No claim is made that SAM can handle any stories other than the ones it was designed for.


## PAM


The theory of scripts maintains that humans use a large number of very detailed scripts. There are often situations, however, which have not been stereotyped into scripts. Descriptions of these unfamiliar events are understood by inferring the goals of the actors in the events and the plans they use for achieving those goals. Standardized plans are held in memory attached to common and specific goals. Specific goals are combined to understand achieving more elaborate goals.

PAM, Plan Applier Mechanism (Schank and Abelson 1977; Wilensky 1978), is meant to be an adjunct to SAM to pick up understanding through goals and plans where scripts leave off. It currently runs as a separate program. Like SAM, it generates paraphrases and summaries of the stories it analyzes.

## References and Further Reading

Abelson, R.P. "Concepts for Representing Mundane Reality in Plans." In *Representation of Understanding*, edited by D.G. Bobrow and A. Collins. New York: Academic Press, 1975.

Bobrow, D.G.; Kaplan, R.M.; Kay, M.; Norman, D.A.; Thompson, H.; and Winograd, T. "GUS, A Frame-Driven Dialog System." *Artificial Intelligence* 8(1977):155-73.

Bobrow, D.G. and Norman, D.A. "Some Principles of Memory Schemata." In *Representation and Understanding*, edited by D.G. Bobrow and A. Collins. New York: Academic Press, 1975.

Bobrow, D.G. and Winograd, T. "KRL, Another Perspective." *Cognitive Science* 3(1979):29-42.

___. "An Overview of KRL, a Knowledge Representation Language." *Cognitive Science* 1(Jan. 1977):3-46.

Bobrow, D.G., Winograd, T. and KRL Research Group. "Experience with KRL-O: One Cycle of a Knowledge Representation Language." In *Proceedings of the International Joint Conference on Artificial Intelligence*. Cambridge, Mass.: MIT, 1977.

Brachman, R.J. "Theoretical Studies in Natural Language Understanding." Annual Report. Cambridge, Mass.: Bolt Berenak and Newman Inc., 1978.

____. "What's in a Concept: Structural Foundations for Semantic Networks." *International Journal of Man-Machine Studies* 9(1977):127- 52.

Collins, A.; H Warnock, E.; Aiello, N.; and Miller, M.L. "Reasoning from Incomplete Knowledge." In *Representation of Understanding*, edited by D.G. Bobrow and A. Collins. New York: Academic Press, 1975.

Kuipers, B.J. "A Frame for Frames: Representing Knowledge for Recognition." In *Representation and Understanding*, edited by D.G. Bobrow and A. Collins. New York: Academic Press, 1975.

Lehnert, W. and Wilks, Y. "A Critical Perspective on KRL." *Cognitive Science* 3(1979):1–28.

Roberts, R.B. and Goldstein, I.P. "The FRL Manual." Memo 409. Cambridge, Mass.: MIT Artificial Intelligence Laboratory, 1977a.

____."The FRL Primer." Memo 408. Cambridge, Mass.: MIT Artificial Intelligence Laboratory, 1977b.

Schank, R. and Abelson, R. "Scripts, Plans and Knowledge." *Advance Papers of the Fourth International Joint Conference on Artificial Intelligence.* Cambridge, Mass.: MIT, 1975.

____. *Scripts, Plans, Goals and Understanding.* Hillsdale, N.J.: Lawrence Erlbaum Associates, 1977.

Wilensky, R. "Why John Married Mary: Understanding Stories Involving Recurring Goals. *Cognitive Science* 2(1978):235–66.

____."PAM–A Program that Infers Intentions." In *Proceedings of the International Joint Conference on Artificial Intelligence.* Cambridge, Mass.: MIT, 1977.

# 7. Discourse

The preceding chapters have been concerned with how a listener decides what a speaker has said. The listener builds a model that he or she hopes is similar to the one built by the speaker. The listener uses various rules to interpret what is heard. The listener is making an implicit assumption that the speaker is following a similar set of rules. The rules are embodied in syntactic analysis, semantic analysis, morphological analysis, and inference. The speaker uses the various classes of rules to encode a concept into words. The listener uses a similar set of rules to decode the string of words into a representation of the concepts. If the rules are sufficiently similar, the concept constructed by the listener will be equivalent to the one that the speaker intended to describe.

## 7.1 Speech Acts

Encoding, decoding and building representations for concepts are a necessary part of communication, but there is more to it than that. When people communicate, they do so for a purpose, whether they are communicating with another person or with a machine.

1) I dub thee Sir Lancelot, Knight of the Round Table.

When King Arthur uttered sentence 1, or its equivalent, one can imagine that the listeners processed it. They identified "I" as the king referring to himself: "Sir Lancelot" referred to the person, whom they probably knew by name, they saw kneeling before the king. The arrangement of the words revealed that the king was doing the dubbing and Lancelot was being dubbed, not the other way around. They also recognized that "dub" refers to a formalized event of conferring a distinction on someone. Through processes perhaps like these, the listeners were each building their models of the idea that the king was trying to get across. But there is more to the sentence than just what is said. By his utterance, King Arthur was actually changing the status of Lancelot.

If anyone else in the realm had said the same words to Lancelot, his status would have remained unchanged. Any listeners hearing an unauthorized pronouncement would use the same rules and go through the same process to determine what the imposter was saying. They would each decode the utterance into a concept very much like the one the king invoked, but with no effect on Lancelot's status.

A speaker's utterance is intended to convey an idea to the listener, and *the speaker expects the listener to do something with the idea.* By saying sentence 1, the king expects all the listeners to change their descriptions of Lancelot, reflecting that he has a new status. The impostor would only expect such an effect through error or misunderstanding.

2) Do you know what time it is?

The effect that a speaker expects to have on a listener cannot necessarily be understood out of context. One normally thinks of sentence 2, for example, as a speaker's request for the listener to tell him or her the time. This is so even though the speaker is literally only asking the listener if he or she is *aware* of the time. If the speaker happens to be the father of a sixteen-year-old girl, and he is greeting her at the door at 3 a.m. as she returns from a date, the expected effect is probably somewhat different. In fact, the father is probably acutely aware of the time. Instead of the time, he wants her to respond with some explanation for her conduct. A response to the question, acceptable to the father, might be, "We had car trouble, Dad."

Linguists have described several kinds of events that occur in discourse called speech acts. The classes of speech acts that we shall discuss here are illocutionary acts and perlocutionary acts. Illocutionary acts are things that the speaker does that indicate how he or she expects the utterance to be used; for example, the speaker may command, question, dub, inform, promise or threaten. Perlocutionary acts are the effects that the speaker actually has on the listener; a speaker may persuade, convince, inspire to action, terrify or exhilarate the listener. Natural language research has used the concept of speech acts primarily for making a distinction between understanding what a speaker has said, and what effects the speaker has or would like to have on the listener.

## 7.2 Speech Acts in Question-Answering Dialogs

Most question-answering programs assume only one kind of transaction between the user and the program: the user is expected to ask a question which the program answers. The programs are deeply committed to this assumption. Every string of words that the user types in is interpreted as a single-sentence question; a query is built on this basis. This is true of LUNAR, LIFER and PLANES. This assumption causes problems with real users because they do not always ask questions.

The author did some performance testing on PLANES. Test users were given problems designed to be typical of the eventual problems that real users would like to solve using the system. Similar tests were done on the Automatic Advisor, as mentioned in chapter 1. One of the interesting results of these tests was the range of utterances made by users that were not database queries. A list of them is given below. Some of the nomenclature may be unfamiliar, but the important point is that users had a much broader range of inputs than just database queries.

1. About the database:
   a. "What do you know?"

   b. "What planes do you know about?" (a query could be done to answer this, but, in **PLANES**, it would be extremely expensive)

   c. "Tell me about f4s."

   d. "Is that everything you know about math 195?"

2. About vocabulary:
   a. "What is a buser?"
   b. "What does howmal mean?"

3. Context setting:
   a. "Now I am talking about the year 1970."
   b. "Year is 1970."
   c. "I am interested in a7's."

4. Reference to discourse objects:
   a. "What was the last plane I talked about?"
   b. "Now combine the two." (meaning combine two tables that were the answers to the last two questions into one table)
   c. "The other ones I just mentioned." (attempt to correct the system after it found an erroneous antecedent for a pronoun)

5. Verifying or summarizing results:
   a. "Then infe 210 and infe 211 must be taken at the same time."
   b. "So all I need is junior standing and math 195."

6. Multiple-query utterances:
   a. "What parts failed and what were the parts removed or installed?"
   b. "How many flights did plane 48 have in dec 1969, and did it have over 50 nor hours?"
   c. "List plane 48 flights and flight hours in december 1969. Were there more than 50 hours not operationally ready?"

7. Multiple-utterance queries:
   a. "How many aircraft flew more than 10 flights in 1973? in 1972? in 1970? List aircraft by number of flights for 1970."
   b. Which parts failed? removed? installed?"

8. Miscellaneous:
   a. "This is a test."
   b. "What time is it?"
   c. "Eat a bag of (obscenity deleted)."
   d. "What's going on here?"

## 7.3 Rules for Organizing Discourse

A conversation is a sequence of speech acts. Propositions are being asserted, questions are being asked, promises may be made and so on. But a conversation is more than a sequence of arbitrary speech acts—they must be related in some way. A conversation must be a coherent sequence of speech acts. The acts each contribute in some way to achieving a goal. The individual speech acts are steps in a plan to achieve the goal.

Interpreting speech acts as steps toward a goal may help to interpret the intended meaning of an utterance:

1) Lefty: Hey Knuckles, you want to go down to Tipsy's and shoot some pool?
   Knuckles: Bubbles is sick.

In example 1, Lefty knows that he has established a goal for Knuckles. Knuckles should answer the question. Lefty will probably assume that Knuckles plans to achieve that goal even if the answer is indirect. Lefty then can consider the fact that Knuckles' wife is sick as either agreeing to play pool or declining the invitation. Knuckles is informing Lefty of his wife's state of health, but he is indirectly informing Lefty that he will be unable to join him. Knowing what kind of response to expect from Knuckles helps Lefty to understand the utterance.

A speaker can concoct a much more elaborate plan than a single sentence. The realization of the plan may consist of a large number of individual speech acts. Writing a book is certainly like that. In order to discuss one concept, a few prerequisite concepts must be discussed first. The prerequisite concepts may have prerequisites of their own. As a result, a planned sequence of informative speech acts (at least the author hopes that they are informative!) are presented in the text. The contribution of the individual speech acts relative to the overall goal of the text gives it coherence. If an author were to describe his new golf clubs in the midst of a discussion of semantics, for example, those statements describing the golf clubs would not contribute to the overall goal of the text, and thus detract from its coherence. The reader, expecting continuity, would come upon the discussion of the golf clubs and think,"What does all this golf club stuff have to do with semantics?"

If the speaker wants to digress momentarily to another subject, there are acceptable ways to do so. The speaker informs the listener of an imminent subject change with a signal like, "Oh, by the way . . ." or, "That reminds me . . ." He can signal a return to the original topic with something like, "Well, back to semantics. . .," "Where were we. . ." or simply, "OK."

The importance of goals and plans relative to speech acts becomes even more pronounced when one considers that an utterance itself does not necessarily specify what speech act it realizes. In the example early in the chapter about conferring knighthood on Lancelot, the same utterance can knight him in one case, when spoken by the king, and have no effect on his status when said by anyone else. For that utterance, the character of the speech act is determined by the sincerity and authority of the speaker. However, in the example where the father asked his daughter about the time, his goal in asking the question determines the kind of speech act it is.

## 7.4 Rules of Dialog

Human dialog is deeply involved with suggesting goals, negotiating them, accepting or rejecting them and finally pursuing them. The goals of the participants in a dialog impose a structure on it. They help establish what gets discussed and in what order.

## CASE STUDY: DIALOG-GAMES

Dialog-games, DG (Levin and Moore 1977; Mann, Moore and Levin 1977), is a goal-centered theory of the structure of dialogs. (The name, dialog-games, refers to a two-person interaction that operates according to conventions known to both participants. This does not suggest, however, that dialog-games are pursued consciously or that they are competitive.) A goal-centered view of dialog is concerned with the function of utterances. *Why* was something said?

A goal-centered view of dialog has several interesting implications. First, it helps explain when and why shifts in the topic occur during a dialog where goals have been achieved. Second, a goal-centered view of dialog motivates the appropriate interpretation of indirect speech acts. Third, it can be used to set expectations for the kind of utterances that are likely to occur, and thereby be used to limit the depth of processing required for the utterance. Fourth, it suggests a cause of problems in man-machine interaction. If human dialog is deeply involved with setting and achieving goals by both parties, then that may help explain why many people find computers difficult or impossible to work with (including current natural language processors!). The machines are totally oblivious to the goal structure of dialog. They perform only on what has been said, without regard for why it has been said.

DGs represent regularities over classes of dialogs. DGs have been written for several situations, but not for all DGs that occur in human dialog. A few implemented DGs are briefly described below:

Helping—Person 1 wants to solve a problem, and interacts with person 2 in an attempt to arrive at a solution.

Action-seeking—Person 1 wants some action performed and interacts with person 2 to get him to perform it.

Information-seeking—Person 1 wants to know some specific information, and interacts with person 2 in order to learn it.

Information-probing—Person 1 wants to know whether person 2 knows some particular information, and interacts with him to find out (Levin and Moore 1977)

Dialog-games consist of parameters, parameter specifications, and components. The parameters of the task-oriented DGs above are a list of the participants and a task. Their parameter specifications include several pieces of information. First, they include constraints on the participants. Second, they specify the top-level goals that the DG attempts to achieve. Third, they indicate the initial conditions for the DG. The initial conditions for the information-seeking DG, for example, include that the seeker does not have the information he or she is seeking and the other participant does have the information. The last structural element of DGs are the components. These are the subgoals that must be achieved in the course of the DG on the way to achieving the main goals. The components are partially ordered to indicate their dependence on one another.

The goals represented by dialog-games are established, pursued and satisfied throughout the course of a conversation. This happens frequently and the transition between goals is usually done smoothly. Both parties are aware of the goals they suggest and accept and achieve goals according to established dialog conventions. Some of the conventions are as familiar as question asking, while others are more indirect, like describing a situation and an unexpected result.

One of the problems of the goal-centered view of dialog is recognizing when goals are being established and when they have been accomplished. The information is implicit in dialogs and is fairly easy for people to recognize. However, since they are a high-level factor in dialog, they are often not represented explicitly in the text. The DG model works by decomposing what is said in the text into elementary propositions and then examining the collections for propositions that suggest DGs. The knowledge about the suggested DGs is then used to examine the dialog further to determine whether all of the parameter specifications either have been satisfied or can be inferred. If the specifications are met, the dialog-game is played.

The following example of a DG is abstracted from Levin and Moore (1977). The help DG has as parameters a HELPER, HELPEE and a TASK. Their parameter specifications indicate that the HELPEE is a person who wants to perform a task that he or she is permitted to do, but is unable to do. A HELPER is a person who is willing and able to enable the HELPEE to do the task. The components of this DG consist of a problem described by the HELPEE and a solution described by the HELPER.

The problem is described as a sequence of commands that did not yield the expected result:

1) L:   Are you there?
2) O:   Yep, what's up?
3) L:   Know anything about the TELNET subsys?
4) O:   Try me.
5) L:   I just connected to [computer site 1] via TELNET, and tried the DIVERT.OUTPUT.STREAM.TO.FILE command.
6)      Strange things happened. Esp., my TELNET typescript is "busy"
7) O:   TELNET.TYPESCRIPT will always be busy until you do a RESET,
8)      but when you do that, be careful not to EXP since that is a temporary file
9) L:   I see . . . it's not enough for me just to do a DISCONNECT?
10) O:  Correct, is that the only problem?

The dialog above illustrates how the help DG is played. Lines 1 and 2 establish the conversation. In line 3, L is bidding for a help DG with L as HELPEE, O as HELPER and using the TELNET SUBSYS as the TASK. The question attempts to determine if O qualifies as HELPER by having the necessary knowledge. In line 4, O accepts the role of HELPER, and, by mutual consent, they are engaged in the help DG. L presents the problem by stating a context in line 5 and the violated expectation in line 6. The solution component is given in line 7, with an additional warning against new problems in line 8. L verifies understanding of the solution in line 9. O bids to terminate the help DG in line 10 since the problem and solution component goals have been achieved.

CASE STUDY: SUSIE SOFTWARE

Susie Software (Brown 1977) is a program that was written to study the structure of conversations. It is built around the idea of conversational exchanges. A conversational exchange is a structural unit of a conversation; for example, a small conversational exchange is a question and an answer, while a debate is a much larger conversational exchange. A conversational exchange would typically involve many individual speech acts from both participants in the conversation.

A conversational exchange is represented by two kinds of expectations. The first is the standard path that the exchange will take if no problems are encountered. The second is the set of recovery paths, which are alternative plans of action taken in case problems do arise. The paths are composed partly of speech acts but also may include procedures that the speaker must execute in order to prepare for a speech act. For example, one conversational exchange in Susie Software is ASK-and-ANSWER. If no problems develop, this exchange will proceed as follows:

1. A asks a question
2. B has the answer in memory
3. B retrieves the answer
4. B gives the answer to A
5. A acknowledges (optional)

This standard path consists of three speech acts (1, 4, 5) and two other acts. There are two problem situations that ASK-and-ANSWER is prepared for with recovery paths:

RECOVERY PATH 1: 1. B states a stipulation.
                    2. A agrees to it.

The first recovery path gives B an alternative to simply answering A's question. Before answering, B may assert a stipulation which A must agree to, or B will not disclose the answer to the question.

The second recovery path accounts for the possibility that B does not know the answer to the question:

RECOVERY PATH 2: 1. B says he doesn't know the answer.

Conversations do not always follow the standard or recovery paths of conversational exchanges. Susie Software is prepared for two contingencies. The first is metadiscussion, or utterances in which the topic of conversation is the conversation itself. Susie recognizes three forms of metadiscussion: (1) suspension of an activity, (2) reactivation of an activity that was previously suspended or concluded, or (3) specification of what the speaker is about to do. These meta-discussion utterances can occur at any time during a conversation.

Susie identifies an utterance as metadiscussion through the use of patterns. The patterns are compared with an internal representation of the utterance (to eliminate the possible variations in surface structure). If the pattern matches, one of three interpretation procedures is assigned: SUSPEND, RESUME and INFORM. The recognition process is somewhat more complex if a metadiscussion utterance is embedded in a sentence. Time phrases are often used when referring to previous events. If the event was part of a conversational exchange that was considered closed, it could be reopened.

The second kind of contingency utterance, an initiator utterance, initiates a new task for Susie. Susie can perform two tasks—writing simple programs to move blocks around on a table and answering questions. One task may temporarily interrupt another. For example, in the midst of a program-writing task, the user may ask a question about the program or about Susie's capabilities. This initiates a question-answering task. When that task is completed, the user will probably return to the program-writing task.

Susie recognizes initiator utterances in the same way that meta-discussion utterances are recognized, by matching an internal representation of the input.

1) Write a program to manipulate blocks for me.
2) Will you write a program to manipulate blocks for me?

3) Can you write a program to manipulate blocks for me?

4) I need a program to manipulate blocks.

Sentences 1-4 can all be interpreted as meaning that the user wants Susie to write a program. Sentence 1 will always be interpreted that way. Sentence 2 can be interpreted as an indirect speech act requesting a program. It may not always be a request; for example, if the speaker does not have the authority to request a program to be written, the listener could reply, "No, you aren't authorized." Similarly, sentence 3 could be asking if the program is capable of writing programs. The point is that the context must be used to discriminate between the speech acts, whether questions or task initiators, to determine the appropriate interpretation. Sentence 4 is even more indirect. The implication is that from the fact that the speaker needs a program, the listener should infer that he or she ought to write one for the speaker.

The examples in the previous paragraph are intended to illustrate that a task initiator, like other utterance types, could assume a variety of surface forms. This is why the matching process uses an internalized form of the sentences which is a more standardized form. In addition to surface form variations, the intended meanings of the utterance may differ with context. The interpretation chosen by Susie depends upon her expectations.

Susie selects speech act interpretations using a stop-on-success strategy. Recall that the important aspects of this strategy are to (1) have all the necessary information that is required to make a selection available when the search begins and (2) order the alternatives before the search begins. Susie's alternative interpretation list is ordered as follows:

1. Metadiscussion
2. Standard path successor steps
3. Recovery path steps
4. Task initiators
5. General failure handlers

If an utterance could be interpreted as either a standard path successor or an initiator of a new task, the successor step would be checked first. The general-failure handlers have not been mentioned previously. As the name implies, they deal with utterances not classified in the preceding steps.

## CASE STUDY: CO-OP

5) Q: How many dairy science students in CS 200 didn't come to class on Wednesday?
   A: None.
6) Q: Are any of the dairy science students in CS 200 getting a failing grade?
   A: No.

The two questions above are loaded—they contain presuppositions that may not be true. They both presuppose that there are, in fact, some dairy science students taking CS 200. The answer "none" to question 5 reinforces that presupposition. It is saying that there are some dairy science students in CS 200, and they all showed up for class on Wednesday. The answer to question 6 also reinforces the presupposition. The way many question answerers work, however, is that a query is built that searches the database for a set. In question 5, each member of the set would be (1) a dairy science student, (2) taking CS 200, (3) absent from class on Wednesday. If the set is empty, most natural language processors would generate a response for the user like "none." A problem arises if the set is empty because there are no dairy science students taking CS 200, or there are no dairy science students at all, or there is no CS 200, or there was no class on Wednesday. If the set is empty for any of these reasons, the answer "none" would be stonewalling.

Stonewalling is the failure to indicate that a presupposition in a question is unjustified. Most question-answering systems are guilty of stonewalling, but one, CO-OP (Joshi, Kaplan and Lee 1977; Kaplan 1978a; Kaplan 1978b; Kaplan and Joshi 1978), gives the user corrective indirect responses to queries like 5 and 6 above. If a query returns an empty set, CO-OP tries to find out why. It corrects the user's mistaken presuppositions if any are found. The responses are called "indirect" because a corrective response is not specifically what the user was expecting. (Kaplan, 1978)

7) Which programmers in Administration work on project 6471?

If the answer to this question is empty, CO-OP begins with the simplest presuppositions, trying to find any that were violated. New database searches are conducted for the sets of programmers, Administration (in the CO-OP database, Administration is a particular group of projects), projects and 6471. If one of these returns an empty set, CO-OP generates a response like:

I don't know of any programmers.

or

I don't know of any 6471.

If the simplest presuppositions are not violated, the more complex ones are tested, like programmers in Administration, programmers work on projects, there is a project 6471. If none of these are empty, they are combined into still larger presuppositions, like there are programmers that work on projects and who work in Administration, there are programmers who work on project 6471.

CO-OP actually does this presupposition checking by forming new database queries and searching the database. Since only the search mechanism is used, which already exists, little additional software is required. The validity of the presuppositions only needs to be verified if the search returns an empty answer, so questions that are not based on false assumptions do not suffer a large computational overhead. One problem is that many database searches need to be conducted. The simple question in example 7 could require up to nine searches in addition to the original query. It should be possible, however, for a query system to be able to keep track of which predicates and combinations of predicates return empty sets in the course of a single database search.

Two more kinds of responses are described with the CO-OP work—suggestive indirect responses and supportive indirect responses. A suggestive indirect response gives the user the answer to a question that is slightly different from the one asked. It is hoped the answer to the altered question is more informative than the answer to the question that was actually asked:

8) Q: Is Knuckles thirty-five years old?
   A: No, he's 29.

The direct (literal) answer to question 8 is no, but that answer is not particularly informative. The questioner may actually want to know how old Knuckles is. Instead of waiting for the user to ask, "How old is he, then?" a system that gives suggestive indirect responses would retrieve this information on its own initiative.

Suggestive indirect responses are somewhat more difficult to deal with than corrective responses. Suggestive ones require a more extensive knowledge of the database to avoid initiating expensive searches of the database that the unfortunate user (who must pay for it) may have no interest in:

9) Q: Are there any more trains to New York this evening?
   A: No, but there are three buses.

Kaplan gives question 9 as an illustration of a question calling for a suggestive indirect response. Two other suggestive responses that seem just as plausible are given below:

10) A: No, but there is one in the morning.
11) A: No, but there is one to Buffalo, one to Trenton, one to Boston, one to . . . .
12) A: No, but there are three buses, two planes and a riverboat.

The most useful answer is the one that satisfies the questioner's needs. Does the questioner want to go to New York, or just get out of town? Is the time important? Perhaps the questioner is just looking for something to while away idle hours. The problem with suggestive responses is in knowing what the questioner really wanted to know as opposed to what was asked.

The third category of indirect responses, supportive indirect responses, includes enough additional information in the response as necessary to make it useful:

13) Q: What are the telephone numbers of the employees of company X?
    A: 344-7645, 393-8881, 236-4444, ...

For most common applications, the response given to this question is inappropriate. It has not been given with enough supporting information to make it useful. Specifically, most users would need the names of the employees associated with their phone numbers. One can imagine situations like telephone canvassing or surveys in which the names may not be required. In most situations, however, the questioner would expect the system to respond with phone numbers and names. As always, there is a trade-off between not wanting to give the user less than is needed, while not giving more than is requested.

## CASE STUDY: SIKLOSSY'S DISCONTINUITIES

Some databases are discontinuous (Siklossy 1977). A small change in the parameters of a query make a dramatic change in the results. If a person books a flight to Europe for May 31, it will cost significantly less than if it were booked for June 1, the very next day! If a child is born on December 31, the parents are allowed an income tax deduction for the entire preceding year. If the child is born one day later, the parents do not get a deduction for the year just ended. These are examples of discontinuities.

Siklossy maintains that an intelligent and responsible question answerer should make discontinuities clear to the asker. He found in studying airline fares that travel agents often do not point out discontinuities of total cost to the traveler even though, when asked, they often show that they are aware of the discontinuities. (To be fair to travel agents, it should be pointed out that they use more heuristics for providing their service than just cost. In planning a recent trip from Champaign, Illinois to Tampa, Florida, the author's agent made a connection through Chicago. When asked whether it would be cheaper to connect through St. Louis, the agent immediately agreed that it would. The ticket was written that way, but a new discontinuity had been introduced. Instead of a one-hour layover in Chicago, there was a four-hour layover in St. Louis. In addition to price, travel agents must consider layovers, ease of finding connecting flights and speed of itinerary preparation. The agents rely heavily on a depth-first search, stopping when the first solution has been found. As a result, a heuristic like "connect through Chicago if possible" may be used for a shorter search.)

There is an implicit assumption with most questions. Unless informed to the contrary, people generally assume that they are dealing with continuous data. For example, in asking for the air fare on a specific date, a person would generally assume that small variations in the departure date will not make much of a change in the fare. If the person books the trip for, say, February 15, the assumption of continuity is certainly valid; the rates are the same on the 13, 14, 16, or 17 of February. But the high-season air fares become effective on June 1. The discontinuity at this date means that a small change, booking for May 31 versus June 1, can make a large change in the total fare.

If the question asker's assumption of continuity is false, the answerer should correct it. This is the same situation as with Kaplan's corrective indirect responses in CO-OP. The only difference is that the continuity assumption is not stated explicitly in the query. However, recognizing that there is a discontinuity "near" the answer to the asker's question is a different task from recognizing a false presupposition explicit in a sentence. Locating discontinuities is primarily a database analysis problem. In contrast, CO-OP's search for violated presuppositions uses the database, but the search is directed by the language of the question. In searching for discontinuities, several questions arise. They will be discussed in the following paragraphs.

What constitutes a discontinuity? Say a type 1 transistor costs $.39 and a roughly similar transistor, type 2, costs $.37. If a question-answering system discovers discontinuities, it must decide whether to pass them on to the user. The user would then have to weigh the relative merits of type 1 to type 2, consider their interchangeability in the application, and so on. If the user is buying only one transistor, he or she would likely just pay the extra two cents. But if the transistor were to be built into a consumer device and the user is considering a purchase of five million transistors, the difference becomes significant: $100,000 worth (which would pay his or her salary for several years!). A discontinuity, then, is not solely a function of the data. It also depends on the user. The same information for different users might not be worth two cents, or it may be worth a small fortune.

When is a discontinuity "near" to a user's question? Once again, the user's attitudes bear on the interpretation. An executive flying from New York to London to close a corporate merger does not care that $50 can be saved by leaving two weeks later; the deal may fall through by then. A vacationer flying to London on a limited budget, who intends to stay there for six months, may be very interested in the reduced fare. For one user, two weeks is near and the suggestion is appreciated. For another, two weeks is totally out of the question so the suggestion may be considered an irrelevant annoyance.

Along what dimensions should discontinuities be considered? Discontinuities often occur in clusters. A car buyer who selects an inexpensive car over an expensive one is taking advantage of a price discontinuity. The buyer, may however, suffer the effects of discontinuities of comfort, quiet and reliability. These discontinuities accompany the price difference. The user's perception designates some discontinuities as paramount, and others as inconsequential.

What if a negative discontinuity is identified? Siklossy maintains that disadvantageous changes should be pointed out by a question answerer as well as advantageous changes. A user who books a flight for May 31 should be informed that a June 1 ticket would increase the fare. The user should be kept informed of the effects of crossing discontinuity boundaries even if he or she is not currently planning to do so.

In some instances, the number of discontinuities may be too large to enumerate. It may be preferable to mention principles rather than specific cases. When flying in Europe, many stopovers may be made at intermediate cities without an additional charge. Instead of listing all the possible combinations, the principle could be described.

Recognizing discontinuities is a process that has the potential of combinatorial explosion. In order to prevent this, the searches must be constrained by as much information as possible. Algorithms for finding discontinuities are just beginning to be studied.

## 7.5 Rules of Written Discourse

### CAUSAL CHAINS IN PARAGRAPHS

Schank (1975) has suggested that one means for understanding the coherence between sentences in a paragraph that describes an episode is through the causal relationships between events. A coherent paragraph or story relates a series of events. The events relate to one another through chains of causal links of which there are four types:

1. Result Causation—an action that causes a change of state. The change of state may be as abstract as generating hurt feelings or wounded pride, or as concrete as a tower that exists after the action of building it.
2. Enablement Causation—a state that allows for an action to have the potential to take place. In order to swim, a person would first have to be in water. The state of being in the water enables swimming.
3. Initiation Causation—any act or state change that can cause an individual to think about a particular thing. Thus, depending on context, hearing footsteps may invoke thoughts of fear, delighted anticipation or memories of past events.
4. Reason Causation—the mental motivation for a person's physical act. For example, the reason why John slugged Mary was that he hated her.

In understanding an episodic paragraph, the user should know that parts of the causal chains are taken from the text, whereas others must be inferred. Establishing causal links between the actions described in a paragraph requires consideration of two kinds of conditions for the actions. The first are absolutely necessary conditions which must be satisfied for the action to occur. The second are reasonably necessary conditions which are probably satisfied for an action to occur. If a reasonably necessary condition is contradicted, the paragraph can still be understood, but it is marked as being peculiar. These peculiarities often become the point of the paragraph. On the other hand, if an absolutely necessary condition is contradicted, the paragraph becomes nonsensical. For example, an absolutely necessary condition for swimming is being in water. A reasonably necessary condition is that the water be at a proper temperature for swimming. We can understand the event of someone swimming in 40°F water, but it seems peculiar. However, if we were told of someone swimming in a desert, we would not understand.

Necessary conditions are of primary importance for connecting the actions and states of a paragraph into a coherent concept. When an action is mentioned in the text, memory is searched for its necessary conditions. If they are not explicitly available from the preceding text, they can be inferred.

Some causal chains lead to deadends. They do not contribute to the understanding of the paragraph as a whole. However, if the paragraph describing an episode is coherent, there must be one causal chain that binds together nearly all of the actions and their causes that the paragraph states.

## STORY GRAMMAR

Just as the jumbled word order in sentences makes the string non-sensical, jumbling the order of sentences in a story makes the resulting collection of sentences a non-story. This suggests that there are structural constraints on the sentences in a story. Rumelhart (1975) has suggested that these constraints can be represented in a grammar for simple stories.

The grammar was described as consisting of a set of syntactic rules, each associated with a semantic rule. Only the syntactic rules will be described here. They are listed below:

```
STORY → SETTING + EPISODE
SETTING → (STATES)*
EPISODE → EVENT + REACTION
EVENT → EPISODE | CHANGE-OF-STATE | ACTION | EVENT
+ EVENT
REACTION → INTERNAL-RESPONSE + OVERT-RESPONSE
INTERNAL-RESPONSE → EMOTION | DESIRE
OVERT-RESPONSE → ACTION | (ATTEMPT)*
ATTEMPT → PLAN + APPLICATION
APPLICATION → (PREACTION)* + ACTION + CONSEQUENCE
PREACTION → SUBGOAL + (ATTEMPT)*
CONSEQUENCE → REACTION | EVENT
```

The grammar fits simple, formally structured stories like fables and fairy tales. The value of a description of the structure of stories is that it helps establish the relationships between the propositions in the story. In addition, when some details have been omitted from the narrative, as inevitably some are, a description of the expected structure can be used to motivate and limit inferencing.

As an example, Rumelhart analyzed one of Aesop's fables, "The Man and the Serpent," given below:

A countryman's son, by accident trod upon a serpent's tail. The serpent turned and bit him. He died. The father, in revenge, got his axe, pursued the serpent, and cut off part of his tail. So the serpent, in revenge, began stinging several of the farmer's cattle. This caused the farmer severe loss. Well, the farmer thought it best to make it up with the serpent. So he brought food and honey to the mouth of its lair, and said to it, "Let's forget and forgive; perhaps you were right in trying to punish my son, and take vengeance

on my cattle, but surely I was right to revenge him; now that
we are both satisfied why should we not be friends again?"
"No, no," said the serpent; "take away your gifts; you can
never forget the death of your son, nor I the loss of my tail."

The setting of this story is not stated explicitly, but can be inferred
from the text. The episode consists of four embedded episodes. At
the top level, the farmer attempts to reconcile his differences with the
serpent because of the loss he has suffered. The loss was the result
of the serpent's reaction to the loss of his tail. Cutting off the serpent's
tail was the reaction to the killing of the countryman's son, which
was the reaction to the son's stepping on the serpent.

The top-level structure is shown in Figure 7.1. The most deeply
embedded event, in which the son steps on the serpent and the
serpent kills him, is expanded in Figure 7.2. Two aspects of the
reaction had to be inferred in the fragment shown in this figure.
Neither the snake's desire for revenge nor his decision to bite the
son were stated explicitly. By contrast, the farmer's desire for
revenge is stated explicitly.

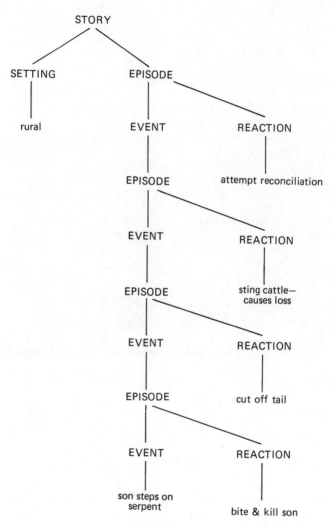

**Figure 7.1**

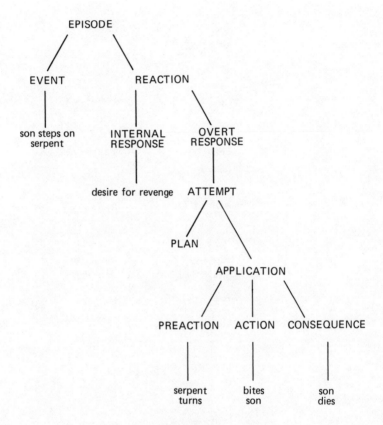

**Figure 7.2**

## References and Further Reading

Brown, G.P. "A Framework for Processing Dialogue." Cambridge Mass.: MIT Laboratory for Computer Science, June 1977.

Joshi, A.K.; Kaplan, S.J.; and Lee, R.M. "Approximate Responses from a Data Base Query System: An Application of Inferencing in Natural Language." In *Proceedings of the International Joint Conference on Artificial Intelligence.* Cambridge, Mass.: MIT, 1977.

Kaplan, S.J. "Indirect Responses to Loaded Questions." In *Proceedings of the Second Workshop on Theoretical Issues in Natural Language Processing.* Urbana, Ill.: University of Illinois, 1978a.

_____. "On the Difference Between Natural Language and High Level Query Languages." In *Proceedings of the ACM 78.* Washington, D.C.: ACM, 1978b.

Kaplan, S.J. and Joshi, A.K. "Cooperative Responses: An Application of Discourse Inference to Database Query Systems." In *Proceedings of the Second Annual Conference of the Canadian Society for Computational Studies of Intelligence.* Toronto, Ontario: 1978.

Levin, J.A. and Moore, J.A. "Dialog-Games: Metacommunications Structures for Natural Language Interaction." *Cognitive Science* 1 (1977):395-420.

Mann, W.C.; Moore, J.A.; and Levin, J.A. "A Comprehensive Model for Human Dialogue." In *Proceedings of the International Joint Conference on Artificial Intelligence.* Cambridge, Mass.: MIT, 1977.

Rumelhart, D.E. "Notes on a Schema for Stories." In *Representation and Understanding*, edited by D.G. Bobrow and A. Collins. New York: Academic Press, 1975.

Schank, R.C. "The Structure of Episodes in Memory." In *Representation of Understanding*, edited by D.G. Bobrow and A. Collins. New York: Academic Press, 1975.

Searle, J. *Speech Acts.* Cambridge, Mass.: University Press, 1970.

Siklossy, L. "Question-Asking Question-Answering." Report TR-71. Austin: University of Texas Department of Computer Sciences, 1977.

# Glossary

**anaphoric**—depending on previous discourse, a pronoun that refers to a previously mentioned concept is a form of anaphoric reference; *see* cataphoric; exophoric

**ATN**—augmented transition network—a heavily used parsing formalism composed of a grammar that is applied in a recurrsive, top-down fashion, and augmented with global registers that are capable of temporarily holding structures for later use

**bottom-up parsing**—synonymous with data-driven parsing; a parsing method that starts with the lowest structures (eg. words) and builds higher level structures from them (eg. noun phrases, prepositional phrases, sentences)

**cataphoric**—depending upon subsequent discourse; in "We asked him, but Knuckles couldn't come," 'him' is cataphoric to Knuckles; relatively rare

**closed classes**—those classes of words that do not readily admit additions, such as pronouns, prepositions, auxiliary verbs and article adjectives (see open classes)

**coercion**—the process of forcing an unusual interpretation on a word or phrase based on its context; this term derives from coercion in computer languages where, for instance, an integer in a floating point expression is coerced into an equivalent floating point number

**conceptual structure**—in generative semantics, conceptual structure is the tree structured representation of meaning of an utterance to which transformations are applied to produce surface structure sentences

**deep structure**–in transformational grammar, the deep structure is the internalized form of sentences to which the transformations are applied to produce the surface structure; deep structure is separated from the knowledge representation by a semantic component (see conceptual structure)

**deterministic parsing**–parsing which requires (or allows) no backtracking; once an interpretation is assigned to a phrase in a deterministic parse, it cannot be altered

**ellipsis**–the omission of words or phrases in an utterance, with the assumption that the listener can use the current context to assume what has been omitted

**exophoric**–depending on the external (non-linguistic) situation for interpretation, as in "Did you hear that explosion?" following an explosion

**extension**–the set of individuals that are instances of a generic concept; the extension of the concept "city" is the set of all cities (see intension)

**frame**–a knowledge cluster that embodies what an individual knows about one particular concept; a frame system is an individual's knowledge about the world represented by frames

**garden path sentences**–sentences that generally force listeners to consciously back up and reinterpret them, such as "I was wary of Ali's punch, but by the third round I realized there was no liquor in it"; sentences that people apparently parse non-deterministically

**generality hierarchy**–a tree structure of concepts, where the most general concepts are closest to the root, and most specific closest to the leaves; more specific concepts generally inherit the characteristics of their ancestors

**heuristic parsing**–technique (generally associated with ATN parsers) of ordering the hypotheses in a top-down parser (arcs in an ATN parser) to try the most likely first, in the hope that the first parse found is the most likely to be correct

**illocutionary act**–the things a speaker does to indicate how his utterance is to be used

**intension**–the intension of a concept X is the set of conditions that must be satisfied in order for a concept to qualify as an X, ie., what it means to be an X (see extension)

**non-deterministic parsing**—parsing which allows decisions to be changed or allow several alternative interpretations to proceed in parallel (see deterministic parsing)

**open classes**—classes of words that readily admit the addition of new members such as nouns, adjectives and verbs (see closed classes)

**parser**—generally intended as a formalism that assigns a structural description to a sentence; also used to describe formalisms that assign a semantic interpretation to a sentence (as in a parser for a semantic grammar)

**perlocutionary acts**—the effects that a speaker actually has on a listener

**phonetic structure**—shows the structure of a sentence as it would actually be pronounced (see surface structure, deep structure, conceptual structure)

**phrase structure grammar**—a set of rules that indicate what and how categories of words and phrases can be combined to construct other categories of phrases

**pragmatic ellipsis**—an omission of information from a syntactically complete sentence that must be assumed from the context

**pragmatics**—the study of the role of contextual knowledge in language; knowledge about the world

**schema**—conceptual structures equivalent to frames

**scripts**—conceptual structures that describe events and sequences of events

**semantic grammar**—a grammar which parses according to semantic categories of words and phrases rather than syntactic categories

**semantic marker** — an attribute assigned to a word or phrase indicating that it describes a concept of a particular semantic class; used as restrictions for the selection of competing semantic interpretations

**semantic net**—a network representation of knowledge; a broad range of knowledge representation formalisms have been called semantic nets, they all involve the designation of conceptual entities linked to one another by named relations

**semantics**—the study of the relationship between symbols and their meanings; sometimes called what is left to linguistics without syntax, most consider it to be the link between syntax and knowledge representation

**speech acts**—actions that are performed through the use of language such as informing, requesting, commanding, etc.

**stonewalling**—giving literal but not complete answers to questions; a characteristic of many question answering systems

**story grammar**—a grammar describing the allowable structure of stories

**substitution**—anaphoric replacement of a word or phrase by a substitute word or phrase like "the green one" for "the green volleyball"; closely related to ellipsis

**surface structure**—shows the structure of a sentence with tense and number represented as separate leaves on the tree (see phonetic structure, deep structure, conceptual structure)

**syntax**—the structural description of a language

**top-down parsing**—synonymous with hypothesis driven parsing, similar to expectation driven parsing; a parsing method that hypothesizes a high level structure (eg. a sentence), then attempts to match (recurrsively) lower level structures to it

**transformational grammar**—a theory of syntax that describes the structure of sentences in the language with a set of recurrsive rules (transformations) that relate pairs of tree structures to one another

**underlying representation**—the internalized representation of meaning of an utterance; like deep structure and conceptual structure, but does not imply commitment to a particular theory of semantics

**well-formed substrings**—substrings that are found through the course of parsing that need not be reparsed in the event of backtracking

# Index

A

Abelson, R. 238, 239
abstract frames 232
ad hoc representation 27
Aiello, N. 239
Airline Guide 165, 179
ambiguity 112
anaphoric 267
approaches to selection 107
Arnold, R. 212
assertions 31
ATN 63,267
ATN arc types 68
augmented transition network 63
Automatic Advisor 4
auxiliary 59

B

backup 67
Barstow, D. 99
Baseball 23
basic frames 232
Bell, A. 212
Berenner, S. 48
blocks world 139
Bobrow, D. 32, 48, 238, 239
Bookchin, B. 212
bottom-up parsing 267
bottom-up and top-down parsing
        compared 71
Brachman, R. 228, 239

Bratley, P. 99
Brown, G. 250, 265
Brown, J. 212
Bruce, B. 136
Bullwinkle, C. 137
Burger, J. 48
Burton, R. 212

C

Cadiou, J. 212
Carney, H. 48
case marker 133
cataphoric 267
causal chains 259
causation,
        enablement 259
        initiation 259
        reason 259
        result 259
Chang, C. 212
Charniak, E. 137
chart parser 75
Chomsky, C. 48
clarification dialog 206
closed classes 51,267
Cocke 79
Codd, E. 212
coercion 9, 267
Collins, A. 239
compiling ATN's 70
complete anaphor 181
concept case frames 198

concept comparison 222
conceptual coverage 11, 14
conceptual prototype 218
conceptual structure 61, 267
context 113
context effect on meaning 105
CO-OP 203, 253
Craig, J. 48, 36

D

Dakin, D. 99
Damerau, F. 99
DEACON 36
deep structure 61, 268
demon 220, 226
deterministic parsing 91, 268
Dialog-Games 246
discontinuities 256
DOCTOR 40

E

Earley 79
ELI 208
ELIZA 40
ellipsis 127, 268
entire system strategy 3
exophoric 268
expectation based parsing 208
expectations 209
extension 229, 268

F

fact retrieval from text 29
Fillmore, C. 132, 137
Finin, T. 68, 99, 137
forced perspective 226
frame 219, 268
frame activation 224, 237
frame deactivation 237
Friedman, J. 100
FRL 226, 231

G

garden path sentences 91, 268
generality hierarchy 221, 268
generalized descriptions 123
Gershman, A. 213
Ginsparg, J. 99
Goldman, N. 213
Goldstein, I. 239
Goodman, B. 214
Green, B. 23, 48
Green, C. 99
Grishman, R. 213
Grosz, B. 137
GUS 234

H

Hadden, G. 99
Hall, B. 100
Halliday, M. 137
Harris, L. 137, 181, 213
Hasan, R. 137
Hayes, P. 137
Hendrix, G. 187, 213
Hershman, R. 213
heuristic parsing 67, 268
Hirschman, L. 213
Hobbs, J. 137

I

illocutionary acts 243, 268
implied relationships 114
implied sets 116
indirect responses,
    corrective 254
    suggestive 254
    supportive 254
individual frames 233
inflections 51, 30
initiator utterance 251
intension 229, 268
isolated phenomena strategy 2

**J**

Joshi, A. 253, 265

**K**

Kaplan, R. 99, 215, 238
Kaplan, S.J. 203, 253, 265
Kasami 79
Kay, M. 75, 99, 238
Kelly, R. 213
kernel sentences 31
keywords 40
Klein, S. 48
KLONE 228
KRL 6–6 221, 231, 234
Kuipers, B. 239
Kuno, S. 99

**L**

large vocabulary problem 202
Laughery, K. 48
LIFER 187, 243
Lee, R. 253, 265
Lehnert, W. 239
Levin, J. 247, 248, 265
Lewis, G. 104
Lindsay, K. 27, 48
LINGOL 77
linguistic coverage 11, 13
Long, B. 48
Longyear, C. 48
lookahead 93
LUNAR 112, 165, 173, 243

**M**

manifestation frames 232
Mann, W. 17, 247, 265
Marcus, M. 92, 99
matching 222
McConlogue, K. 48
metadiscussion utterance 251

methodology 3
methods 219
MICROPLANNER 139
Miller, H. 213
Miller, M. 239
modality 231
modals 59
modifier attachment 111, 179
Moore, J. 137, 247, 248, 265
morphemes 61
morphology 51
multiple word senses 103
Nash-Webber, B. 99, 137, 215
natural languages 1
necessary conditions
    absolutely 260
    reasonably 260
Newell, A. 137
Norman, D. 238
non-deterministic parsing 91, 269
noun-noun modification 7, 112

**O**

Oetinger, A. 99
open classes 51, 269
oracle 79

**P**

PAM 235, 237
parallel parsing 68
parser defined 52, 269
PARSIFAL 91
perfect 59
perlocutionary acts 243, 269
Petrick, S. 17, 100
phonetic structure 56, 269
phrase structure parsing 89, 269
PLANES 129, 195, 243
pragmatic ellipsis 129, 199, 197, 269
pragmatics 51, 269
Preference Semantics 183
Pratt, V. 100

procedurally encoded knowledge 141
progressive 59
pronouns 9, 116
PROTOSYNTHEX 29
PROTOSYNTHEX II 31
prototype 232
PSI 82

Q

quantification 125, 166, 169, 180

R

Raze, C. 213
Reader 82
recovery path 250
reference list 9, 117, 181
reference to events 119
Reiter, R. 137
RENDEZVOUS 202
rewrite rules 37
Rieger, C. 213
Riesbeck, C. 213
ring structures 37
Roberts, R. 239
Robinson, J. 100
ROBOT 181
Roussopoulos, N. 212
Rubin, A. 214

S

Sacerdoti, E. 213, 214
SAD-SAM 27
Sagalowicz, D. 213
Sager, N. 213, 214
SAM 108, 235
Samlowski, W. 137
Schank, R. 138, 214, 239, 235, 265
schema 219, 269
scripts 219, 235, 269
Searle J. 265
selection, approaches to 107

semantic density 183
semantic grammar 52, 185, 269
semantic grammars and ATNs 70
semantic marker 8, 106, 269
semantic net 4, 229, 269
semantics 51, 101, 269
semi-anaphor 180
servants 226
Sheridan, P. 138
SHRDLU 139
Sidner, C. 138
Siklossy, L. 256, 265
Simmons, R. 29, 48
Slocum, J. 213
smart quantifiers 130
SOPHIE 184
specialization frames 233
speech acts 243, 270
stereotype 218
standard path 250
stop-on-success 108
stonewalling 253, 270
story grammar 260, 270
string transformations 90
structural ellipsis 128
STUDENT 32
substitution 126, 270
substructure ellipsis 128
suffix stripping 29
suffixes, and lexical class 30
superstructure ellipsis 128
surface structure 58, 270
Susie Software 250
syntactic structure 55
syntax defined 50, 270
SYNTHEX 29

T

templates 33, 40, 170
Tennant, H. 17
Thompson, B. 138
Thompson, F. 138
Thompson, H. 238

top-down parsing 71, 270
TQA 89
trace theory 94
transfer ability 166
transformational analysis 89
transformational grammar 89, 94,
      106, 270
translation 21, 183
try-all-possibilities 110

U

underlying structure 61, 270
unmentioned concepts 122

V

Van Lehn, K. 138
verb tables 39
viewpoints 225

W

Walker, D. 100
Waltz, D. 214
Warnock, E. 239
Watt, W. 18
weak implication 32
Webber, B. 138
weights on arcs 67
well-formed substrings 67, 270
Weizenbaum, J. 48, 40
Wilensky, R. 239
Wilks, Y. 18, 100, 138, 183, 214, 239
Winograd, T. 215, 238
Wolf, A. 48
Woods, W. 18, 100, 130, 138, 215
word sense selection 103, 183, 237

Y

Younger 79

Z

Zwicky, A. 100